T0309940

Real Estate Finance in
the New Economy

Real Estate Finance in the New Economy

Piyush Tiwari
Faculty of Architecture, Building and Planning
University of Melbourne, Australia

Michael White
School of Architecture, Design and the Built Environment
Nottingham Trent University, UK

This edition first published 2014
© 2014 John Wiley & Sons, Ltd

Registered Office
John Wiley & Sons, Ltd, The Atrium, Southern Gate, Chichester, West Sussex, PO19 8SQ,
United Kingdom.

Editorial Offices
9600 Garsington Road, Oxford, OX4 2DQ, United Kingdom.
The Atrium, Southern Gate, Chichester, West Sussex, PO19 8SQ, United Kingdom.

For details of our global editorial offices, for customer services and for information about how
to apply for permission to reuse the copyright material in this book please see our website at
www.wiley.com/wiley-blackwell.

The right of the author to be identified as the author of this work has been asserted in
accordance with the UK Copyright, Designs and Patents Act 1988.

All rights reserved. No part of this publication may be reproduced, stored in a retrieval
system, or transmitted, in any form or by any means, electronic, mechanical, photocopying,
recording or otherwise, except as permitted by the UK Copyright, Designs and Patents
Act 1988, without the prior permission of the publisher.

Designations used by companies to distinguish their products are often claimed as
trademarks. All brand names and product names used in this book are trade names, service
marks, trademarks or registered trademarks of their respective owners. The publisher is not
associated with any product or vendor mentioned in this book.

Limit of Liability/Disclaimer of Warranty: While the publisher and author(s) have used their
best efforts in preparing this book, they make no representations or warranties with respect
to the accuracy or completeness of the contents of this book and specifically disclaim any
implied warranties of merchantability or fitness for a particular purpose. It is sold on the
understanding that the publisher is not engaged in rendering professional services and neither
the publisher nor the author shall be liable for damages arising herefrom. If professional
advice or other expert assistance is required, the services of a competent professional should
be sought.

Library of Congress Cataloging-in-Publication Data

Tiwari, Piyush.
  Real estate finance in the new economy / PiyushTiwari, Michael White.
      pages   cm
  Includes bibliographical references and index.
  ISBN 978-1-4051-5871-8 (cloth)
1. Real estate investment.   I. White, Michael, 1965–   II. Title.
  HD1382.5.T593 2014
  332.63'24–dc23

                                                 2013041260

A catalogue record for this book is available from the British Library.

Wiley also publishes its books in a variety of electronic formats. Some content that appears
in print may not be available in electronic books.

Cover design by Garth Stewart
Cover image credit: iStock photo

Set in 10/13pt Trump Mediaeval by SPi Publisher Services, Pondicherry, India
Printed and bound in Singapore by Markono Print Media Pte Ltd

1   2014

 The Royal Institution of Chartered Surveyors is the mark of property professionalism worldwide, promoting best practice, regulation and consumer protection for business and the community. It is the home of property related knowledge and is an impartial advisor to governments and global organisations. It is committed to the promotion of research in support of the efficient and effective operation of land and property markets worldwide.

Real Estate Issues

Series Managing Editors

Clare Eriksson	Head of Research, Royal Institution of Chartered Surveyors
John Henneberry	Department of Town & Regional Planning, University of Sheffield
K.W. Chau	Chair Professor, Department of Real Estate and Construction, The University of Hong Kong
Elaine Worzala	Director of the Carter Real Estate Center, Department of Economics and
	Finance, School of Business and Economics, College of Charleston

Real Estate Issues is an international book series presenting the latest thinking into how real estate markets operate. The books have a strong theoretical basis – providing the underpinning for the development of new ideas.

The books are inclusive in nature, drawing both upon established techniques for real estate market analysis and on those from other academic disciplines as appropriate. The series embraces a comparative approach, allowing theory and practice to be put forward and tested for their applicability and relevance to the understanding of new situations. It does not seek to impose solutions, but rather provides a more effective means by which solutions can be found. It will not make any presumptions as to the importance of real estate markets but will uncover and present, through the clarity of the thinking, the real significance of the operation of real estate markets.

Further information on the *Real Estate Issues* series can be found at:
http://eu.wiley.com/WileyCDA/Section/id-380013.html

Books in the series

Greenfields, Brownfields & Housing Development
Adams & Watkins
9780632063871

Planning, Public Policy & Property Markets
Adams, Watkins & White
9781405124300

Housing & Welfare in Southern Europe
Allen, Barlow, Léal, Maloutas & Padovani
9781405103077

Markets & Institutions in Real Estate & Construction
Ball
9781405110990

Building Cycles: Growth & Instability
Barras
9781405130011

Neighbourhood Renewal & Housing Markets: Community Engagement in the US and UK
Beider
9781405134101

Mortgage Markets Worldwide
Ben-Shahar, Leung & Ong
9781405132107

The Cost of Land Use Decisions: Applying Transaction Cost Economics to Planning & Development
Buitelaar
9781405151238

Urban Regeneration & Social Sustainability: Best Practice from European Cities
Colantonio & Dixon
9781405194198

Urban Regeneration in Europe
Couch, Fraser & Percy
9780632058419

Urban Sprawl in Europe: Landscapes, Land-Use Change & Policy
Couch, Leontidou & Petschel-Held
9781405139175

Transforming Private Landlords
Crook & Kemp
9781405184151

Real Estate & the New Economy: The Impact of Information and Communications Technology
Dixon, McAllister, Marston & Snow
9781405117784

Economics & Land Use Planning
Evans
9781405118613

Economics, Real Estate & the Supply of Land
Evans
9781405118620

Management of Privatised Housing: International Policies & Practice
Gruis, Tsenkova & Nieboer
9781405181884

Development & Developers: Perspectives on Property
Guy & Henneberry
9780632058426

The Right to Buy: Analysis & Evaluation of a Housing Policy
Jones & Murie
9781405131971

Housing Markets & Planning Policy
Jones & Watkins
9781405175203

Office Markets & Public Policy
Jones
9781405199766

Challenges of the Housing Economy: An International Perspective
Jones, White & Dunse
9780470672334

Mass Appraisal Methods: An International Perspective for Property Valuers
Kauko & d'Amato
9781405180979

Economics of the Mortgage Market: Perspectives on Household Decision Making
Leece
9781405114615

Towers of Capital: Office Markets & International Financial Services
Lizieri
9781405156721

Making Housing More Affordable: The Role of Intermediate Tenures
Monk & Whitehead
9781405147149

Global Trends in Real Estate Finance
Newell & Sieracki
9781405151283

Housing Economics & Public Policy
O'Sullivan & Gibb
9780632064618

International Real Estate: An Institutional Approach
Seabrooke, Kent & How
9781405103084

Urban Design in the Real Estate Development Process: Policy Tools & Property Decisions
Tiesdell & Adams
9781405192194

Real Estate Finance in the New Economy
Tiwari & White
9781405158718

British Housebuilders: History & Analysis
Wellings
9781405149181

Contents

Preface

Investment in real estate assets has increased significantly over the past two decades. As an asset class, real estate has become important for both national and international investors. The past two decades have also witnessed increased economic integration across the globe and integration of financial markets. Debt financing for real estate investment rose rapidly until the financial crisis.

This book has been written against the background of the crisis and turbulence in world markets. Real estate values have fallen in developed countries, and while less exposed to the crisis, asset values have also been volatile in the emerging markets of East Asia. The financial turbulence has called into question policies that encouraged the integration of world economies and liberalisation of financial markets.

The book begins by setting the context for the discussion real estate financing. We discuss internationalisation and the growth of foreign direct investment. Following this, the evolution of international real estate markets is examined. As real estate markets grow, there is also a development of indirect (or securitised) investment vehicles starting in the United States and also being seen in the United Kingdom, other European countries and, more recently, by markets in Asia-Pacific. This begins to strengthen the link between real estate and the finance system, and debt-based products begin to be developed. We then examine the flow of funds into real estate markets from investors who view real estate as another asset class alongside bonds and equity. Financial innovation is discussed and the new products defined and listed. Risk in real estate investment is highlighted, and following this we examine the relationship between real estate financing, asset price bubbles and the macroeconomy. World integration of financial markets causes us to examine international macroeconomy volatility and interconnectedness.

The financial crisis is discussed, and we focus on mispricing that occurred in asset markets, including the underestimation of risk that led to economic actors paying too much for real estate before the crisis occurred. We also discuss whether risk is overestimated after the initial crisis, implying that prices and investment have fallen to a level below what they should be. The importance of debt finance and its attractiveness is also examined. The availability of finance and its cyclical impacts are discussed.

We conclude by discussing real estate finance in the new world economy. This new economy is a much more uncertain place that viewed from the perspective from before the financial crisis. The new economy, we argue, embodies an assumption in favour of policies associated with neo-economic liberalism and simplistic rules for monetary authorities. But these policy rules we find are time-inconsistent. Perverse incentives caused excessive risk taking in financial markets, and mortgage-backed products were highly complex, difficult to rate for risk and hence were inaccurately overpriced. The role of real estate has been significant in recent cyclical fluctuations. The financial methods that have been used in real estate have increased volatility in macroeconomies. Policy makers may not be able to afford to ignore asset price inflation and thus would need to review the narrow remit given to independent monetary authorities.

Acknowledgements

We would like to thank Pushpa and Anushka, and Irene and James for all the support, understanding and encouragement during those long hours which we spent writing the book chapters. We would also like to thank Madeleine and Beth at Wiley for their patience in waiting for the final chapters to be delivered.

1

International Economic Developments since the 1970s

Introduction

Financial deregulation that has taken place over the last quarter century has meant that large flows of funds can move quickly around the world seeking out the highest risk-adjusted return for investors. Real estate is increasingly seen as another asset that can be used in portfolios for diversification purposes, and a variety of investment vehicles in real estate have emerged. This book seeks to examine the financing of real estate investment and development within the context of an increasingly integrated international world economy and financial system. The approach adopted in the book is based on three questions:

- How real estate's financial structure – the mixture of real estate financial instruments, markets and intermediaries operating in an economy – changes as economy grows and becomes internationalised
- How the developments in real estate finance – quality and quantity of real estate financial instruments, markets and intermediaries – impact economic growth
- How real estate's financial structure influences economic development

The exposure of the financial sector to real estate has become clearly visible in the last few years. Linked to this, the international integration of the

Real Estate Finance in the New Economy, First Edition. Piyush Tiwari and Michael White.
© 2014 John Wiley & Sons, Ltd. Published 2014 by John Wiley & Sons, Ltd.

financial sector has also become highly apparent. The extent of financial integration and the scale and structure of the international financial markets today are significantly different from the 1970s when the earliest waves of internationalisation of real estate companies began.

In this chapter, international economic developments over the past 40 years are reviewed. This period is one of substantial change in the patterns of world trade and financial flows. Such change is set in the context of classical and contemporary trade theories. The globalisation of production and the increasing integration of different countries into the global system of trade are examined. This period also sees the development of world trading blocs such as the European Union (EU), the North American Free Trade Agreement (NAFTA) and a more loose affiliation of the Association of Southeast Asian Nations (ASEAN) together with Japan, South Korea and more recently China.

International trade theories: Setting the scene

In the asset market, investors invest in property in anticipation of realising returns. Property generates income (in the form of rent) and capital (in the form of change in capital values over time) returns for investors. Investors in the property asset market are both national and international. The nature of capital flows in property is of two types: (i) portfolio investment, where an investor resident in one country invests in stocks, bonds and other financial instruments related to property in the other country, and (ii) foreign direct investment (FDI), where an investor based in one country acquires property in the other country with the intention of managing it.

The development market is the market where developers combine land, material, capital and expertise to generate new space. Developers may be either national or international. In recent years, a number of international developers have been involved in development overseas. And finally, there is the user or occupation market. Their demand for space reflects economic fundamentals in that their demand is a derived demand for the use to which the space is put, being able to generate revenue from the sale of their product/service in the final market for goods and services. This occupier base may be local, regional, national or international.

There are three types of issues to consider: (i) internationalisation of economies through trade and FDI, which have implications for demand for real estate space; (ii) international capital flows in assets, including real estate; and (iii) internationalisation of real estate production processes and organisations. This chapter will explore various theoretical models that have been used in the economic literature to explain international trade in goods and services, capital and internationalisation of organisational structure.

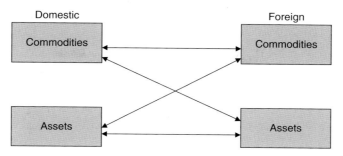

Figure 1.1   Types of international transactions.

International goods and capital flows

International trade in goods and capital flows are among the forms of transaction (other examples being trade in labour, technology, etc.) that take place between economic agents in different countries. Economic theory suggests that economic agents (consumers, producers, governments, etc.) can benefit from specialisation in production of certain commodities and exchange these 'products' for other goods and services. It is impossible for a country to be self-reliant without reducing its standard of living. There are three possible types of international transactions, as illustrated in Figure 1.1.

Residents of different countries could trade commodities for other commodities, or they could trade commodities for assets (i.e. that is for future commodities), or they could trade assets for other assets. All three types of exchange lead to gains from trade.

But, why does trade happen and how can trade between nations be explained theoretically?

Reasons for trade

There are five basic reasons why trade may take place between countries:

Differences in technology   Advantageous trade can occur between countries if the countries differ in their technological abilities to produce commodities. Technology refers to the techniques used to convert resources (land, labour, capital) into outputs. The basis for trade in this Ricardian trade theory of comparative advantage is differences in technology.

Differences in resource endowments   Advantageous trade can occur between countries if the countries differ in their endowments of resources. Resource endowments refer to the skills and abilities of a country's workforce, the natural resources available within its borders (minerals, farmland, etc.) and the sophistication of its capital stock (machinery, infrastructure, communications systems). The basis for trade in this pure exchange model and the Heckscher–Ohlin (H–O) trade model is differences in resource endowments.

Differences in demand   Advantageous trade can occur between countries if demands or preferences differ between countries. Individuals in different countries may have different preferences or demands for various products. The Chinese are likely to demand more rice than the Germans, even if facing the same price. Scots might demand more whisky, and the Japanese more fish, than Americans would, even if they all faced the same prices.

Existence of economies of scale in production   The existence of economies of scale in production is sufficient to generate advantageous trade between two countries. Economies of scale refer to a production process in which production costs fall as the scale of production rises. This feature of production is also known as 'increasing returns to scale'. This can also be linked to agglomeration economies in particular industries in certain locations (e.g. international finance in London or New York).

Existence of government policies   Government taxation and subsidy programmes can generate advantages in the production of certain products. In these circumstances, advantageous trade may arise simply because of differences in government policies across countries.

Differences in return on capital   Trade in capital may happen if the real return on capital across different countries varies. This may happen if demand for capital in present and future time periods differs among different countries.

   The main reason for trade to take place is that countries find it advantageous to trade. As mentioned previously, it is impossible for any country to be self-reliant without reducing its standard of living. This can be understood from the following simple illustration. Suppose that there is one good that the world produces and there is one good that the world consumes. This good can be produced by all countries; however, each country can decide whether to produce the good domestically or import it (partially or fully). Figure 1.2 presents the market equilibrium for the good under (i) no trade and (ii) trade scenarios.

   In economics, the demand curve describes the quantity of a good that a household or a firm chooses to buy at a given price. Similarly, the supply curve describes the quantity of good that a household or firm would like to sell at a particular price. If demands of individual households in a country

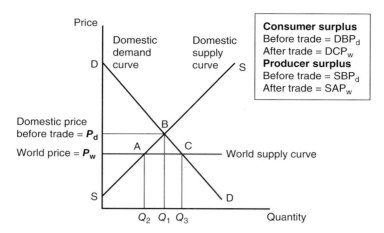

Figure 1.2 Demand, supply and market equilibrium.

are aggregated, we can obtain an aggregate demand curve that tells us the total quantity of that good demanded at each possible price. Similarly, an aggregate supply curve would tell us the total quantity of a good that would be supplied by a country at each possible price.

Consider first the case of a closed country (which means that this country does not engage in trade with foreign countries). Figure 1.2 plots the price on the vertical axis and quantity on the horizontal axis. The downward-sloping line DD is the aggregate domestic demand curve for the whole country, and the upward-sloping line SS is the aggregate domestic supply curve. The point of intersection of demand and supply curve is the market equilibrium. This point determines the price that will be paid and accepted in the market. The point is labelled as B, for equilibrium, the corresponding price P_d is the equilibrium price, and quantity Q_1 is the equilibrium quantity.

Now, suppose the country which was closed to trade opens its borders (removes restrictions that were not permitting trade to happen. Restrictions in the real world could take many forms, such as import tariffs, export restriction or quantity quotas) so that trade in goods and services can take place. The supply curve that the country faces now is the horizontal world supply curve. The world supply curve is horizontal because competition would prevent prices rising above this level. If prices rose, producers around the world would take this opportunity to expand their market and increase their production, thereby bringing the equilibrium price to P_d.

The supply curve that the country faces is not the original upward-sloping curve but the horizontal world supply curve. The demand curve, which depends on domestic preferences, does not change. The new demand–supply equilibrium will be at point C. Note that at this point the equilibrium price of the good is $P_w < P_d$. Consumers demand quantity Q_3. What happens to domestic producers? Does production shift abroad? The answer to this question is complicated by political economy of trade and the extent to which trade is protected by the country. However, in the aforementioned example, when there are no restrictions on trade after the opening up of the economy, the domestic producers could supply goods at world price up to a quantity Q_2 because their marginal cost of production up to Q_2 is less than or equal to the world price. Above Q_2, the marginal cost of production would exceed the market price at which goods can be sold (=world price), so that producers would find it unprofitable to produce. The country with demand Q_3 would produce Q_2 domestically and import (=$Q_3 - Q_2$) from the world market.

To understand the impact of trade on producers and consumers, let's use an economic concept called 'surplus'. Consumer surplus is the amount that consumers benefit by being able to purchase the good for a price that is less than they are willing to pay. For example, for all quantities supplied less than the equilibrium quantity, consumers are willing to pay higher than the equilibrium price. By paying equilibrium price, their surplus before trade is DBPd. The producer surplus is the amount by which producers benefit by selling at a market price mechanism that is higher than they would be willing to sell for. In the autarky (no trade) case, producer surplus is SBPd. Note that producer surplus flows through to owners of factors of production (labour, capital, land), unlike economic profit, which is 0 under perfect competition. If market for labour and capital is also perfectly competitive, producer surplus ends up as economic rent to the owners of scarce resources like land.

Let us see how trade affects the welfare of consumers and producers. The trade has opened up opportunities to buy goods at a lower price. For domestic consumers, trade is welfare enhancing. For domestic producers, however, the revenue has declined as they face price competition and find it unviable to produce more than Q_2. Consumers' surplus, which was DBPd before trade, has increased to DCPw. Producers' surplus, however, has declined from SBPd to SAPw.

International trade is generally beneficial to nations; however, it is quite possible that trade may hurt some groups within the nation (in the aforementioned example, the welfare of producers has been affected). In other words, international trade has strong impact on the distribution of income. International trade can adversely affect owners of resources that are 'specific' to industries that compete with imports and cannot find alternative ways to redeploy these resources to alternative use (Krugman and Obstfeld, 2000, chapter 3). Trade could also affect the distribution of income between broad groups, between workers and owners of resources (Krugman and Obstfeld, 2000, chapter 4).

Theoretical models of trade

Economic discussion suggesting that trade is advantageous dates back to Adam Smith's *The Wealth of Nations*. In this early economics treatise, dating back to the eighteenth century, Adam Smith argues: 'If a foreign country can supply with a commodity cheaper than we ourselves can make it, better buy it of them with some part of the produce of our own industry, employed in a way in which we have some advantage'. The theory which Adam Smith proposed is based on the concept of *absolute advantage* in production. The idea here is simple and intuitive. If our country can produce some set of goods at lower cost than a foreign country, and if the foreign country can produce some other set of goods at a lower cost than we can produce them, then clearly it would be best for us to trade our relatively cheaper goods for their relatively cheaper goods. In this way, both countries may gain from trade. However, if one country has absolute advantage in all goods, should other countries engage in trade with this country? The answer is not obvious from an absolute advantage model.

The theory of comparative advantage

British economist David Ricardo proposed a comparative advantage theory in 1817 in his book *On the Principles of Political Economy and Taxation*. The fundamental idea of the Ricardian model of comparative advantage is that the basis of trade is differences in technology. Ricardo demonstrated, using an example with two countries, two goods and one country having productive advantage in both the goods, that the world output could be improved if each country specialised in the production of the good for which their opportunity cost was lowest. If appropriate terms of trade were then chosen, both countries could end up with more of both goods.

If there are two countries producing two goods and one country has productive advantage in both goods, to benefit from specialisation and free trade, the country with advantage in both goods should specialise and trade the good which it is 'most best' at producing, while the other should specialise and trade the good which it is 'least worse' at producing.

A simple way to demonstrate that countries can gain from trade is through a numerical example. Ricardo demonstrated using a two-country, two-good example, a country can gain from trade even if it has technological disadvantage in producing both goods. Let us assume that there are two countries, the United Kingdom and the United States; two goods, whisky and computers; and one factor of production, labour. Suppose the United Kingdom has absolute advantage in production of both these goods. Suppose, in the United Kingdom, the labour requirement to produce one unit of

Table 1.1   Summary of hypothetical inputs required for production.

Goods	United Kingdom – labour per unit	United States – labour per unit	Opportunity cost – United Kingdom	Opportunity cost – United States
Whisky	1	6	0.5	2
Computer	2	3	2	0.5

whisky is one and the labour requirement to produce one unit of computer is two. The United States can produce one unit of whisky by employing six units of labour and one unit of computer by employing three units of labour. Total available labour in each of these countries is 24 units. By assumption, the United Kingdom is more efficient in producing both goods, as the labour required to produce one unit of whisky in the United Kingdom is less than the labour required to produce one unit of whisky in the United States and the labour required to produce one unit of computer in the United Kingdom is less than the labour required to produce one unit of computer in the United States. In order to produce whisky, the United Kingdom must produce fewer computers. Economists use a term called opportunity cost to describe such trade-offs. The opportunity cost of whisky in terms of computers is the number of computers that could have been produced with the resources used to produce given units of whisky. The opportunity cost of whisky in the United Kingdom is 0.5, as this is the number of units of computer whose production is to be given up to produce one unit of whisky in the United Kingdom. The opportunity cost of computer in the United Kingdom is two units of whisky. The opportunity cost of whisky in the United States is two units of computers, and the opportunity cost of computer in the United States is 0.5 units of whisky. Table 1.1 summarises the aforementioned discussion.

Suppose that 24 labour units are available in both the United Kingdom and the United States. The production possibility frontiers (PPF) for both these countries are plotted in Figure 1.3. PPF is a graph that shows the different quantities of two goods that an economy could efficiently produce with limited productive resources. The PPF for the United Kingdom lies outside that for the United States. Since the size of both economies is assumed to be same (both have 24 units of labour), the United Kingdom has absolute advantage over the United States, because the United Kingdom can produce any possible combination of whisky and computer far more efficiently than the United States. The levels of production at points that will lie below the PPF make inefficient use of resources, and points above the PPF are infeasible. Points along the curve describe the trade-off between the two goods, that is, the opportunity cost. The opportunity cost of producing whisky is lower in the United Kingdom than in the United States. The United Kingdom has a comparative advantage in producing

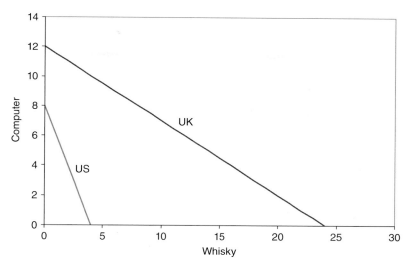

Figure 1.3 Production possibility frontier.

Table 1.2 Consumption and production in autarky.

	Whisky	Computers
United Kingdom	18	3
United States	2	4
World total	20	7

whisky. Again, looking at Table 1.2, one can see that the opportunity cost of producing computers is lower in the United States than in the United Kingdom. This means that the United States has a comparative advantage in producing computers.

With full employment and efficient use of available technologies, production would occur at some point on the PPF. The level at which the economy would produce depends on the consumer demand for goods. Suppose the United Kingdom and the United States do not engage in trade (a situation known in economics as 'autarky'). Producers will produce at a level which consumers demand at prevailing prices. In autarky, this would mean that supply would equal demand. Let us assume that the consumption demand for whisky in the United Kingdom is six units and consumption demand for computers is nine units. This would be the point at which the United Kingdom would produce and would be represented by a point on the PPF. Suppose the demand for whisky in the United States is two units and the demand for computers is four units. Producers in the United States would produce at these levels, and this would be represented as a point on the PPF for the United States. In autarky, the total world output of whisky is eight

Table 1.3 Production with specialisation in the comparative advantage good.

	Whisky	Computers
United Kingdom	24	0
United States	0	8
World total	24	8

Table 1.4 Consumption and production after trade.

	Whisky		Computers	
	Consumption	Production	Consumption*	Production
United Kingdom	20	24	3.5	0
United States	4	0	4.5	8
World total	24	24	8	8

*Assuming that consumption of 0.5 computer is possible.

units and the output of computers is 13 units. Table 1.2 presents the level of output in the United Kingdom and the United States in autarky.

Suppose that the United Kingdom and the United States each specialises in the commodity in which it has comparative advantage. The output levels are represented in Table 1.3.

Table 1.3 indicates that if the United Kingdom and the United States each specialise in a commodity in which it has comparative advantage, world output increases. The countries, however, would not benefit unless trade were permitted. These levels of production were possible even in autarky, but countries were not producing at these levels because both goods were demanded by the residents of these countries. Production would match the consumption within a country if no trade were permitted.

Let us allow for trade. There is a surplus whisky production of four units and surplus computer production of one unit. If we allow this surplus to be split equally between the United Kingdom and the United States, their consumption of goods will be at the levels shown in Table 1.4.

As can be seen from Table 1.4, consumption of goods in both countries has increased with trade rather than autarky. The aforementioned numerical example illustrates that even under circumstances where one country had absolute advantage in production of both the goods, if countries specialised in production of goods in which they had comparative advantage and trade, world output would increase. Both countries would gain from trade.

The aforementioned example demonstrates only one possible outcome of the model. The conclusions presented previously are more likely possibilities rather than generalised results. It is quite possible that, with a different choice of production/consumption points in autarky, world output might not rise for both goods upon specialisation. This would mean that, even after trade, both countries might not gain. Moreover, in the aforementioned example, we assumed a term of trade that generated the conclusion described previously: that both countries benefit from trade. Under a very different assumption regarding terms of trade, the conclusion may be that only one country benefits from trade. Even if the country has more of both goods, the distribution of these may not be uniform across all consumers. Some consumers within a country may benefit, while others may not benefit at all.

These questions could be answered by describing the model more fully, which is beyond the scope of this book (a detailed model is presented in Krugman and Obstfeld, 2000, chapters 2 and 3); however, the conclusions that emerge from generalisation suggest that the proposition that trade is beneficial is 'unqualified'. The benefits from trade for a country could be thought of as an indirect method of production. Instead of producing a good for itself, the country could produce another good and trade with another country for the desired good. Whenever a good is imported, it is true that this indirect production requires less labour than when the good is produced domestically. Trade also enlarges the consumption possibilities of a country.

The Heckscher–Ohlin trade model

The basis for trade in a comparative advantage model is the difference in efficiency in production of goods and services across countries. However, if, say, both countries had the same production efficiency, would trade still be possible? An answer to this question is provided by another important theory called the H–O trade model, proposed by two Swedish economists. The rationale for trade in the H–O model is the difference in resources between countries. The H–O model emphasises the interplay between the proportions in which different factors of production are available in different countries and the proportions in which they are used in producing different goods. We develop the H–O model by using a simple example of two economies which can produce two goods using two factors of production, and we start with an autarky case, that is, these two economies do not trade. This is a convenient starting point, as it will be interesting to see what happens when the assumption regarding no trade is lifted.

Assumptions

In our simple model, there are two countries (England and Portugal) which can produce two goods (cloth and wine). Production of goods requires two inputs (labour measured in hours and land measured in acres). England has

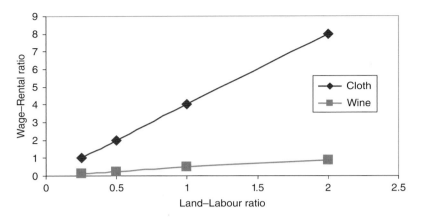

Figure 1.4   Factor prices and input choice in China.

a total labour stock of 500 hours, and Portugal has a total labour stock of 200 hours. England has a land area of 1000 acres and Portugal's land area is 600 acres:

England uses 0.5 acres to produce 1 metre of cloth.
England uses 1 hour to produce 1 metre of cloth.
England uses 2 acres to produce 1 gallon of wine.
England uses 0.5 hours to produce 1 gallon of wine.
Total supply of land in England = 1000 acres.
Total supply of labour in England = 500 hours.

An important point to bear in mind here is the use of word 'uses' instead of 'requires' as in the Ricardian model. The reason for this change in the play of words is that in a two-factor economy, there is a possibility of choice in the use of inputs. For example, English cloth producers may be able to produce more cloth per acre of land by employing more labour. The factor combination choice that producers would make would depend on the relative cost of land and labour. If land rent is high and wages are low, producers use less land and more labour per unit of output. If wages are high and land rents low, they use more land and less labour per unit of output. Assume that the costs in both countries are represented in U.S. dollar terms rather than on their domestic currency basis. Suppose that the wage rate per hour of labour in England is $2 and land rent per acre in England is $4, and the input choices made previously are dependent on the ratio of these two-factor prices. The land rent to wage ratio is 2 (obtained by dividing $4/$2). There is a relation between wage–rental ratio and land–labour ratio, as shown in Figure 1.4. The curve for cloth lies to the left of the curve for wine, indicating that, at any given factor price, production of wine will always use a higher ratio of

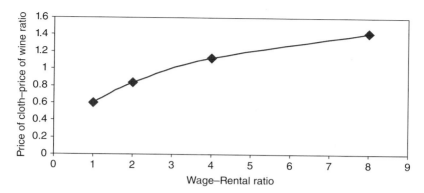

Figure 1.5 Factor prices and goods prices in China.

land than production of cloth. Wine is more land intensive than cloth, and cloth is more labour intensive than wine.

To start with the autarky case, England and Portugal don't engage in trade, and England will produce both commodities. Competition in each sector will ensure that the price of each good equals its cost of production (economic profit is 0 under perfect competition). The cost of production depends on the factor prices. If land rent is higher, production cost of the good that is land intensive will be higher. For a closed economy, if relative factor prices increase, the increase in the price of the commodity intensive in that factor is higher than the increase in the price of the other commodity, which does not use this factor as intensively in its production. There is a direct relationship between wage–rental ratio and price of cloth (P_c)/price of wine (P_w) ratio, shown by the upward-sloping curve in Figure 1.5. It is easy to draw this curve. For each wage–rental ratio, assume that the rents do not change and only the wage rate changes. Calculate wage rate for each level of wage–rental ratio by multiplying the ratio by rent. After calculating wage rate, production cost in each sector can be calculated by multiplying per unit of output by factor prices by respective factor inputs and by adding these factor costs per unit of output together. In a competitive market, production cost would equal price. For each wage–rental level, the ratio P_c/P_w can be obtained by dividing price of cloth by price of wine.

In our example, if the wage rate increased and the level of land rent remained the same, the price of cloth relative to the price of wine would increase more rapidly because cloth production requires more labour per unit of output than wine. The way to see this is to put Figure 1.4 and Figure 1.5 together (see Figure 1.6).

An interesting relation between price of cloth/price of wine, land–labour ratio and wage–rental ratio emerges. If the relative price of cloth were to rise, this would also raise wages relative to land rent, as can be seen from the

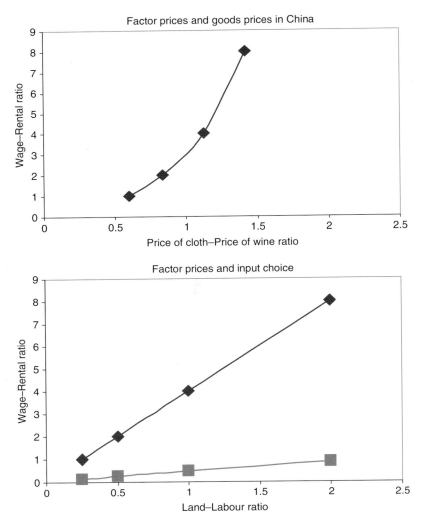

Figure 1.6   Wage–rental ratios.

left figure. A rise in wage–rental ratio would cause an increase in land–labour ratio, and both the sectors would shift their factor use towards land. Another important observation that could be made from the left figure is that an increase in price of cloth/price of wine ratio would lead to an increase in wages far larger than an increase in land rent.

Let us put together the story of two goods and two factors in the economy. Taking the relative price of cloth to wine as given, we can determine the wage–rental ratio which in turn would determine the land–labour ratio in the production of cloth and wine, as discussed earlier. The total factor endowments of labour and land in England are fixed, and we assume that

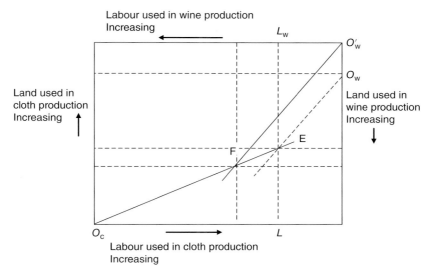

Figure 1.7   Resource allocation for production of two goods for the two countries.
Source: Krugman and Obstfeld (2009) © 2009. Printed and electronically reproduced by permission of Pearson Educational, Inc.

England would employ its supply of labour and land fully. Full employment of factors would determine the factor allocation across sectors.

The factor allocation across sectors could be shown using the box diagram (Figure 1.7).

Figure 1.7 is a convenient representation of allocation of resources across two goods in a two-factor economy. Total labour supply in the economy is plotted as the horizontal axis, and total land supply is plotted as the vertical axis. The resource allocation for wine production is shown with its origin at O_c, and the resource allocation for cloth production is shown with its origin at O_w. The allocation of resources across the two sectors is represented by point E. At this equilibrium allocation, $O_c L_c$ is the labour used in production of cloth, and $O_c R_c$ is the land used in the production of cloth. $O_w L_w$ is the labour used in production of wine and $O_w R_w$ is the land used in production of wine. The total endowment of labour in England is $500 = O_w L_w + O_c L_{c'}$ and the total endowment of land is $1000 = O_w R_w + O_c R_{c'}$. The point E has been determined from Figure 1.7. Given the cloth to wine prices, we can determine the rent to wage ratio in cloth production on the left side of the figure. Projecting rent to wage ratio in cloth production to the right side of the figure gives the land–labour ratio for cloth production. A straight line drawn from $O_{c'}$ in Figure 1.7, with the calculated land–labour ratio for cloth production as slope, is the line on which point E must lie. A similar straight line can be drawn from Ow once the slope of land–labour ratio in wine production is known. E is the point where these two lines intersect.

Suppose the land availability in England increases, holding both good prices and labour supply fixed. The increased supply of land makes the box taller. The origin for production of wine shifts from O_w to O'_w. Again, drawing the land–labour slope line originating at O'_w, one can see that the equilibrium point has shifted from E to F. This has important implications because it suggests that the land and labour use in production of cloth has reduced. It also suggests that land and labour use in production of wine has increased. With increased land supply, the possibility of producing wine increases substantially, and the economy shifts its production to wine production. An economy would tend to be relatively effective at producing goods that are intensive in the factors with which the country is relatively well endowed (Krugman and Obstfeld, 2000, chapter 4).

A similar description of the other two-factor economy, Portugal, can be offered. Suppose residents in England and Portugal have similar tastes and therefore these economies have identical demand for cloth and wine when faced with similar relative price of the two goods. Both these economies have similar technologies for producing wine and cloth. This means that the land–labour ratio to produce one unit of wine or cloth is the same in England and Portugal. The assumptions made previously with regard to England and Portugal suggest that England is labour abundant in comparison to Portugal, because the land–labour ratio in England is 2, while the land–labour ratio in Portugal is 3. Production of cloth is more labour intensive than production of wine. The English PPF relative to Portugal is shifted more in the direction of cloth than in the direction of wine. Other things being equal, England would have a higher ratio of cloth to wine.

With trade, the relative price of cloth in terms of wine would be the same across England and Portugal. Since England and Portugal differ in factor abundances, for any ratio of price of cloth to wine, English production would be skewed towards cloth production. Portugal would specialise in the production of wine.

The H–O model suggests that the reason for trade is factor endowment. A country which is abundant in labour should specialise in production of goods that are labour intensive, and a country which is capital intensive should specialise in production of commodities that are capital intensive. Both these countries would benefit from trade.

The inter-temporal trade model

The exchange of goods and services is one of the ways in which economies trade with each other. The other mode of trade is through the movement of capital. International capital transactions are substantial and take many forms through which economic agents in one country provide productive capital to agents in other countries. The mode of capital transfer is through

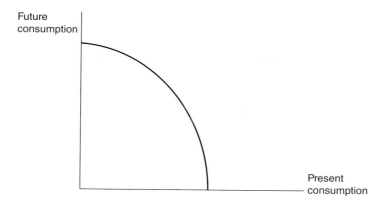

Figure 1.8   Inter-temporal PPF.
Source: Adapted from Krugman and Obstfeld (2000).

financial transactions. For example, economic agents resident in the United Kingdom buy stocks of firms resident in Hong Kong. It is like saying that residents in the United Kingdom provide loans to residents in Hong Kong. Two points that need to be borne in mind in this example are as follows: (i) the loan provided today would not be repaid until the next period, and (ii) UK residents investing in Hong Kong dollars would be repaid in Hong Kong dollars. This means that they would have to exchange their domestic currency, pounds sterling, for Hong Kong dollars, and when they were repaid in the next period in Hong Kong dollars, they would exchange these for pounds sterling and repatriate them to the United Kingdom. Expectations about exchange rate become an important part of international capital transfer decisions. Another example where this is also relevant is the purchase of U.S. government debt by China. If the Chinese currency appreciated (or was revalued), they would receive a lower domestic currency return from their U.S. debt purchases.

International borrowing and lending can be interpreted as a type of international trade – trade of present goods for goods in the future. Consider an economy that produces one good and exists for two periods – the present and the future. The economy faces a trade-off in the production of the consumption good between the present and future periods. The inter-temporal PPF for the economy is shown in Figure 1.8.

The inter-temporal production possibility curves of different countries would differ from each other. For some countries, these would reflect production possibilities that are biased towards present output and for others production possibilities that are biased towards future output. Suppose there are two countries, domestic and foreign, with different inter-temporal PPFs. Domestic's production possibilities are biased towards present output, and foreign's are biased towards future output. In the absence of international borrowing and lending, the relative price of future consumption will be higher in domestic than foreign.

However, with trade, domestic would export present consumption and import future consumption. The price of future consumption to present consumption is a function of real interest rate. Under the assumption that real interest rate is positive, the price of future consumption is lower than the price of present consumption. If trade in capital is permitted, the relative price of future consumption and world interest rate will be determined by the world relative supply and demand of future consumption (Krugman and Obstfeld, 2000, p. 169). A country that has comparative advantage in production of future consumption would have a lower production cost of future consumption. With trade in capital permitted, this country would offer a higher interest rate than the one where the production costs of future consumption are not as low. This would in turn mean that countries who borrow in the international market are those where opportunities exist.

International trade in capital and the role of international capital markets

Capital markets are markets where people, companies and governments with more funds than they need (because they save some of their income) transfer those funds to people, companies or governments who have a shortage of funds (because they spend more than their income). The two major capital markets are for stocks and bonds. Companies issue securities on the capital markets to raise capital for productive uses. Investors (savers – people, companies and governments) with surplus funds (savings) invest in these securities in anticipation of cash flows in the future. Recent developments in financial engineering have led to development and trading of a wide variety of financial and physical capital (assets) including stocks, bonds (government and corporate), bank deposits denominated in different currencies, commodities (such as petroleum, wheat, bauxite, gold), derivatives (forward contracts, futures contracts, swaps, options contracts, etc.), real estate and land, securities and derivatives backed by real estate assets (such as mortgage-backed securities, real estate investment trusts securities) and factories and equipment. The role of capital markets is to promote economic efficiency by channelling money from those who do not have an immediate use for it to those who do. The physical places where stocks, bonds and other derivatives are bought, sold and traded are called stock exchanges. Stock exchanges play a very important role in capital transfer, as they provide the regulation of company listings, a price-forming mechanism, the supervision of trading, the authorisation of members, the settlement of transactions and the publication of trade data and price. Examples of major stock exchanges are the New York Stock Exchange

(NYSE), the National Association of Securities Dealers Automated Quotations (NASDAQ), the London Stock Exchange (LSE), the Tokyo Stock Exchange (TSE), the Hong Kong Stock Exchange, the Singapore Stock Exchange and stock exchanges in many other cities.

International capital markets are a group of markets (in New York, London, Tokyo, Singapore and many other financial cities) that trade different types of financial and physical assets. Though individual country capital markets are regulated by domestic regulatory authorities, there is increasing evidence of capital flows into foreign assets traded on foreign capital markets. During the 1980s and 1990s, it became quite common for multinational companies to seek a listing on several foreign stock exchanges. The reasons for listing on foreign stock exchanges could have been to attract wider investor interests or because local exchanges were small for the ambitions of the company. Multinational companies conduct their operations and businesses in local currency (different from their domestic currency), and, to hedge against currency risk, they often prefer to raise capital from local markets in local currency by listing on local stock exchanges. One of the consequences of these developments has been the expansion in primary issues and secondary market trading in nondomestic equities. Foreign listing requires compliance with foreign accounting and listing regulations. However, companies are willing to bear that risk because of the advantages associated with accessing larger capital markets. German automobile major Daimler–Benz accepted the U.S. accounting rules, stricter than those in Germany, to be able to list on New York.

It may, however, be emphasised here that, though capital markets have become internationalised, there is no one single market. In essence, the international capital market is a number of closely integrated markets which conduct any transaction with an international dimension. Examples of assets traded on international capital markets are foreign exchange, internationally traded stocks and bonds (Eurobonds), American Depository Receipts (ADRs) or Global Depository Receipts (GDRs) issued by public enterprises in developing and transitional economies.

The Dunning eclectic paradigm

Traditional trade models are able to explain international capital flows, but the explanation is only partial. Borrowing and lending, as envisaged in the inter-temporal trade model described earlier, are only one of the ways through which capital movements occur. The World Trade Organization (WTO) recognises two types of capital flows: (i) portfolio investment of the type described in the inter-temporal trade model, where an investor resident in one country invests in stocks, bonds and other financial instruments in the other country, and (ii) FDI, where an investor based in one country acquires assets in the other country with the intention of managing them. FDI involves the transfer of much more than capital alone. Technological expertise, marketing and management skills and other firm-specific resources are transferred to the host country as well. Each country has its own way of defining whether a particular investment should be classified as an FDI or a foreign portfolio investment. When measuring foreign invest- ment flows, UNCTAD defines FDI as investments involving ownerships of more than 10%. Investments of less than 10% are classified as portfolio investments. Portfolio investors, with a small minority holding in the investment, exercise very little, if any, control in the asset and thus are typically passive investors.

Traditional trade theories find it difficult to explain the ways in which FDI finances the production that is undertaken by transnational corporations (TNCs). Traditional trade theorists were less concerned with explanations of the composition of goods and factors actually traded across boundaries than with theorising on what would happen in the real world if certain condi- tions were present. The H–O model, discussed previously, asserted that, provided certain conditions were met, countries would specialise in the production of goods which required relatively large inputs of resources with which they were comparatively well endowed and would export these in exchange for others which required relatively large inputs of factors with which they were comparatively poorly endowed. Among the conditions were that countries had two homogeneous inputs, labour and capital, both of which were locationally immobile. Inputs were converted into outputs by the most efficient and internationally identical technologies. All enterprises were price-takers, and there were no barriers to trade and no transaction costs. International tastes were similar. These assumptions and their impli- cations have been criticised in the literature. Under the conditions of factor immobility, identical technologies and perfect competition, the only possible form of international involvement is through international trade; production by one country's enterprises for a foreign market must be undertaken within the exporting country; and all enterprises have equal access to location- specific endowments.

One of the deductions of the H–O model is that trade will equalise factor prices. Replacing the assumption of factor immobility with that of immobil- ity of goods, it may be shown that movement of factors also responds to resource endowments. This was used to explain the international (portfolio) capital movements in terms of relative prices or differential interest rates. For many years, trade theory and capital theory paralleled each other, but eventually, the two were formally integrated into the factor price equalisa- tion theorem by Samuelson (1948) and Mundell (1957). Simply stated, the theorem says that when the prices of the output goods are equalised between countries as they move to free trade, then the prices of the factors (capital and labour) will also be equalised between countries. This implies that free trade will equalise the wages of workers and the rents earned on capital throughout the world. The theorem derives from the assumptions of the H–O model, the most critical of which is the assumption that the two countries share the same production technology and that markets are perfectly competitive. Over the last four decades, trade models introduced more realism to traditional trade theories in an attempt to explain observed trade flows (Dunning, 2000).

Another important development observed in international capital flows has been growth and composition of FDI or production financed by such investment. Earlier explanations based on either location theory or investment theory did not quite convincingly explain the 'non-trade' nature of involvement of FDI flows. FDI flows have raised the 'non-trade' nature of international engagement of a country alongside trade, which needs to be explained. A country may engage economically with the outside world by letting economic agents (irrespective of their nationality) use resources located within its boundaries to produce goods and services for sale outside its boundaries or may import resources or products based on those resources located in other countries. This has been the view of traditional trade theories. However, when we view the involvement of a country's economic agents in servicing foreign markets with goods and services, irrespective of where resources needed to do this are located or used, and the extent to which its own economic agents are supplied goods by foreign-owned firms, irrespective of where the production is undertaken, explanations based on geographical boundaries become insufficient. A country's economic space is perceived more in terms of the markets exploited by its institutions than its geographical boundaries. Economic involvement of one country's enterprises in another may be for the purposes of supplying both foreign and domestic markets. Production for a particular foreign market may be wholly or partly located in the home country, in the foreign market, in a third country or in a combination of the three. The capability of a home country's enterprise to supply either a foreign or a domestic market from a foreign production base depends on its possessing certain resource endowments not available to, or not utilised by, another country's enterprises. These endowments include both tangible assets (such as natural resources, labour, capital) and intangible assets (such as knowledge, organisation and entrepreneurial skills, access to markets). Such endowments could be purely location specific to the home country; in other words, they have to be used where they are located and are available to all firms, or they could be ownership specific, that is, internal to the enterprise of the home country but capable of being used with other resources in the home country or elsewhere.

For some kinds of trade, it is sufficient for the exporting countries to have a location endowment advantage over the importing country. Trade envisaged by the Ricardian or H–O trade model is of this type. Trade in highly skill-intensive or sophisticated consumer goods is based more on ownership advantages of exporting firms. This, however, presupposes that these advantages are better used in combination with location-specific endowments in the exporting country rather than in the importing (or a third) country. Where, however, location-specific endowments favour the importing (or a third) country, foreign production will replace trade. Foreign production, then, implies that location-specific endowments favour a foreign country, but ownership-specific endowments favour the home country's firms. Advantages associated with ownership-specific endowments are sufficient to overcome the cost of producing in a foreign environment.

John Dunning (1977) proposed an eclectic paradigm to explain international capital flows which take the form of FDI. The focus of the paradigm is to explain why firms choose the FDI route to participate in foreign markets rather than employing seemingly more convenient means of market participation such as strategic alliances, joint ventures or management contracts. Dunning argued that FDI is the most effective vehicle for serving foreign markets when the firm possesses an ordered series of advantages that arise under conditions of imperfect competition.

According to Dunning, to undertake production in foreign markets, the firm must first have some competitive advantages in its home market that are specific to the firm. These advantages arise out of inputs which an enterprise may create for itself – certain types of technology and organisation skills – or can purchase from other institutions, but over which, in doing so, it acquires some proprietary right of use. Such ownership-specific inputs may take the form of legally protected rights (such as patents, brand names, trademarks) or of a commercial monopoly through acquisition of a particular raw material essential to the production of the product or of exclusive control over particular market outlets, or there may be scale advantages. Firms that engage in production at international locations operate in different location-specific environments, from which they may derive additional ownership advantages – such as their ability to engage in international transfer pricing, to shift liquid assets between currency areas to hedge against exchange rate risk and to reduce the impact of institutional risk in a country by operating parallel production capacity in other countries. Although the origin of ownership advantages may be linked to location-specific endowments, their use is not so defined. The ability of enterprises to acquire ownership endowments is clearly not unrelated to the endowment specific to the countries in which they operate and particularly their country of origin. But whatever the significance of the country of origin of such inputs, they are worth separating from those which are location specific, because the enterprise possessing them can exploit them wherever it wishes, usually at a minimal transfer cost.

The possession of ownership advantages determines which firms will supply a particular foreign market, and the pattern of location endowments explains whether the firm will supply the market by exports or by local production. Whatever route the firm chooses, it could (i) supply the foreign market by selling or leasing its ownership advantages to a firm located in a foreign market or (ii) internalise its capital, technology and management skills within itself to produce goods. TNCs internalise the production of goods rather than externalising the use of ownership advantages by engaging in portfolio investment, licensing, management contracts, etc. Dunning (1977) argues that enterprises internalise their ownership endowments to avoid the disadvantages, or capitalise on the imperfections, of one or the other of the two main external mechanisms of resource allocation – the market and the public (government) system of resource allocation. Market imperfections arise wherever negotiation or transaction costs are high or information about a product is not fully available or is costly to acquire. Public intervention in the allocation of resources may also encourage firms to internalise their activities.

Based on this, Dunning proposed three sets of advantages (OLI advantages) that lead enterprises to locate part of their production process in a foreign market. These are:

Ownership (O advantage): A firm's O advantage must be unique to the firm, and it must be possible for those advantages to be transferred abroad. As discussed earlier, O advantages largely take the form of common governance or the possession of intangible assets, such as specific know-how, proprietary technology, patents or brand loyalty, which are exclusive or specific to the firm possessing them. The greater the O advantages of enterprises, the more incentive firms have to exploit those advantages in foreign markets.

Location (L advantage): Location advantages are due to economic differences among countries and may take many forms. The host country may offer such features as low-cost labour, skilled labour, better access to raw materials or a large market. In addition, it may simply offer the opportunity for a firm to make a defensive investment to prevent its competitors from gaining a foothold. In the absence of L advantages such as these, there would be no incentive for the firm to engage in FDI, and foreign markets would be best served entirely by exports.

Internalisation (I advantage): When O and L advantages exist, internalisation advantages allow the firm to minimise transaction costs and other agency costs that would likely occur if the firm were to engage in some other form of market penetration strategy, such as a joint venture or strategic alliance. This would mean that the cost of directly managing and controlling all activities of the enterprise would be less than the cost of operating in any other manner. By direct entry, the cost of monitoring foreign partners, having information filtered through third parties, dealing with foreign financial institutions, etc., would be mitigated. If the firm had the ability to effectively exert control over its value chain, it would be more beneficial to the firm to utilise its I advantages than to enter into leasing, franchising or other types of arrangements.

Porter's model of competitive advantage of nations

The reasons for trade among nations in Ricardo's comparative advantage model or the H–O model are differences in the following factor endowments: land, location, labour, natural resources and local population size. These factor endowments are largely inherited and difficult to influence. Traditional models, though interesting in understanding the rationale for trade, offer a rather passive view of national economic opportunity. Singapore has very little of these factor endowments but is a very important global trade part-ner. Dubai has emerged as a global city without boasting many of the factor endowments necessary for comparative advantage.

Porter (1990) argues that competitiveness of nations and industrial growth can hardly be built on the aforementioned passive factors. According to him, the most important definition of the competitiveness of nations is 'national productivity' (Porter, 1990, p. 6). Porter proposed that the competitiveness of nations depends on four broad attributes (four diamonds) of the national location, namely, factor conditions, demand conditions, related and sup-porting industries and firms and strategy and rivalry.

Porter's factor conditions require that a nation has to have an appropriate supply of factors to be successful. These factors are land, labour and capital, but the interpretation of these is far more specific than suggested by comparative advantage or the H–O model. While interpreting factors, Porter looks at these at highly disaggregated levels. Distinctions are drawn between basic factors, such as climate and unskilled labour, and advanced factors, such as highly skilled labour and infrastructure. Basic factors are not sufficient for competitiveness, and the nation has to create advanced factors. Similarly, there is a distinction between generalised factors and specialised factors. Generalised factors can be deployed in a wide range of industries, while specialised factors are industry specific. Abundance of a factor supply does help in building competitive industry, as in the case of Denmark's success in furniture due to the availability of a pool of trained graduate furniture designers (Porter, 1990, p. 78; Davies and Ellis, 2000). The lack of availability of factors could also prove to be a boon in disguise by creating an environment for innovation if a nation wants to achieve competitiveness. Italy's high cost of capital and energy and shortages of basic raw materials led its steel producers to develop mini steel mill technology, in which Italy is the world leader (Porter, 1990, p. 82; Davies and Ellis, 2000).

Porter offers three demand conditions for a nation's competitiveness. He suggests that a country would be competitive in an industry which is more important at home than anywhere else. An example is Swedish industries, which are highly competitive in high-voltage electricity distribution over long distances. The reason for their competitiveness is their experience in the home market in supplying electricity to distant and remote locations where energy-intensive paper and steel industries are located. The second condition is that demanding home consumers force companies to meet high standards. Americans' desire for convenience led to a fast-food revolution, which has spread to other countries as well (Davies and Ellis, 2000). The third condition is that firms in the home market anticipate the needs of consumers in other countries. Japanese consumers and government forced firms to produce energy-saving products even before energy costs became important (Davies and Ellis, 2000). These three conditions are not necessarily dependent on the size of the domestic market, but force industries to innovate, giving them an edge over others in international competition, though a large domestic market which supported the aforementioned three demand conditions would be highly supportive of international competitiveness.

Porter argues that a nation's industries will be better able to compete in the international market if there are clusters of industries in the home economy, which are linked vertically and horizontally through demand, supply, technology, distribution and consumer networks. California has an IT and ITES cluster, which has helped firms located there become internationally competitive.

The fourth attribute for the competitiveness of nations proposed by Porter is concerned with the strategies and structures of domestic firms and the extent of rivalry between them. If the business environment favours family-run firms, the nation will specialise in industries that do not experience economies of scale, as in Italy. If the executives are dominated by engineers, the nation will have competitive advantage in those sectors that require high-technology content, as in Germany. If the institutional structures for raising capital favour returns in the short term, the nation will be successful in industries which offer short-term returns. In addition to strategies and structures, Porter argues for the importance of rivalry of firms in domestic markets. This is important for innovation and leads to competitiveness internationally.

In addition to these four attributes, two other factors, chance and government, also play a very important role (Davies and Ellis, 2000).

Chance refers to events, such as war, which offer opportunities to firms. Government plays a role through policies. Proactive government policies in Dubai have contributed to the business competitiveness of Dubai in the world market.

Another important feature of Porter's theory is that nations follow an evolutionary path of industrial development, moving from the factor-driven to the investment-driven, to the innovation-driven and finally to the wealth-driven stage. For competitiveness, attributes have to be compatible with the stage of development (Porter, 1990). For prosperity to be reached and sustained, a nation must reach the innovation-driven stage of development (Davies and Ellis, 2000). This implies that comparative advantage in terms of factors is not sufficient for international success; a nation's industries must upgrade through innovation, product differentiation, branding and marketing. However, since Porter's model first appeared, a number of criticisms have also been voiced (see Davies and Ellis, 2000, for review). These authors argue that the suggestion in Porter's model that strong four diamonds at home are necessary conditions for a nation's competitiveness has major drawbacks. This argument was attacked as inappropriate at a time when the world economy has become increasingly globalised and TNCs[1] are becoming increasingly important. Dunning (1993) argues that during the 1990s 'an increasing proportion of the assets of firms in a particular country are either acquired from or are located in, another country'. This in turn questions the importance of strong four diamonds in the home base for the competitiveness of these firms. Porter's model is unable to explain the organisation structure of TNCs that locate their production processes in more than one country. Porter's model suggests that outward FDI[2] is a sign of competitive strength in a nation's industry, while inward FDI indicates that 'the process of competitive up-grading is not entirely healthy' (Davies and Ellis, 2000). Authors such as Lau (1994) argue that capital would flow to locations where it is highly productive, in which case inward FDI is a strength of competitiveness rather than a weakness. English success can largely be attributed to inward FDI (Lin and Song, 1997). England has also used its comparative advantage in labour-oriented sectors for development rather than pursuing the 'upgrading' strategy of Porter (Lin and Song, 1997).

Traditional trade models and Porter's competitive advantage model are insufficient on their own to explain fully the reasons for some of the complex patterns of trade observed in capital and goods, such as FDI and the growth of TNCs. The pursuit of a better explanation has led to another interesting model (better referred to as a paradigm) used in international business literature, referred to as Dunning's eclectic paradigm, to explain the location of FDI and TNCs.

Trading blocs and globalisation

Current patterns of world trade have been influenced by the existence of world (regional) trading blocs such as the EU, NAFTA and ASEAN. Some of these, particularly the EU, have been shown to have trade-creating and trade-diverting impacts (El Agraa 2007) where it encourages intra-member trading but discourages trade with countries outside its boundaries. This is a characteristic of a customs union (having a common external tariff) but is less significant for other less restrictive trading blocs.

Trading blocs also link to the presence of TNCs that have headquarters in, for example, the United States or Japan. These corporations play a significant role in FDI flows with the largest 100 providing 33% of the world stock of FDI of $2 trillion (early 1990s). They also can account for a significant proportion of international trade. For example, they made up over 75% of U.S. international trade by the end of the 1980s.

They have been a major force for world economic integration as they have opened facilities in a greater number of countries, often chasing lower costs of production. Hence, newly industrialising nations have been created as producers have manufacturing out of higher cost economies (these becoming more service orientated). This process can be seen within each trading bloc. Thus, production has moved from the United States to Mexico, from Western to Eastern Europe and from Japan to other countries in East Asia. This development has often occurred in waves, first from Japan to South Korea and Taiwan, then into Malaysia and Thailand and then into China and the Philippines.

As a consequence, more countries have been integrated into global systems of trade and international financial flows. The latter have also grown substantially and faster than trade itself. Its growth has been made possible by the policies of financial deregulation that have been adopted in many countries around the world. Its inception comes from the earlier period after the breakdown of the Bretton Woods system of fixed exchange rates. After the turbulence of the 1970s, the international economy has come to be characterised by deregulation, integration, structural and spatial changes and high capital mobility. There has also been the development of a more competitive finance industry that could be argued has led to excessive lending to the property industry. Overexposure has affected the stability of financial systems. This has been seen in Thailand in the Asian financial crisis where the stability of the banking sector was interlinked with lending to speculative real estate development. More recently, the exposure of a number of banks to real estate has been witnessed in different countries. The scale of these problems has led to a much more cautious lending environment and concerns about asset bases of financial institutions.

Increased capital mobility internationally has also affected asset prices globally and has strengthened the link between property and the macro-economy. Essentially, the volatility of the real estate sector has a larger impact on asset values, and since the financial sector can permit borrowing against such asset values, there are more significant impacts on consumption growth and GDP than there would have been without financial deregulation and ability for leverage.

Conclusions

This chapter has examined the different theories of international trade. Paradoxically, perhaps the increase in trade is often an increase within the trading blocs themselves rather than between them, and most trade of TNCs remains within their home trading blocs. However, dominating trade flows are flows of international finance. Consequent upon deregulation and deliberate policy by different governments, these financial flows make it harder for individual governments to ignore the globalised financial system of pursued policies that this system does not support. It is against this background that new financial products have been developed that aid investment in real estate assets across the globe.

Notes

1 A TNC is an enterprise that controls assets of other entities in economies other than its home economy, usually by owning a certain equity capital stake (usually at least 10% of ordinary shares). A foreign affiliate or direct investment enterprise is an enterprise in which a foreign direct investor, resident in another economy, owns a stake that permits a lasting interest in the management of that enterprise.
2 FDI is an investment involving a long-term relationship and lasting interest in, and control by, a resident entity in one economy in an enterprise resident in another economy. In FDI, the investor exerts significant influence on the management of the enterprise resident in the other economy. The ownership level required for a direct investment to exist is 10% of the voting shares (UNCTAD, 2004).

References

Davies, H. and Ellis, P. (2000) Porter's competitive advantage of nations: time for final judgement? *Journal of Management Studies*, **37** (8), 1189–1213.
Dunning, J.H. (1977) Trade location of economic activity and the multinational enterprise a search for an eclectic paradigm. In: *The International Allocation of Economic Activity* (eds B. Ohlin, P.O. Hesselborn and P.J. Wiskman). Macmillan, London.
Dunning, J.H. (1993) Internationalising Porter's 'diamond'. *Management International Review*, **2**, 7–15.

Dunning, J.H. (2000) The eclectic paradigm as an envelope for economic and business theories of MNE activity. *International Business Review*, **9**, 163–190.

El Agraa, A.M. (2007) *The European Union: Economics and Policies.* Cambridge University Press, Cambridge.

Krugman, P.R. and Obstfeld, M. (2000) *International Economics*, 5th edn. Addison-Wesley/Longman, Reading.

Krugman, P.R. and Obstfeld, M. (2009) *International Economics: Theory and Policy*, 8th edn. Pearson Addison-Wesley, Boston.

Lau, L. (1994) The competitive advantage of Taiwan. *Journal of Far Eastern Business*, **1** (1), 90–112.

Lin, X. and Song, H. (1997) China and the multinationals – a winning combination. *Long Range Planning*, **30** (1), 74–83.

Mundell, R. (1957) International trade and factor mobility. *American Economic Review*, **47** (2), 321–335.

Porter, M.E. (1990) *The Competitive Advantage of Nations.* Macmillan, London.

Ricardo, D. (1817) *On the Principles of Political Economy and Taxation.* John Murray, London.

Samuelson, P.A. (1948, June) International trade and equalization of factor prices. *Economic Journal*, **58**.

UNCTAD (2004) *World Investment Report: The Shift Toward Services.* UN Publication, Geneva.

2

International Real Estate Markets: Evolution

Introduction

In a market economy, market competition ensures efficient allocation of resources (goods, services, capital and labour) among the various users. Market forces of demand and supply interact to determine the market clearing price of the resources and how they are allocated. Property is both a consumption (use) and an investment good. In the market for the use of property, property resources are allocated to various users that can broadly be divided into households and businesses. Users compete for physical location and space, and competition among them determines who gains the use of space and how much they must bid for its use. Capital for investment in property is allocated in the capital markets. Participants in the capital markets invest in stocks, bonds, mutual funds, private business enterprises, mortgage contracts, property and other assets with the expectation of receiving financial returns on their investments. Investment opportunities that yield the highest returns, considering risk, will attract a flow of capital. Property as an asset competes with a diverse set of investment opportunities to attract investment. Government affects property markets in a number of ways through planning, legal, taxation, subsidy and a host of other regulations. The value of the property is determined through the interaction of three functional divisions: the property use market, financial markets and government. Property values determined in this way become a guide to

Real Estate Finance in the New Economy, First Edition. Piyush Tiwari and Michael White.
© 2014 John Wiley & Sons, Ltd. Published 2014 by John Wiley & Sons, Ltd.

property developers. When market values exceed the cost of production of new properties, developers are inclined to build, thereby adding to the supply of space and simultaneously to the supply of investible property assets.

This chapter presents an overview of property market activity in an international context. To simplify the presentation, the market activity is discussed in the context of three property submarkets: (i) use market, (ii) investment market and (iii) development. This chapter also presents an overview of the trends in financing property investment. The description in this chapter relies heavily on data information from various research reports published by real estate service providers such as CBRE (various years), Jones Lang LaSalle (various years), RREEF (various years), PwC (various years) and other sources that are individually referenced.

The discussion of the international context is incomplete without discussing the motivation for internationalisation of property markets. Internationalisation of the use market is closely linked with globalisation of economic activities, evidenced through growth of Transnational Corporations (TNCs) and substantial growth in foreign direct investment (FDI) and trade. All these lead to greater demand for space, and this demand shifts across national boundaries. Globalisation has also led to increased capital mobility for investment across countries. Property, as well as being one of the asset classes, is also a recipient of cross-border investment. Bardhan *et al.* (2008) describe two transmission mechanisms through which globalisation affects property rents and values. They argue that economic openness leads to higher local productivity and output, which increases the demand for non-tradeable goods such as property. Elasticity of supply in property markets is low, which causes rents and values to increase disproportionately. Another argument put forward by these authors is based on the Balassa–Samuelson hypothesis, which states that increasing internationalisation leads to asymmetric increase in productivity of tradeable goods vis-à-vis non-tradeable goods. The impact of higher productivity is that wages in the tradeable sector rise, and assuming that the labour within the economy is mobile between the tradeable and non-tradeable sectors, this raises wages in the entire economy. The relative price of property, a non-tradeable sector, will also rise.

If the markets are opaque, they offer opportunities for excess returns over risk-free rate for investors investing in property. With increasing international financial integration, the opportunity for excess returns will eventually reduce, thereby diminishing arbitrage opportunities, if they exist. Country and currency risk-adjusted returns will equalise across various property markets. Studies have been conducted to explain the forces that drive differences in property returns across countries/regions. Hamelink and Hoesli (2004), in their study on property security returns in 21 countries, find that country, scale and value/growth factors are important in explaining returns. Eichholtz *et al.* (1998), Eichholtz and Huisman (1999), Ling and Naranjo (2002) and Bond *et al.* (2003) find that country-specific variables play an important role in determining differences in property returns across countries.

If country-specific variables are an important determinant of property returns, could diversification benefits, in a mixed- or single-asset portfolio context, be achieved through investing in international property? A number of studies have been conducted on the interrelationship between property markets across national boundaries, particularly from the point of view of examining the international property investment diversification potential. Conover *et al.* (2002) show that foreign property investment provides diversification benefits beyond those obtainable from foreign stocks. Liu and Mei (1998) find that inclusion of international property securities in a portfolio improves risk-adjusted returns, after accounting for currency risk. A similar result was found by Hamelink and Hoesli (2004), who claim that portfolio diversification benefits are created by including property assets in a mixed-asset portfolio. A contrasting view, however, was given by Stevenson (2000), who found that the potential diversification benefits that could arise from investing in property securities are not generally statistically significant.

The research, as presented earlier , is inconclusive at one level but on the other hand raises an important aspect to be explored further – trends in international property investment and investor profile. In addition to market activity, this chapter also presents changing trends in international property investment and investor profile.

Size of property market

Estimating the size of property markets is problematic due to their largely fragmented and private nature. Various researchers have made attempts to estimate the size of the market (see, e.g. ULI and PwC, 2007; Key and Law, 2005; DTZ, 2006/2007). RREEF (2007) estimated that the size of global property market (total[1] stock) was around US$26 trillion in December 2006. Due to data limitations, it is difficult to assess the composition of total stock by property type. RREEF (2008) reports the share of various property types with a caveat. Figure 2.1 presents the estimated size of global property market by property type as of 2007.

In markets for which data exists (in the form of a local index prepared by the Investment Property Databank (IPD)), such as the United States or Europe, the majority of investment-grade property is in retail (30–50%, depending on the country) or offices (35–50%, again a function of country). The share of industrial and other property types is small.

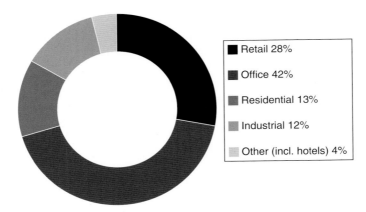

Figure 2.1   Size of global property market by property type, 2007.
Source: ING Real Estate (2008), global vision 2008. Reproduced by permission of CBRE.

Of the total stock of nearly US$26 trillion, nearly US$10 trillion (invested stock) was owned by professional property investors such as funds, property managers, private investment vehicles, listed companies, and institutions. The rest was owner-occupied, termed investible because it may over time become owned by institutions. Most of the invested stock is located in the matured markets of America and Europe. Of the total stock of US$9.5 trillion in America, nearly US$4.7 trillion is already invested (RREEF, 2007). In Europe, US$3.2 trillion worth of stock out of a total of US$9.2 trillion is already invested (RREEF, 2007). Asia has the smallest proportion of the total stock that is invested. Of the total US$5.9 trillion worth of property, only US$1.9 trillion worth of stock is invested. The size of the ten largest property markets is presented in Figure 2.2.

The United States dominates the global invested property market with a share of 48% of the total. Europe and Asia follow the United States, with a share of 33% and 19%, respectively. Within Europe, the Western countries dominate, with the four largest markets of Germany, the United Kingdom, France and Italy representing nearly 70% of the total. In Asia-Pacific, the more mature economies of Japan, Australia, Hong Kong and Singapore account for 80% of the total (RREEF, 2007).

Emerging markets in Europe and Asia have a small, but the fastest growing, share in invested property. Central and Eastern Europe accounts for 5% of the value of the European property stock. In Asia, China and India have grown dramatically in recent years, and their invested stock represents around 10% of the regional total.

Besides the differences in the size of the market, these markets differ in the share taken by different property types. Highly mature markets like the United States, the United Kingdom and Australia have a high share of retail

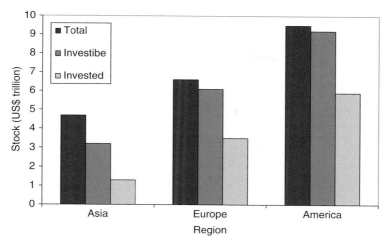

Figure 2.2 Region-wise size of real estate markets (as of December 2006).
Source: RREEF (2007), the future size of the global real estate market. Reproduced by permission of RREEF.

property space, reflecting the maturity and concentration of retail industry in these countries. RREEF (2007) estimates that nearly 56% of invested stock in Australia by the end of 2006 was in retail. The share of retail in total invested stock in the United Kingdom and the United States was around 47% and 20%, respectively, by the end of 2006.

In the mature economies of Western Europe (e.g. Germany, France and Scandinavian countries) and Asia (e.g. Japan), office markets tend to dominate the invested market. This reflects the importance of the service economy in these countries and the relative immaturity of retail and logistics markets. Emerging economies, on the other hand, display a relatively high share of retail and logistics in their total invested stock (though the overall level of stock is very small), reflecting the export orientation- and manufacturing-dominated economic structure.

User market

The user market for commercial property mirrors the economic picture of the city. Evidence of property use market activity can be seen from indicators such as rental levels, the market's position on rental cycles and vacancy levels. As discussed earlier, most of the investment-grade commercial property stock is located in matured economies. The emerging markets' share is fairly small but is becoming increasingly important as rapid economic growth is driving demand for space from domestic and international users.

For users in the property market, space is cost. The position of a property market on a rental cycle vis-à-vis other markets reflects both the opportunity and the challenges for users. Businesses evaluate the cost of space in their decision to locate offices.

Rental evidence as of May 2008 for key office markets is presented in Table 2.1.

Some interesting observations can be drawn from the aforementioned table:

(1) It is obvious that the rents (occupancy cost) differ substantially across different markets. However, the more important message that comes out of the table is that it is not necessarily the matured markets that are expensive. Neither are they located in the same geographical region. Among the top five most expensive markets, three are in Asia and two in Europe. From the standpoint of market maturity, Moscow and Mumbai are classified as emerging, while Tokyo is mature and London is a highly mature market (JLL, 2008).

(2) Another point to note from the aforementioned table is the growth in rents. Markets like Moscow, Ho Chi Minh City and Singapore have seen a change in rental to the extent of around 100% over May 2007. Markets in the United Kingdom have seen rental growth in single digits, and rents in London City have in fact declined over the last year.

(3) The third point that emerges from the aforementioned table is the differences in lease term and rent-free period across markets. Lease terms vary from 25 years in Dublin to 2 years in Ho Chi Minh City. A general observation that could be made is that matured markets usually have longer leases, with the exception of Singapore in Table 4.1, which is a matured market but has a lease term of 3 years. Rent-free period depends on the market conditions. In a weak market, landlords offer incentives in the form of rent-free periods, and in a strong market, precisely the reverse would happen.

It is also important to note that the currency units for rental values presented in the aforementioned table are in US$. Rents are paid in the local market in local currencies. Though it is convenient to show rents in US$ here, growth rates in local currency would be very different from the growth rates in US$ terms.

The differences across markets are further compounded when one makes comparisons across various property types. As an example, in many markets, the lease terms for retail and office markets differ substantially (Table 2.2). Lease terms for retail and industrial properties are usually longer than for office property.

Table 2.1   Rents and vacancy levels in key office markets.

Market	Rent (US$/ SF/annum)	% change over 12 months	Typical lease term (years)	Typical rent-free period (months)
London (West End), UK	299.54	24.2	10–15	9
Moscow, Russia	232.37	92.7	7	6
Tokyo (inner city), Japan	220.25	35.9	5	1
Mumbai, India	210.97	52.4	3+3+3	1
Tokyo (outer central), Japan	175.35	22.2	5	1
London (city), UK	164.18	−0.9	10	15–18
New Delhi, India	145.16	24.9	3+3+3	1
Paris, France	141.98	27.1	3/6/9	3–6
Singapore	139.31	105	3	1
Dubai, UAE	128.49	43.4	3–5	1
Hong Kong	126.79	30.4	3 or 6	2–3
Dublin, Ireland	126.60	18.9	25	3
New York, Midtown, US	103.43	22.7		
Paris La Defense, France	103.20	39.3	3/6/9	3–6
Birmingham, UK	100.38	15.0	10	15
Oslo, Norway	97.30	89.3	5–10	0
Madrid, Spain	96.64	23.3	3–5	1–2
Zurich, Switzerland	92.99	37.3	5+5	1–3
Luxembourg	92.78	34.6	3/6/9	12
Edinburgh, UK	92.43	4.2	10	12
Manchester, UK	87.46	2.5	10	12
Stockholm, Sweden	86.69	38.3	3–5	2–3
Ho Chi Minh City, Vietnam	85.84	94.4	2	1
Milan, Italy	85.41	25.3	6+6	6
Abu Dhabi, UAE	84.14	10.3	3+	1
Frankfurt am Main, Germany	82.63	35.9	5+5	3–5
Bristol, UK	81.49	18.7	10	12
Glasgow, UK	80.50	2.6	10	12
Geneva, Switzerland	78.43	32.1	5	0–3
Warsaw, Poland	76.55	57.4	3–5	1–6
Leeds, UK	76.53	2.7	10/15	18
Rio de Janeiro, Brazil	74.60	35.6	5	1–2
Athens, Greece	73.79	40.0	12	0–2
Aberdeen, UK	72.55	7.2	10+5	9
Sao Paulo, Brazil	71.41	44.0	5	3
Seoul, South Korea	71.40	−0.4	2–3	1–2
Rome, Italy	71.18	41.3	6+6	6
Sydney (core), Australia	68.52	13.9	8	9.9
Shanghai (Pudong) China	68.45	25.5	2–3	1–2
Munich, Germany	67.55	22.9	5+5	3–6
Perth, Australia	66.58	48.9	5	0.0
Calgary, Canada	66.27	19.5		
Brussels, Belgium	64.77	16.2	3/6/9	12
Liverpool, UK	64.60	31.8	5/10	15
Barcelona, Spain	64.43	30.0	3+2	2
Brisbane, Australia	63.32	35.2	5	1.0
Toronto, Canada	62.44	19.5		
Los Angeles, USA	62.06	18.6		
Jersey, UK	61.46	1.4	15	18
Shanghai (Puxi), China	61.26	25.0	2–3	1–2

Source: Reproduced by permission of CBRE Research, including CBRE (2008).

Table 2.2   Typical lease lengths of European retail and office properties.

	Retail (years)	Office (years)
Netherlands	5	5–10
Belgium	9	3–9
France	9–12	6–12
Germany	10	5–10
Spain	10–15	3–5
UK	10–15	10–15
Sweden	3–5	3–5

Source: Reproduced by permission of CBRE and ING Real Estate (2008), global retail markets.

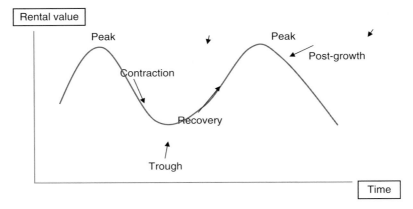

Figure 2.3   Property market rental cycle.
Source: Authors' own stylised graph.

At a given point in time, different markets face different conditions regarding rental growth. Property consultants depict the position of a market using a diagrammatic representation (such as the property clock by JLL and the property cycle by RREEF) of the markets with an indicative position of the market at a particular point in time. Though these diagrams do not indicate either the level of growth in rental values or the peak and amplitude of the property cycle, these are useful ways of presenting the direction in which future rents are expected to move. Figure 2.3 is the representation of a property cycle. In the recovery phase vacancy rates fall and rents initially stabilise and then begin to rise. The growth phase is characterised by low and declining vacancy rates and rising rents that support construction of new space. The post-growth phase is characterised by low but increasing vacancy rates and rising to flattening rents. The contraction phase witnesses high or increasing vacancy levels and declining rents.

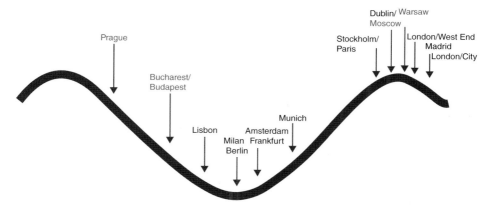

Figure 2.4   European office rental cycle (October 2007).
Source: RREEF (2007), RREEF global real estate insights 2007, October 2007.
Reproduced by permission of RREEF.
Note: Cites marked in grey represent the Central and Eastern European markets.

The retail market also has cycles (the underlying driver of retails is consumer demand, which is affected by the economy), but these are not as pronounced as the office market cycles.

The position of various European markets on the office market cycle as of October 2007 is presented in Figure 2.4.

Figure 2.4 illustrates the office market conditions that these cities are facing. For example, the rents in Milan (Italy) and Berlin (Germany) had bottomed out, and rents in these markets would be expected to start recovering. Budapest (Hungary) and Lisbon (Portugal) were still witnessing declining rents. Warsaw (Poland), Moscow (Russia), Dublin (Ireland), Stockholm (Sweden) and Paris (France) had reached/almost reached the peak on rental cycle. Rents in London (United Kingdom) and Madrid (Spain) had started to decline. Using data for any point in time, this graph can be used to provide a snapshot of the positions of different locations in relation to each other and in relation to their position in the stylised rental cycle. It should not be taken to imply that the amplitude of fluctuation is the same in each city nor that each phase of the cycle is identical in duration.

Figure 2.5 presents a rental cycle for industrial property in Europe. An important observation that could be made here is that the positions on the property cycle for different asset types do not necessarily coincide. For example, the office market in Munich is in the recovery phase, but the industrial property market is in the post-growth stage. Even though the main driver for all property types is growth in the economy, market micro-structures (such as supply conditions, economic competition from other markets and economic structural changes) also play an important role.

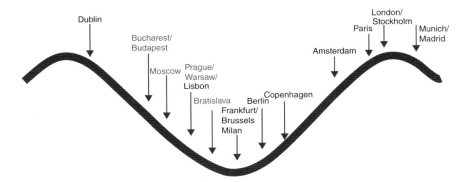

Figure 2.5   European industrial property rental cycle (October 2007).
Source: RREEF (2007), RREEF global real estate insights 2007, October 2007.
Reproduced by permission of RREEF.
Note: Cities marked in grey represent the Central and Eastern European markets.

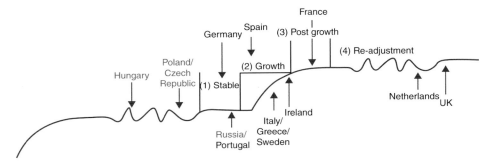

Figure 2.6   European retail property rental cycle (October 2007).
Source: RREEF (2007), RREEF global real estate insights 2007, October.
Reproduced by permission of RREEF.
Note: Cities marked in grey represent the Central and Eastern European markets.

The European retail property cycle as of October 2007 is presented in Figure 2.6. The position of a market in the retail rental cycle is a function of economy and market microstructure. According to RREEF (2007), Western Europe witnessed strong economic growth during the first half of 2007, which led to good performance from European shopping centre markets. Strong retailer demand and lack of good-quality shopping centre space had created a positive rental environment for retail, with some exceptions, most particularly in the United Kingdom and the Netherlands. The UK retail market had been experiencing rising interest rates, falling house prices, weakening consumer spending and an increase in new supply. Slowing rental growth reflected these conditions. The retail market in the Netherlands had been wavering between readjustment and stability due to an ample amount of new supply and retail price deflation. Greece, Spain, Sweden and Ireland were at an attractive stage of their growth cycles. Ireland and Spain

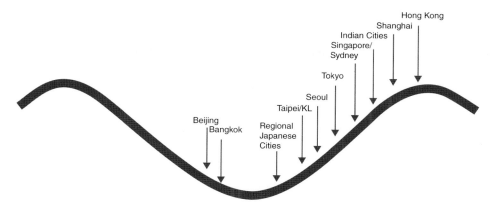

Figure 2.7   Asian office property rental cycle (October 2007).
Source: RREEF (2007), RREEF global real estate insights 2007, October.
Reproduced by permission of RREEF.

were benefiting from rapidly expanding economies in recent years. Retail property rents benefited from rapid expansion of foreign retailers. A shortage of good quality of supply in France and the improving economic outlook in Germany boosted the retail market performance in both countries.

European rental cycles differ in amplitude and timing from those of Asia-Pacific. Rental cycles have been quite pronounced in the cities of Asia-Pacific, where economic conditions have changed quite dramatically in the past. During the financial crisis of 1997, many of the Asia-Pacific economies suffered. Following 1997, rents in the office market had declined to around a third by 1999 in the CBD of Beijing. By 1999, Hong Kong had also seen a fall in office property rents to a third of its 1995 peak rent levels. Though rental levels have recovered since then, they have not reached the peak levels that were witnessed during the first half of the 1990s. Office property rental levels in Tokyo (Japan) remained subdued since 1996. Rents in Tokyo started to increase after 2004 in response to the recovery in the Japanese economy. Rents in the Singapore office market softened after the 1997 financial crisis. However, the market started to recover by the end of 1999. By 2001, rents had increased by nearly 20% from their levels in 1999. The cycle was repeated with the SARS outbreak, which affected Singaporean economy quite badly, and rents fell sharply. The rental cycle for the office market in Asia-Pacific is shown in Figure 2.7. Asian office markets have experienced a strong growth cycle. The economic fundamentals are strong, as Asian economies have been growing rapidly, and this is attracting external capital into property in this region. There is also a huge pipeline of new supply in markets such as Australia, India, Singapore and Hong Kong, which should soften the rental values in the near future. Beijing (China) and Bangkok (Thailand) are in the contraction phase.

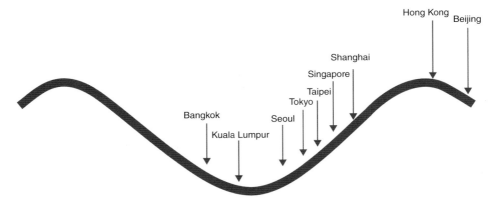

Figure 2.8   Retail property rental cycle in Asia-Pacific (October 2007).
Source: RREEF (2007), RREEF global real estate insights 2007, October.
Reproduced by permission of RREEF.

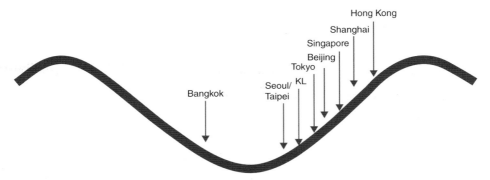

Figure 2.9   Asia-Pacific industrial property rental cycle.
Source: RREEF (2007), RREEF Global real estate insights 2007, October.
Reproduced by permission of RREEF.

Economic growth and rising level of affluence are driving retail demand in Asia-Pacific. This is reflected in the retail rental cycle (Figure 2.8). Most markets, except Bangkok (Thailand) and Kuala Lumpur (Malaysia), are in the growth phase of the cycle.

Figure 2.9 presents an industrial property rental cycle in Asia-Pacific. The economic structure of the region is manufacturing based and export oriented. There is a shortage of good-quality industrial property, as this sector is in its stage of emergence in most parts of the Asia-Pacific region.

Investment market

In recent years, property investment activity has increased substantially (Figure 2.10). During 2007, capital flow in global property markets amounted to US$795 billion (RREEF, 2008). However, a large proportion of this activity

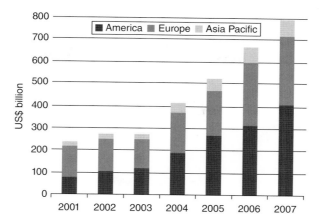

Figure 2.10 Property investment market activity.
Source: RREEF (2008), global real estate investment and performance 2007 and 2008.
Reproduced by permission of RREEF.

is concentrated in the United States (around half) and Europe (around a third). The size of the property investment market in Asia-Pacific is small but increasing in importance, particularly in the listed property investment market, where Asia-Pacific leads the way. Nearly 15% of the Asia-Pacific investment market is in listed securities compared with the global average of 9%.

The United States and Continental Europe have had a long tradition of property investment, with highly developed direct and indirect property markets. The diversity of investors includes institutional investors, private national buyers and foreign investors. The active investment market in Asia-Pacific only emerged from the mid-1980s (Walker and Flanagan, 1991). A large part of the real assets in Asia-Pacific is owner-occupied, but the direct property investment market is growing rapidly. This region has witnessed far more activity in listed property investment market than the United States or Europe since the 1980s. In the earlier phase, the listed securities market was dominated by real estate developers. The property market collapse in many Asia-Pacific countries during the Asian financial crisis of 1997, and the dominance of developers, made the listed property market volatile. However, since 2002, Japan, Singapore and several other countries introduced Real Estate Investment Trusts (REITs), which has helped in stabilising the listed securities market.

Property investment activity has become global, and the share of cross-border investment has increased more than fourfold since 2001 (Figure 2.11), amounting to nearly 28% of the total investment. Europe witnesses a large share of cross-border investment activity within the European Union (EU) countries. The share of cross-border investment activity is also increasing in the United States and Asia-Pacific. In 2007, the share of cross-border investment in the United States was 21% and in Asia-Pacific 12%.

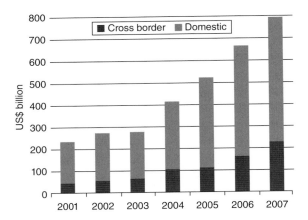

Figure 2.11   Property investment by origin.
Source: RREEF (2008), global real estate investment and performance 2007 and 2008.
Reproduced by permission of RREEF.

Investment behaviour has changed substantially over the last 10 years.
Literature has long argued that in a mixed-asset portfolio context, it is possible
to diversify risk by investing in international real assets because individual
country returns are less than perfectly correlated (Hoesli and MacGregor,
2000). However, studies such as Geurts and Jaffe (1996) did not find much
evidence of international diversification, and they attributed the lack of
international diversification to investors' home asset bias. Investors
understand their home market well but face formal and informal barriers
when they invest abroad. These barriers in turn discourage cross-border
investment. In recent years, due to globalisation of economic activities,
convergence of political and economic structures (e.g. due to the enlargement
of the EU), convergence in property market practices and increased market
transparency, cross-border activity has increased. Capital from the United
States and the United Kingdom was at the forefront of cross-border investment
in 2007 (RREEF, 2008), amounting to nearly 40% of total global cross-border
investment. With better understanding, increased confidence and development
of diverse property investment products across the globe, a large proportion of
investment has become cross-continental (Table 2.3). The destination of
capital flows depends on investors' risk and return preferences. While a large
proportion of the American capital has flown into emerging markets, the UK
capital has been largely concentrated on mature markets in Asia and Europe.

Overall, the performance of property markets had been quite robust until the
first half of 2007, though there had been variations across different markets.
Huge capital inflows in property have led to declining cap rates (Figure 2.12),
and the trend in movement of cap rates in all regions has been southwards.

There have been variations at the individual market level, as shown in
Figure 2.13; some markets, like Seoul (South Korea), have seen far greater

Table 2.3   Cross-continental investment activity 2007, US$ billion.

Sources of capital	Destination of activity		
	America	**Europe**	**Asia-Pacific**
America		46.1	12.6
Europe	21.0		1.3
Asia-Pacific	14.0	7.7	
Total cross-continent	35.0	53.9	13.9
Total cross-border	48.1	150.5	25.8
Total transaction	410.0	307.5	75.6

Source: RREEF (2008), global real estate investment and performance 2007 and 2008.

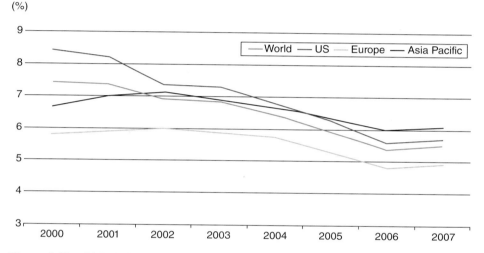

Figure 2.12   Global office cap rate trends.
Source: RREEF (2008), global real estate investment and performance 2007 and 2008.
Reproduced by permission of RREEF.
Note: Aggregate weighted average performance based on 24 global markets – 10 in the United States, 10 in Europe and 4 in Asia-Pacific.

compression than other markets (like Tokyo, Japan) located in the same region. Cap rates in Hong Kong have in fact moved outwards.

Property investment has delivered better returns than other asset classes, with far lower volatility over the last 10 years in all markets (Table 2.4).

Property securities have outperformed direct real estate returns. Caution must, however, be exercised in interpreting these numbers, as the averages conceal marked variations over time and from market to market. Japan, for example, has seen negative performance in the late 1990s (RREEF, 2007).

Region-wise direct property returns are shown in Figure 2.14. The total property return during 2005 and 2006 was around 16–17%, though this level of return is unlikely to be achieved during 2007 and 2008.

Total return has two components: income returns and growth in values. During recent years, the share of value growth in total returns has increased

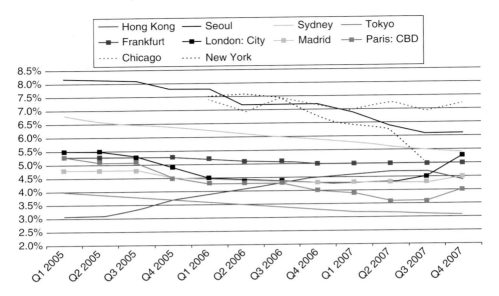

Figure 2.13   Cap rate movement across major office markets.
Source: RREEF (2008), global real estate investment and performance 2007 and 2008.
Reproduced by permission of RREEF.

Table 2.4   Risk and return for various asset classes.

	Direct property	Equities	Property securities	Bonds
Europe				
Return	9.5%	10.1%	19.0%	5.9%
Risk	1.8%	21.4%	16.7%	4.7%
Return/risk	5.3	0.5	1.1	1.3
North America				
Return	12.7%	8.3%	14.9%	6.1%
Risk	4.3%	20.1%	19.0%	5.3%
Return/risk	3.0	0.4	0.8	1.2
Asia-Pacific				
Return	4.3%	3.8%	12.7%	
Risk	8.6%	24.0%	21.8%	
Return/risk	0.49	0.16	0.58	

Source: Reproduced by permission of CBRE and RREEF (2007), global real estate insights 2007.
Note: Europe: All property total returns is a weighted average of Germany, France, Spain, Ireland,
Italy, the Netherlands and the United Kingdom.
North America: All property total returns is a weighted average of Canada and the United States.
Asia-Pacific: All property total returns is a weighted average of Australia, South Korea, China,
Japan, Singapore, New Zealand and Hong Kong.

substantially, as evidenced by the cap rate compression in Figure 2.10. Value
growth in the United States, France, Spain and Sweden has averaged 60% of
returns. High share of value growth in total returns has increased investment risk and has shifted the risk towards the end of the holding period.

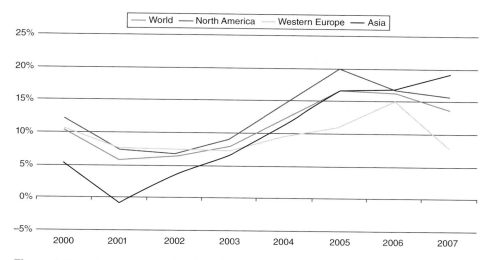

Figure 2.14 Direct all property total returns.
Source: RREEF (2008), global real estate investment and performance 2007 and 2008.
Reproduced by permission of RREEF.

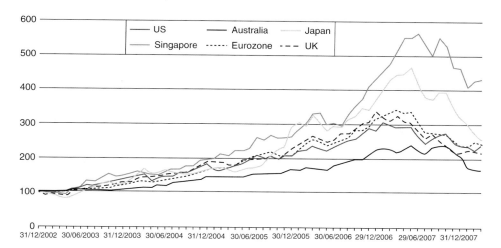

Figure 2.15 Property security returns across major markets.
Source: RREEF (2008), global real estate investment and performance 2007 and 2008.
Reproduced by permission of RREEF.
Note: Real estate securities returns indexed to end 2002 = 100 in local currencies.

Indirect public and private property investment markets have developed and grown substantially around the world. As demonstrated by Figure 2.13, until the first half of 2007, property security returns across major markets were phenomenal. During the latter half of 2007, capital flows in property declined due to the credit crunch, leading to a decline in property security returns. An interesting observation from Figure 2.15 is the simultaneity of the movement of property returns across various markets located in Asia, Europe and America.

Investor profile

Nearly 93% of global commercial property is privately owned, though there are some regional differences – for example, Hong Kong and Australia have 10–12% public ownership. A number of public and private investment vehicles have emerged that have facilitated investment in property. There are differences between public and private vehicles for investment in property. Public vehicles have the advantage of being highly liquid, diversifiable and gearable and have limited liability. There are disadvantages as well; since they are traded on stock markets, they tend to have high correlation with equity markets. Usually, the cost of valuation of publicly traded property is high. Private vehicles offer higher leverage and have limited liability for investors and potential for stock market diversification. Their disadvantage is that they are less liquid.

During the last two decades, public vehicles have gained popularity because of their liquidity. These vehicles have provided mechanisms for institutions and individuals to get exposure to property quickly and in a cost-effective way. Some investors, such as institutional investors, prefer continuous pricing of their assets, and public vehicles provide that feature as they are traded on stock markets.

One of the reasons for the strong performance of property from 2001 until recently has been due to phenomenal investor interest in this asset class from a range of investors including pension funds, REITs, leveraged buyers and retail investors (RREEF, 2008). Property as an asset has become an important component of a mixed-asset portfolio for both individual and institutional investors. Figure 2.16 presents the current and target allocation of investment to property by pension funds in select countries.

In most countries, the allocation of funds by pension funds for property is expected to grow. Substantial growth is expected in countries like Japan, where investors are seeking to allocate as much as 8% to property.

In addition to institutional investors, two other groups of investors that have been active in the property investment market are Sovereign Wealth Funds (SWFs) and equity-rich individuals (high net worth individuals (HNWIs)). SWFs control huge sums of capital and at the moment have low or no allocation to property. However, as reported by RREEF (2008), this is changing, and there is a significant potential for a share of these funds to be invested in property. HNWIs comprise a diverse group – retail-driven investors in German open-end funds and Australian wholesale funds, HNWIs from the Middle East, Asia and Eastern Europe. As indicated by Figure 2.17,

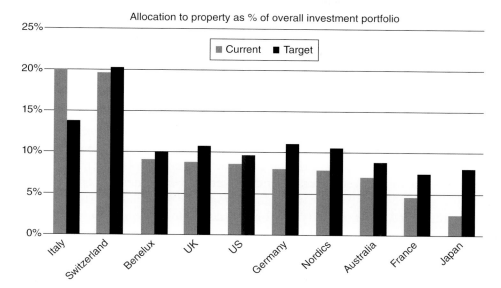

Figure 2.16   Pension funds allocation for property asset.
Source: RREEF (2008), global real estate investment and performance 2007 and 2008.
Reproduced by permission of RREEF.

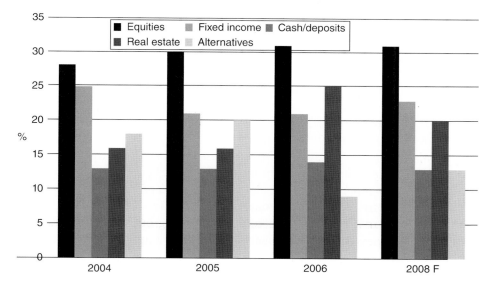

Figure 2.17   Middle Eastern HNWIs asset allocation 2004–2008.
Source: RREEF (2008), global real estate investment and performance 2007 and 2008.
Reproduced by permission of RREEF.

their allocation for property (an example of asset allocation of Middle Eastern HNWIs) has been increasing.

With the increasing diversity of investors interested in property, the profile of investors has also changed. The change in profile, however, differs from market to market and is a function of local conditions. The New York office market has witnessed an increase in the share of private investors in 2005 compared with 2001. The increased share of private investors has been due to repricing of risk by investors following September 2001, which led to an increase in the share of local buyers, and national buyers such as institutional investors moved to other locations. The London office market has witnessed a substantial increase in the share of investment in office stock by foreign investors. American, Irish, German and Middle Eastern investors have increased their activity in this market. Hong Kong office stock is largely under public ownership. However, the trend indicates that the share of REITs and foreign investor ownership is increasing.

Development

Development activity is triggered by current and expected use and investment market activities. The prevailing regulatory and planning regime, the availability of construction finance and other resources constrain development activity.

It is often difficult to obtain information on completions from published sources. While availability of information on other property market indicators, such as rental growth, total return and yields, has become easier as real estate service providers and property data agencies like IPD have started to compile them and publish them, development pipeline and completions for various markets are still not reported for easy access as are other indicators. It is also important to note the cyclical nature of development activity. Barras (1994) presents a conceptual model for building cycles. He argues that building booms and busts are generated by the interaction of the business cycle, the credit cycle and the long cycle of development in the property market. Figure 2.18 presents the evolution of shopping centre stock in five matured property markets.

The five countries covered in Figure 2.18 house over 3000 shopping centres with a gross lettable area of 64 million square metres (62% of all shopping centres in Europe). As discussed earlier, the economy is also a driver for shopping centres, but rental cycles are not as pronounced as for office or logistic property. As shown in Table 2.2, retail leases are either longer than or similar to office leases. Moreover, shopping centres are less volatile than other commercial property sectors (Figure 2.19). These factors have led to significant interest in retail sectors from investors and developers. Planning restrictions have influenced the supply of new shopping centres in the last decade in the United Kingdom and France. In these countries, out-of-town

Precentage of total stock

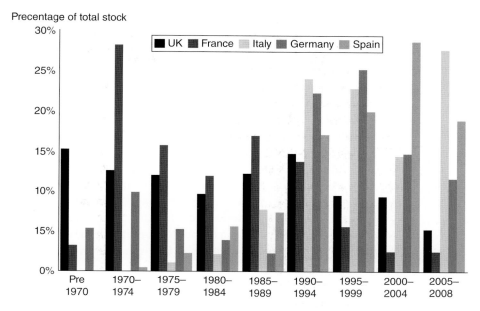

Figure 2.18 New shopping centre completions as percentage of total stock.
Source: JLL (2008), the big five: shopping centre investment in core Western Europe.
Reproduced by permission of Jones Lang LaSalle.

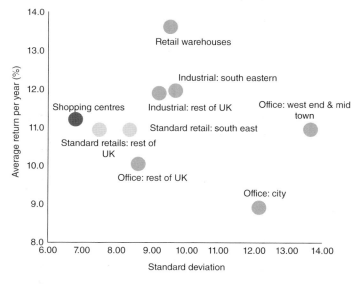

Figure 2.19 Risk and return for commercial property sectors in the United Kingdom
(1981–2007).
Source: JLL (2008), the big five: shopping centre investment in core Western Europe.
Reproduced by permission of Jones Lang LaSalle.

centres were restricted in order to regenerate town centre retailing through extensions or redevelopments. Barcelona in Spain has imposed a moratorium on new shopping centre development. Despite these measures, new stock has continued to increase.

The specialist nature of the retail sector has led to the appearance of sector specialists, though generic investors and institutions are also actively involved. The ownership structure differs from country to country. While the UK market has seen a diverse range of owners (mainly REITs), France, Italy and Spain have seen a large proportion of retail assets owned by sector specialists.

An important trend in the development sector has been the internationalisation of property developers. There are a number of property developers who have entered foreign markets. Hong Kong Land has developed properties in Singapore, Thailand, Macau, Indonesia and Vietnam as well as its home market of Hong Kong. British Land has undertaken major development projects in Spain, though their main focus is the UK market. The American developer Hines has expanded far beyond the U.S. market to China, Spain, Germany, Brazil, etc. Another developer, Goodman, has developed properties in Europe and Asia-Pacific. Globalisation and market integration have opened opportunities beyond the home market. The demand for high-specification buildings has also led developers with domain knowledge to export to other markets. Saturation and competition in the domestic market also push developers overseas.

Financing of property

Globally, the institutional property industry has been transformed substantially over the last five decades. The changing needs of capital users and providers, regulatory shifts, advances in financial engineering and risk management methodologies and new opportunities created by cyclical and secular changes have led to a wide array of investment vehicles and strategies (Conner and Liang, 2003). Institutional investment in property started with mortgages and direct property and then gradually expanded into public securities (like REITs and shares of listed companies) and opportunistic and value-added investments (Conner and Liang, 2003). Developments in risk management tools and the sustained performance of property markets have attracted institutional investors to private equity investments in real estate companies.

There are four sources of capital for commercial real estate. These are private equity, private debt, public equity and public debt. Whole mortgages are private mortgage investments (debt) typically provided by banks and financial institutions to property developers or investors in real estate. Mortgages are nonrecourse loans which stay on the balance sheet of lenders for the full term or until repayment. A number of structured debt instruments have been developed which provide depth to simple mortgages and exploit the risk–return

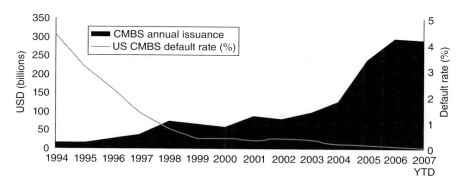

Figure 2.20 Global CMBS issuance and default rate.
Source: ING Real Estate (2008), global vision. Reproduced by permission of CBRE.

characteristics of property investments. Structured debt investments, such as commercial mortgage-backed securities (CMBS), synthetic mortgages and hybrid vehicles, are categorised under public and private markets. Innovation in risk measurement, which has allowed structuring of investments according to risk–return profile, has permitted the structured debt market to create fundamentally different instruments that appeal to different investors. Public securities include REITs, stocks of listed property companies, and, in select international markets, publicly listed property unit trusts. Traditionally, private equity in real estate used to be direct investment in properties. Private equity as mentioned in Figure 2.22 has the traditional meaning. This definition, however, is different from private equity investment outside the real estate industry, where private equity means entity-level investment. Later in this chapter, private equity refers to this definition and private equity means entity-level investments in real estate companies.

Private debt accounted for $4.25 trillion in 2005, private equity $450 billion. Public debt accounted for $254 billion in 2007. . The global trend indicates that though private debt is the major source of investment in property, the public capital markets also contribute nearly US$1 trillion. Private equity has emerged as an important source of capital for property investment. The scope of private equity that has been raised during the last 2–3 years goes beyond the traditional definition of private equity and includes various forms of capital markets arbitrage between different segments (public, private, equity, debt) of the property's capital base.

Public sources of capital (debt and equity) have also become an important source of finance for property investment. The public debt market, comprising corporate bonds and CMBS, is an important source of capital. Figure 2.20 presents the volume of global CMBS issuance. From nearly no CMBS issuance during the early 1990s, the volume of global CMBS issuance had grown to US$254 billion during January–November 2007. Of this total volume, nearly 75% is attributable to the United States. Other markets, though small, are

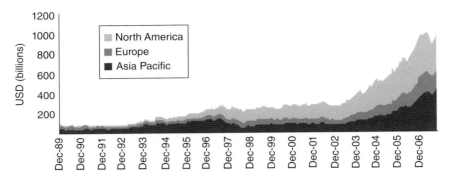

Figure 2.21   Market capitalisation of listed property globally.
Source: ING Real Estate (2008), global vision. Reproduced by permission of CBRE.

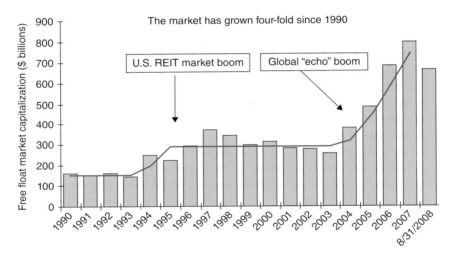

Figure 2.22   Global REITs market capitalisation.
Source: CBRE research, including CBRE (2008). Reproduced by permission of CBRE.

becoming increasingly important. According to ING Real Estate (2008), during the 12 months to November 2007, US$30.8 billion of collateral based in the United Kingdom and another US$47.6 billion in Continental Europe had been securitised through CMBS, while Japan (US$7.8 billion), Canada (US$4.1 billion) and Australia (US$2.6 billion) were the other significant CMBS markets. The default rate on CMBS has been low (Figure 2.20), and this has contributed to the growth of the market for these securities.

Public equity has emerged as an important source of finance for property investment, and the market for listed property has grown substantially since the early 1990s (Figure 2.21), as an increasing number of countries are adopting REITs or REIT-like structures. By December 2006, the market capitalisation of listed property stood at around US$1 trillion, of which REITs accounted for nearly 70% (Figure 2.22).

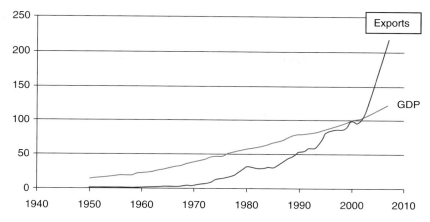

Figure 2.23 World merchandise exports and GDP (in value terms). *Source*: World Trade Data.

International real estate activity and trade models

Explaining international real estate activity is complex and requires explanation at the subsector level (use, investment and development). Real estate space is a local input in the production and supply of goods and services. Demand drivers in the user market are national and international, but the supply drivers are largely local, though the national allegiance of suppliers could be international. Explanation of international activity in the user market requires an explanation of demand drivers, which are international in nature in this market. Increased exports lead to the expansion of domestic production. Increased domestic production increases the demand for industrial space. Imports also have an impact on demand for real estate space. Goods imported need to be marketed and distributed, boosting the demand for retail space. Global trade has increased substantially over the last half-century (Figure 2.23). During 1950–2007, while the world GDP (in value terms) increased by around eight times, world exports of merchandise (in value terms) grew by 217 times. There are certain features of trade that need to be discussed. While world exports grew from US$5.6 trillion in 1997 to US$13.95 trillion in 2007, the profile of exporting nations/regions also changed dramatically during these 10 years. Three decades ago, a large part of world trade took place within the triad of North America, Europe and Japan. However, the geography of trade has changed since then. Europe is still the largest exporter in the world, but its share in global exports decreased from 43% in 1997 to 41% in 2007. North America's share in world exports also declined from 18% in 1997 to 13% in 2007. Asia's share increased from 27% to 29% during the same period. The dominance of Japan as the sole exporting nation in Asia has been challenged by China and recently by Korea and India. Japan's share of exports in Asia declined from 27% in 1997 to 17% in 2007, while China's share increased from 12% in 1997 to 29% in 2007. Other regions, such as the Middle East Commonwealth of Independent States (CIS), have grown their exports substantially.

Regional trading blocs have played an important role in trade. A regional trade bloc is a type of intergovernmental agreement, often part of a regional intergovernmental organisation, where regional barriers to trade (tariffs and nontariff barriers) are reduced or eliminated among the participating states (Schott, 1991). Trade liberalisation since 1980s has led to phenomenal growth in trade, but a large part of trade takes place within nations of various regional trading blocs. In 2007, nearly 68% of exports from the nations of the EU (the EU comprises 27 countries: Austria, Belgium, Bulgaria, Cyprus, the Czech Republic, Denmark, Estonia, Finland, France, Germany, Greece, Hungary, Ireland, Italy, Latvia, Lithuania, Luxembourg, Malta, the Netherlands, Poland, Portugal, Romania, Slovakia, Slovenia, Spain, Sweden, the United Kingdom) were to countries within the EU, and around 64% of imports by EU nations were of goods and services produced by nations in the EU. Nearly half of the exports and a third of imports from NAFTA countries (the United States, Canada and Mexico) were to/ from NAFTA countries. Another important regional trade bloc is ASEAN. However, ASEAN nations (Brunei Darussalam, Cambodia, Indonesia, Lao PDR, Malaysia, Myanmar, the Philippines, Singapore, Thailand and Vietnam) are less connected with each other in terms of trade than the EU and NAFTA. There are many other regional trade blocs (such as MERCOSUR or the Andean community), but the size of trade by these blocs is quite small. Among these regional trade blocs, EU nations have been by far the most connected, for the reason that the integration of nations within this bloc is wider than trade liberalisation. The formation of the EU is based on convergence of governance (related to European community policies, foreign and security policies and justice and home affairs), the legal system (which is based on treaties among member nations. These treaties give power to set policy goals and establish institutions with the necessary legal power to implement them) and the economy. Economic integration within the EU has led to the establishment of a single economic market across the territory of all its members. The single market allows free circulation of goods, capital, people and services across the Union. There is a common application of an external tariff on all goods entering the market. Many countries in the EU have adopted the euro as their currency and have transferred the power to formulate monetary policies to the European Central Bank. Institutionally, the EU has converged to a greater degree and this has led to increased internal trade within this bloc. Regional distribution and the nature of trade have a profound impact on the nature and location of real estate space required. Traditional trade theories are successful in explaining the reasons for trade between countries but are rather weak in explaining the location of origination and destination of trade at subnational level and the role of institutions in determining trade flows.

Porter's model of competitive advantage of nations suggests that countries having four diamonds would grow economically. A corollary to this would be that these countries would have a higher demand for real estate space. Porter's model also discusses the role of government and chance in a nation's competitiveness. This argument could be extended further to argue the importance of facilitating institutional framework for economic growth. Real estate markets operate within a three-level hierarchy of institutions (Keogh and D'Arcy, 1999). These institutions are (i) at the top of the hierarchy and broader society-level institutions such as legal, political, economic and social; (ii) in the middle, real estate market-level institutions, which are far more local, such as legal and conventional aspects of property rights, legal and conventional aspects of land use and development and decentralised and informal institutions that affect real estate markets; and (iii) at the bottom of the hierarchy, an organisation of real estate markets itself according bundling and unbundling of rights associated with real estate, such as use, investment, development and other services involved in this market, including real estate service providers, financial service providers, professional bodies and government and nongovernmental institutions. Real estate market institutions at the middle and bottom of the hierarchy are local, though operating within the top level of the hierarchy of institutions. These institutions could be influenced by government policies and other market forces at the local, regional and national levels.

Another important global economic trend is the growth of FDI. FDI inflows increased from US$55 billion dollars in 1980 to US$1305 billion in 2006. As a percentage of world GDP, FDI inflows grew from around 0.75% of GDP in 1980 to more than 3.5% of GDP in 2006 (UNCTAD, 2008). In recent years, real estate companies have also been direct recipients of FDI. The geography of FDI has changed quite substantially over the last three decades. Up until the1980s, most of the FDI inflows were from and to developed economies (North America, developed Europe and Japan). The share of Asia minus Japan was less than 1% in 1980. By 2006, the Asian region (Asia excluding Japan) was the destination for nearly 20% of FDI inflows. The share of developed nations has declined to 66%. Transitional economies have become a major destination for FDI inflows (Figure 2.24).

The inflow of FDI investment has an expansionary effect on the economic output, and it also influences the organisation and management of the

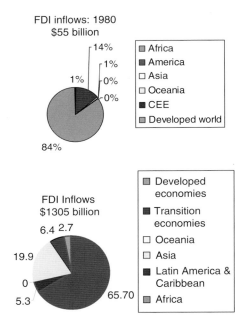

Figure 2.24 FDI inflows.
Source: UNCTAD Development and Globalization: facts and figures (2008).

recipient industry. The share of the services sector as recipient of FDI has increased from 49% in 1990 to 66% in 2005 (UNCTAD, 2008). The impact of FDI on real estate space is in terms of expansion in demand as well as the nature of the space demanded, particularly since the international investor has management and organisational control which influences decisions related to the quality of space required.

Another important global trend in production of goods and services has been the growth of TNCs and their foreign affiliates. There were 78 000 TNCs and 780 000 foreign affiliates in 2005. Most large TNCs are head-quartered in developed countries. According to the UNCTAD World Investment Report (2008), from 1990 to 2006, the value of assets of foreign affiliates increased five times (US$51 trillion in 2006), sales three times (US$25 trillion in 2006) and employment two times (US$73 million in 2006). The growth of TNCs and their foreign affiliates leads to increased integration of economic and business practices. This also generates demand for high-quality real estate space, occupation and management practices which are different from those of domestic firms. As discussed earlier, the organisation of the international production structure of TNCs is better explained by Dunning's eclectic paradigm. The global demands of TNCs and their foreign affiliates for real estate are better served by real estate firms that are global in nature. This has led to the emergence of real estate

TNCs in the development sector and real estate services sector during the last 30 years. Chapter will explain the internationalisation of real estate service providers in detail.

Real estate user demand generates interest for investment. The basic idea behind international investment in real estate could be explained by an inter-temporal trade model. Evidence presented in Chapter indicates that international investment in real estate has increased substantially. As discussed in Chapter , international real estate provides diversification benefits in mixed asset and real estate only portfolios. Real estate asset is like any other asset, but management of real estate requires a different focus from, say, stocks or bonds. Direct real estate has a long-term investment horizon, while stocks or bonds have a short-term investment horizon. Management of direct real estate investment involves a host of integration and ongoing management issues (Tripathy, 2008). The skills required to manage a global real estate portfolio are diverse – ranging from managing information to managing investor relationships to managing multiple bank relationships to understanding of tax structures across different countries to understanding of components of real estate investment that enhance value (Tripathy, 2008). Real estate investment requires local market knowledge – understanding of political, regulatory and tax structures – as well as under-standing of global investors' needs for standardisation of processes and control, reporting standards and data standards. Management of real estate investment has led to the emergence of global asset managers with real estate capabilities. There are push and pull factors that have led to the globalisation of asset managers. Squeezing margins at home, competition and market saturation have caused domestic asset managers to look overseas. Internationalisation of investment clients, market expansion abroad, liberalisation of financial markets, maturity of investment culture, better governance and regulatory structures and so on have been pull factors for asset management firms to go overseas. Dunning's 'OLI' paradigm is well equipped to explain why global asset management firms establish part of their organisational functions abroad.

Conclusions

The overview presented in this chapter of property use, investment, finance and development markets indicates that substantial internationalisation has happened. Globalisation of economic activities has generated a demand for space that shifts across national boundaries. Globalisation of economies has also led to international capital flows in assets, including property. A number of debt- or equity-based instruments have emerged, which have facilitated investment in commercial properties. Though property is still largely financed by private debt and equity, the role of public markets as a provider of debt and equity has increased substantially. Among the regions, most of the invested commercial properties are located in North America and Europe. Asia, despite strong economic growth, has a relatively low proportion of invested commercial properties. Internationalisation of property markets is leading to convergence of market practices, as evidenced by aligning of lease terms. The availability of market data and information differs from market to market. Market maturity plays an important role in shaping the landscape of the geography of property investment. The size of the investable stock and the underexposure of stock in some countries to the investment market suggest that long-term growth potential exists.

Note

1 'Total' stock refers to the overall stock of commercial real estate. 'Investible' stock means investment-grade properties. This stock might currently be institutionally owned or owner-occupied, but, in time, it should all become 'institutional'. This is smaller than the total stock as much commercial real estate is of too poor a quality to become institutional or will always remain owner-occupied. 'Invested' stock, or the current stock, refers to those properties which are currently owned by professional real estate investors for investment purposes (adapted from RREEF, 2007).

References

Bardhan, A., Edelstein, R. and Tsang, D. (2008) Global financial integration and real estate security returns. *Real Estate Economics*, **36** (2), 285–311.

Bond, S., Karolyi, G.A. and Sanders, A.B. (2003) International real estate returns: A multifactor multicountry approach. *Real Estate Economics*, **31** (3), 481–500.

CBRE (2008) *Global Market Rents May 2008: Office Rents and Occupancy Costs Worldwide*, CB Richard Ellis, Los Angeles.

Conner, P. and Liang, Y. (2003), The Expanding Frontier of Institutional Real Estate, May, Pramerica Real Estate Investor, Pramerica Financial, Parsippany.

Conover, C., Friday, H. and Sirmans, G. (2002) Diversification benefits from foreign real estate investments. *The Journal of Real Estate Portfolio Management*, **8** (1), 17–25.

DTZ (2006/2007) *Money into Property: Global*, June, DTZ Research, London.

Eichholtz, P. and Huisman, R. (1999) The cross section of global property share returns. In: *A Global Perspective on Real Estate Cycles* (eds S.J. Brown and C.H. Liu). Boston, Kluwer Academic Publishers.

Eichholtz, P., Huisman, R., Koedijk, K. and Schuin, L. (1998) Continental factors in international real estate returns. *Real Estate Economics*, **26**, 493–509.

Geurts, T. and Jaffe, A. (1996) Risk and real estate investment: an international perspective. *Journal of Real Estate Research*, **11** (2), 117–130.

Hamelink, F. and Hoesli, M. (2004) What factors determine international real estate security returns? *Real Estate Economics*, **32**, 437–462.

Hoesli, M. and MacGregor, B. (2000) *Property Investment. Principles and Practice of Portfolio Management*. Pearson Education Ltd, Harlow.

ING Real Estate (2008) Global vision 2008. www.ingrealestate.com (accessed 16 October 2013).

JLL (2008) *Asia Pacific Property Digest*, First Quarter.

Keogh, G. and D'Arcy, E. (1999) Property market efficiency: an institutional economics perspective. *Urban Studies*, **36**, 2401–2414.

Key, T. and Law, V. (2005) The size of the UK market. *IPF Seminar*, City University, London, May.

Ling, D.C. and Naranjo, A. (2002) Commercial real estate return performance: A cross country analysis. *Journal of Real Estate Finance and Economics*, **24**, 119–142.

Liu, C.H. and Mei, J. (1998) The predictability of international real estate markets, exchange rate risks and diversification consequences. *Real Estate Economics*, **26**, 3–39.

RREEF (2007) *Global Real Estate Insights*. RREEF Research, London.

RREEF (2008) *Global Real Estate Investment and Performance 2007 and 2008*. RREEF Limited, London.

Schott, J.J. (1991) Trading blocs and the world trading system. *World Economy*, **14** (1), 1–17.

Stevenson, S. (2000) International real estate diversification: empirical tests using hedged indices. *Journal of Real Estate Research*, **19** (1/2), 105–131.

Tripathy, M. (2008) *Managing a Global Real Estate Portfolio*, Deloitte Development LLC, New York.

ULI and PwC (2007) *Emerging Trends in Real Estate*. PricewaterhouseCoppers, Washington, DC.

UNCTAD (2008) *World Investment Report (WIR): Transnational Corporations and the Infrastructure Challenge*. UNCTAD, Geneva.

Walker, A. and Flanagan, R. (eds.) (1991) *Property and Construction in Asia Pacific: Hong Kong, Japan, Singapore*. BSP Professional Books, Oxford.

3

Financial Systems, Flow of Funds to Property and Innovations

Introduction

The purpose of this chapter is to discuss how funds flow to property. Who are the investors? Who are the intermediaries, and what mechanisms do they use to channelise funds from investors into property?

These mechanisms have evolved within the financial systems as a way to allocate risk associated with financing property to those who can assume them for returns in commensuration with the risk. Figure 3.1 shows the flow of funds to property, though it may be flagged here that property is only a small component of overall investment space. In a simplified scenario, domestic or foreign economic agents such as households, firms and government with surplus financial resources in present time (in terms of savings) can invest in those domestic or foreign opportunities (including property) that require these resources to carry out economic activities and earn risk-adjusted return on their investment in the future. These economic agents could invest directly in these opportunities (such as housing and office buildings for own use purposes) or channelise their savings into various opportunities through primary capital markets or through secondary financial sectors such as banks, pension funds and insurance companies for investment in income-generating properties.

The purpose of the financial system and financing mechanisms is to reduce impediments and create opportunities for the flow of funds from

Real Estate Finance in the New Economy, First Edition. Piyush Tiwari and Michael White.
© 2014 John Wiley & Sons, Ltd. Published 2014 by John Wiley & Sons, Ltd.

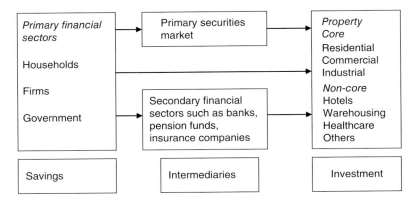

Figure 3.1   Flow of funds to property.

investors to investment opportunities. Property has its own specific characteristics. An objective of this chapter is to discuss how the financial system
(and financing mechanisms) have evolved in response to the characteristics
of property asset class and to what extent various mechanisms have been
able to address the specificities of property.

Bank-based and market-based financial systems

The mechanisms for financing assets that develop in a country depend on
the regulatory and institutional environment within which financial system
operates. There are two types of systems: (i) market-based and (ii) bank-
based financing system. This does not mean that the mechanisms that
would evolve in a country would conform only to one system or the other.
It means that one of these two systems would have predominant influence
in the evolution of financial mechanisms through which resources would be
mobilised and investments will take place. Mechanisms conforming to the
other system will exist in a meaningful but to a lesser extent. The differences
between the two financial systems arise from the way savings are mobilised;
investments are identified, made and monitored; and risks are managed.

The other difference is from the legal perspective. In a bank-based economy (Germany and Japan), laws governing financial systems are enacted and
implemented by the government. These are based mainly on the civil law
rather than the common law. Market-based financial systems are found
most often in countries (the United States and the United Kingdom) that
employ a common law legal system. Common law is less defined and can
vary from case to case. Instead of government enacting and implementing
the laws governing financial system, common law-based regulation is
implemented through courts.

In a market-based system, primary securities markets play the dominant role. Banks in such a system are less dependent upon interest from loans and gain much of their revenue through fee-based services. In contrast, in a bank-based financial system, banks play a major role in channelising financial flows to investment opportunities through loans. Interests earned on loans form the major part of their income. In a market-based system, a number of non-banking sources for investments exist. Investments by private systems and government often compete with those of the bank.

In a pure bank-based system, banks mobilise capital, identify good projects, monitor managers and manage risk. The risk management, information dissemination, corporate control and capital allocation are all left to market forces in a market-based system. In a well-developed market, any information that is available is revealed quickly in the public markets, which reduces the transaction costs. Some view this as a shortcoming of market-based system as the incentives for individual investors to acquire information decline (Stiglitz, 1985). Standardisation becomes the key, and in this context, there may not be enough incentives to identify innovative investment opportunities. In a bank-based system, banks form long-run relationships with borrowers (firms), information is private, and investments are custom made.

There are other concerns which proponents of the bank-based system identify with the market-based system. Liquid markets create a myopic investor climate where investors have fewer incentives to exert rigorous corporate control (Bhide, 1993). However, powerful banks with close relationships with firms can more effectively obtain information about firms and manage their loans/investments to these firms than markets. The view against bank-based system is that powerful banks can stifle innovation by extracting informational rents and protecting established firms with close bank–firm ties from competition (Rajan, 1992). Moreover, in the absence of appropriate regulatory restrictions, they may collude with firm managers against other creditors and impede efficient corporate governance (Wenger and Kaserer, 1998). Market-based systems will reduce these inherent inefficiencies associated with bank-based systems.

Levine (2001) minimises the importance of the bank-based versus market-based debate. He argues that financial arrangements comprising contracts, markets and intermediaries arise to ameliorate market imperfections and provide financial services. Financial arrangements emerge to assess potential investment opportunities, exert corporate control, facilitate risk management, enhance liquidity and ease savings mobilisation (Levine 2001). Finance is a set of contracts. These contracts are defined and made effective by legal rights and enforcement mechanisms. From this perspective, a well-functioning legal system facilitates the operation of both market- and bank-based systems. While focusing on legal systems, it is not inconsistent with banks or markets playing an important role in the economy. With financial innovations and their export that has accompanied globalisation, the coexistence of bank-based and market-based system has further got reinforced.

The mechanisms that develop for financing or investment in an asset take root in the efficiency of the market. Though a detailed discussion on market efficiency is out of the scope of the present book, it is important to mention the key elements of an efficient market. According to Fama (1970), an efficient financial market is one in which security prices always fully reflect the available information. This hypothesis rests on three arguments which progressively rely on weaker assumptions. First, investors are assumed to be rational and hence value securities rationally for its fundamental value. Any new information is quickly factored in the price. As a result, all available information is captured in the price. Second, to the extent that some investors are not rational, their trades are random and therefore cancel each other out without affecting prices. Third, to the extent that investors are irrational in similar ways, they are met in the market by arbitrageurs who eliminate their influence on prices (Shleifer, 2000).

Given the aforementioned definition of the efficient markets, property markets are not efficient. Trading on this asset is infrequent (one property does only few times during its life), transactions take time to materialise, and the transaction costs are high. Information on transaction price, rental and lease terms are highly private, and hence, third party valuation plays a key role in guiding buyers' and sellers' decisions. Participants in the market are few and most deals are negotiated deals. Property being local in nature, laws and local planning regulations play a very important role in determining the value of the property. Importance to understand these local norms for the participants makes the market thin.

The role of financial system is to evolve mechanisms that can take into account characteristics of property asset class and create opportunities for investors to invest in this asset class. Hence, the question to ask in case of property investment is what bank-based and market-based mechanisms have evolved for channelising savings from the real economy for financing of property development and investment in property as an asset class. As would be discussed later, to a large extent, property is financed through debt instruments, mainly debt from commercial banks. In the last two to two and half decades, innovations in financial mechanisms have taken place to enhance the role of the market-based financing in the sector. Figure 3.2 presents the flow of funds to the property.

Though various mechanisms would be discussed in detail in the next section, it is important to observe here that both bank-based and market-based systems are operative in any economy. The extent to which an economy is able to use these mechanisms depends on the depth and maturity of its

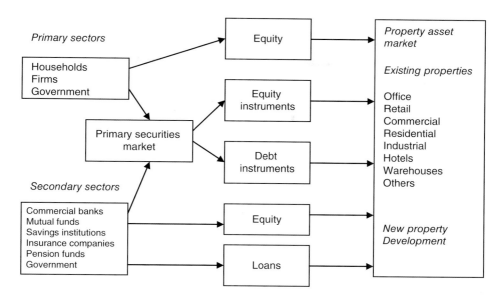

Figure 3.2   Typical flow of funds to property.

banking system and primary markets as well as regulatory environment within which intermediaries and investors operate. It is also important to observe from the aforementioned figure that in a fully developed system, bank-based and market-based systems interact and innovate to provide mechanisms to fund property assets and new developments.

Property investors and intermediaries

There are four major types of investors: institutional investors, unregulated investors, households and proprietors and corporations. Motives for investment in property differ for different investors. Even for investors in the same type, as described earlier, motives could differ. There are those who invest in property for financial reasons, that is, they are looking for a return on their investment, and there are those whose intention is to invest in property for occupation purposes. Figure 3.3 presents the further breakdown of investors in each type.

Following are the two distinct and mutually exclusive investment objectives (Geltner *et al.* 2007): (i) the growth (savings) objective, which implies a relatively long time horizon with no immediate or likely intermediate need to use the cash being invested, and (ii) the income (current cash flow) objective, which implies that the investor has short-term and ongoing cash requirements from his investments. There are other considerations that affect investors in the property markets. Risk is an important factor in the

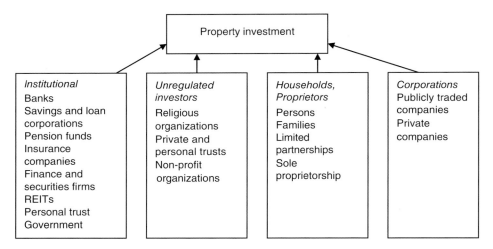

Figure 3.3   Commercial real estate investors.

decision for investment in real estate. This arises from the concern that future investment performance may vary over time in a manner that is not entirely predictable at the time of investment. Time horizon, for which investor wants to stay invested, itself is a factor. Liquidity, that is, the ease with which the asset could be bought or sold at full value without much affecting the price of the asset, is another consideration. Investor expertise and management burden that investment in property pose determines the ability and desire of investor to invest in property. Minimum size of investment required also determines the willingness and ability of an investor to invest in property.

Considering that investor space is heterogeneous, an elaborate investment system with a number of intermediaries and mechanisms through which funds flow to property has emerged. While the investment mechanisms will be discussed in the next section, it is interesting to see the range of intermediaries that operates in the property investment markets (Figure 3.4). These intermediaries are the conduits between investors and investment, and the investment mechanisms are the products through which investment is made.

Investment mechanisms

Figure 3.5 presents a highly simplified version of real estate investment system with main mechanisms depicted there. The figure does not cover investment mechanisms exhaustively, as given the range of possibilities that exists, it will be highly ambitious to attempt here.

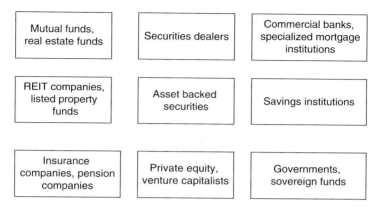

Figure 3.4   Intermediaries in the property investment market.

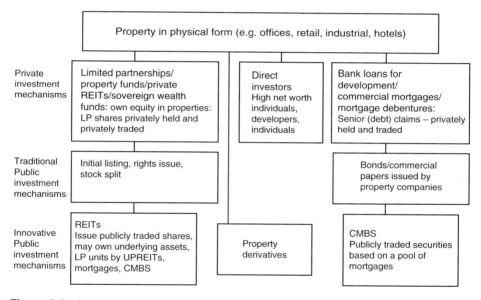

Figure 3.5   Investment mechanisms.

Private investment mechanisms

Debt   The private investment mechanisms (Figure 3.5) for debt and equity are the traditional ways of financing property during its development phase and later when it is an income-generating asset. These two together form the major share of investment flow in property. The finance for development is short term and takes the form of a loan or an overdraft facility. Since during the time the construction is on, there is no cash flow to repay the debt, the repayment is a bullet payment of accumulated interest and principal at the time of when the project development ends. In the United

Kingdom, 30 years ago, the term of the loan coincided with the length of the construction period, but later, lenders have started to look at the loan period up to the first rent review (usually after 5 years of completion of project) as the expectation is that the property would have stabilised and a better value for refinancing or sale could be achieved for owners at this stage. The loan for development is provided by one bank or a syndicate of banks.

In the United Kingdom, which is a market-based system, during the property boom period of 1980s, property companies were able to assemble a panel of banks with the help of an underwriter who would compete on interest rates for an opportunity to lend. Property companies had the opportunity to raise debt finance on very competitive rates from different lenders up to an agreed limit (Lizieri *et al.*, 2001). However, during the 1990s, when the property downturn began, the lending market became very conservative in their lending (Lizieri *et al.*, 2001). These loans from banks are secured on company assets or development project assets and/or other fixed and floating charges that borrowers could provide. During 1970s, the interest rates used to be fixed but the interest rate risk for lenders was too high to assume, and hence, these were replaced by floating rates based on London Interbank Borrowing Rate (LIBOR) or some other floating rates plus a margin that banks charged to assume risks associated with the development and the borrower (Lizieri *et al.*, 2001). In that sense from the risk perspective, each development project and borrower is different and the interest rates charged to them is different. This is where complication arises, and the importance of a bank-based system assumes importance as banks with relation with borrowers are supposedly able to assess their risks better.

Commercial mortgages represent the senior claim on any cash flow (called senior debt) that is generated by stabilised property (i.e. development is over and property has been let out and is receiving cash flows in the form of rent and other incomes) and provide lenders/investors (typically banks or insurance companies) with fixed tenured, contractually fixed cash flow streams. Traditionally, the mortgage is a long-term loan (typically 15–25 years tenure) kept as a 'whole loan' on the balance sheet of investors to maturity, meaning that it is not broken into small homogeneous shares or units such as corporate bonds that are traded on stock exchanges. However, over the last three–four decades, a number of variants of mortgages have also emerged first in response to the low loan-to-value (LTV) ratio for property lending and the low valuation accorded to property for lending purposes (the practice is that the property is valued on the basis of 'vacant possession') and the second the comfort that banks have gained with property investment. As per the Basel Accord, commercial property lending carries full risk weighting, and hence, other types of mortgage instruments have emerged that combine the balance-sheet and off-balance-sheet lending. These mortgage instruments, more prevalent in the United States, take the form of profit sharing mortgages such as participating or convertible mortgages. These mortgages are usually more prevalent during weaker markets to unlock more capital for borrowers.

Participation loans, also called equity participation loans, are a combination of loan and equity that a lender take in a project. Though it is called equity participation, but the lender does not acquire ownership interest in the project. Lender's interest is only limited to the participation in the cash flows, and this participation kicks in only after property has starting generating cash flows (Brueggeman and Fisher, 2008). Lenders receive a percentage of potential gross income or net operating income or cash flow after regular debt service, as may be agreed for their participation. In return for receiving participation, lenders charge lower interest rates on their loans. Participations are highly negotiable between lenders and borrowers, and there is no standard way of structuring them (Brueggeman and Fisher, 2008).

A convertible mortgage gives lenders an option to purchase full or partial interest in the property at the end of some specified time period. This purchase option allows lenders to convert their mortgage to equity ownership. Lenders may view this as a combination of mortgage loan and purchase of a call option, which gives them an option to acquire full or partial equity interest for a predetermined price on the option's expiration date (Brueggeman and Fisher, 2008). Here again, lenders accept a lower interest rate in exchange for the conversion option.

Equity   The source of equity capital for property development and asset investment is provided by two types of investors: those who want to actively involve in management and operation of underlying property asset such as property companies (e.g. developers, institutions and high net worth individuals) and others who want to invest in property to diversify their investment portfolios but do not want hands on involvement. A number of mechanisms have emerged to meet the needs of these investors with the needs for equity for property investment. Examples of these passive equity investment mechanisms are units in real estate equity funds such as real estate limited partnerships (RELPs), commingled real estate funds (CREFs) and private Real Estate Investment Trusts (REITs – whose units are not publicly traded); companies; and mutual funds, though passive equity investment mechanisms provide investors with an ownership interests in the underlying asset but give limited governance authority over the assets and are not traded in the liquid public exchanges.

The greater part of the pan-European market is concentrated in non-REIT form including limited partnerships, companies and mutual fund vehicles. REITs are quite popular in the United States. Partnerships are very popular as they allow even the most complex arrangements to be structured through a partnership agreement rather than under a company law (Brown, 2003).

The fund sponsor for a real estate equity fund is usually an affiliate of a developer or professional investment organisation. The investors generally provide most, if not all, of the investment. The structure of the fund has at least one general partner and any number of limited partners. The general partners, who are the fund sponsors, provide 'sweat equity' and have the responsibility for management of partnership assets. They may have a small equity contribution. Limited partners are very restricted in management of a joint venture, and their personal liability is limited. However, limited partners insist on having approval rights over a variety of major decisions ranging from refinancings, sales, leases and budgets to insurance, service contracts and litigations (Larkin *et al.*, 2003). Some funds also have investment committees that include limited partners with role to provide advice to general partners on issues such as conflicts of interest and valuation of fund assets (Larkin *et al.*, 2003).

The legal form of the fund is largely determined by the tax efficiency of the form chosen and familiarity of the fund structure to prospective investors (Larkin *et al.*, 2003). These funds though structured to be tax efficient, are not generally tax shelters, in that they do not attempt to accelerate tax deductions to shelter unrelated incomes (Larkin *et al.*, 2003). The investment objectives of real estate private equity funds can be either capital appreciation or income. The investment cycle varies depending on the strategy of the fund, target assets and needs of the investors. For example, while real estate opportunity funds typically have 2–3-year investment period, 1–2-year monitoring period, a fund organised for acquisition of a typical asset may just have duration of 2–3 years. These funds will typically leverage each real estate investment by borrowing money to finance a portion of the purchase price and securing the debt by granting direct lien on the property assets owned by the fund.

RELPs were popular in the United States prior to 1986 due to tax advantages associated with them. Passive investors could offset their other incomes with property (tax) loss from investment in limited partnerships. With these advantages gone with the Tax Reform Act of 1986, their popularity has declined. Moreover, many of the funds in the United States were organised under the laws of the State of Delaware or tax heavens like Cayman Islands. In Europe, though, there is no one jurisdiction of choice for real estate private equity funds, and the choice of jurisdiction depends on the nature of investors, tax residency of the investor and the likely jurisdiction of the property assets (Larkin *et al.*, 2003).

Another important source of equity capital, in recent times, is the Sovereign Wealth Funds (SWFs). These funds are wholly owned government entities that invest nation's surplus wealth in broad array of investments overseas. A number of governments, such as Abu Dhabi, Qatar, Kuwait, Norway, Singapore, Australia and China, have floated these funds. SWFs are commonly active investors or passive asset managers. Though the asset holding of SWFs is not easily available, their property holdings are about 5–10%. A number of SWFs have taken controlling positions in large property assets (Langford *et al.*, 2009).

Public investment mechanisms

Property companies and developers access markets by issuing bonds and commercial paper for debt and through initial public offer (IPO) or rights issue or stock split for equity funding. The problem, however, is that given the risk perceived by the market (arising from concerns about true value of underlying property and cyclical nature of property markets) for investment in property, very few companies are able to issue unsecured debt paper that would obtain the highest ratings. The same problem is faced with the equity offers of property companies. The view is that the property companies are valued on the basis of discounted net asset value. Markets trade property securities at a heavy discount to net asset value (NAV) (due to reasons such as contingent capital gains tax liability, valuation uncertainty, hidden management cost, illiquidity of the underlying asset), which averaged 25% in the long run in the United Kingdom (Lizieri *et al.*, 2001). Property stocks are usually considered as value stock and are also affected by the cyclicity of general stock markets. During the stock market downturn of the late 1990s in the United Kingdom, property stocks performed badly even compared to other value stocks, which led some public property companies (such as MEPC) to delist their stocks and others to buy back shares (Lizieri *et al.*, 2001). A similar trend is observed in India, where large property company stocks (such as DLF, Unitech) are being traded at a heavy discount since 2007, which has led to the postponement of some property companies' decision to raise equity capital from public markets.

Other mechanisms

There are some other mechanisms as well through which property is financed. One of them, sale and leaseback, is common and takes many forms. Many non-property companies, whose core business is not property, have owner-occupied properties for their use, enter in a sale and leaseback type of arrangement with property companies. Non-property companies sell the ownership interest in the property to a property company and take long-term lease on it. The reason for entering in such an arrangement is that it allows them to free up financial resources locked in property for their core business, trim down their balance sheet by reducing asset size and also gain from tax shield as lease payments are expenses for tax purposes. From the perspective of the market as well, non-property companies that hold too much of property assets face problems. The asset value of their properties may not be fully reflected in company's market capitalisation. For a number of major retailers, a big problem is that their property assets are valued far in excess of the retailers' market capitalisation, posing a threat of takeover and asset stripping. The problem is further complicated for companies whose required rate of return is higher than what property can (notionally) generate. These would motivate companies to unlock the capital from property assets.

Another form of sale and leaseback is where the property company sells the completed development to an institution and takes long-term lease. The company expects to gain from profit rent from subletting. The risk and profit sharing structure between the institution and the property company varies from a fixed rent to an agreed sharing of any rental uplift (Lizieri *et al.*, 2001). Another type of financing arrangement that exists is the sale and leaseback of land. These are done to increase the proportion of financing in a development project. The land is sold to an investor and is leased back. Here, the developer/investor owns the building and leases back the land from another investor. By doing this, 100% financing of land is obtained and the building is financing on usual lender's property finance loan terms.

Innovations

The major innovations have been around the development of public investment vehicles for investment in property asset class. These have taken the form of asset-backed securities (ABS), commercial mortgage-backed securities (CMBS), REITs and property derivatives. While ABS and CMBS are debt vehicles, REITs are equity investment vehicles.

In ABS or CMBS, the issuer, usually a special purpose vehicle, offers bonds or commercial paper to the capital markets. Cash flows from a single or a pool of property assets (such as rental income or loan repayments) is used to pay the coupon and capital redemption payment on the bonds or commercial paper. Some charge on underlying property assets provides security against default. The mechanism of CMBS is briefly discussed in Appendix 4.1.

There are several advantages to a lender from CMBS and to a firm from ABS. By securitising loans (in case of CMBS) or rental income and value streams (in case of ABS), the exposure to specific risk associated with property reduces. For lenders, the securitised loan portfolio moves off their balance sheet, thereby improving their capital adequacy and solvency ratios. For firms, ABS allows them to raise capital secured on value and income stream of their property assets while retaining the ownership. Issuing ABS or CMBS on public markets allows firms and lenders to tap a new source of capital. In case of CMBS, there are also opportunities to earn profits from arrangement and service fee and from the spread between the interest on loans and coupon payable on bond or commercial papers. For firms, ABS is a cheaper source of borrowing. The cost of these borrowing could further reduce as in case of tenanted properties, the rating of the bond depends on the tenant covenants rather than the rating of the firm issuing securities.

There are a number of advantages to investors too. They are able to gain exposure to a market that faces huge entry barriers and high transaction costs. Investment in securities allows them to benefit from liquid and marketable nature of this asset. Moreover, since the underlying asset is a pool of loans or pool of properties, the specific risk to an investor reduces. It is also claimed that for ABS or CMBS, the transaction, monitoring and management costs for an investor are lower than those associated with investing in direct property.

These advantages, however, come at a cost. ABS or CMBS reduce the flexibility for the issuer in managing their securitised portfolio. There are also costs associated with arrangement, underwriting, rating and credit enhancement of a bond or commercial paper.

Lizieri *et al.* (2001) argue that asset-backed securitisation offers further potential for innovation, which could be explored. Underlying any lease, there are three sources of cash flows. The first is base rent, which given strong tenant covenants is a secure stream of income. The second is the possibility of a rental uplift at the time of rent review (in the United Kingdom where lease agreements specify upward-only rent revisions at the time of rent reviews, the possibility of rental uplift are far more secure compared to the United States where rent revisions are linked to the prevailing market conditions). This stream of income would appeal to certain investors who have larger appetite for risk but would require a higher return. The third class of cash flows arises from the fact that property has a residual value at the end of the lease which is still more speculative investment but would appeal to certain investors. These income streams could be sold to investors as income strips. The first, which is based on base rent, would attract institutional investors. There is a role for brokerage in the development of this market. Initial costs may be high due to costs involved in structuring these products and legal fees.

REITs, discussed briefly in Appendix 4.1, provide tax-efficient vehicles for equity investment in property. These allow subdivision of ownership of single property or developments.

The development in property derivatives has been slow partly due to lack of transparency and infrequent data. In the United Kingdom, over the last few years, property derivatives based on IPD income return and capital growth have emerged. These derivatives, one called Property Index Certificates and the other called Property Index Forwards, are synthetic investment vehicles offering opportunities for low-cost exposure to property market.

Economic assessment of investment mechanisms

The focus of this section is on the role that private and public innovative investment mechanisms such as sales and leaseback, asset and mortgage-backed securitisation and REITs have played in financing property. Chapter 4 shows that the flow of funds to property through public markets using securitisation and REITs has increased substantially over the last 20 years. A number of these innovations, though originated in the United States, have been exported to other economies. However, how well have these instruments been able to overcome the limitations of property asset class (namely, lumpy investment, inelastic supply in the space market, infrequent transactions, huge transaction cost, information asymmetry, a somewhat rigid valuation system that does not allow innovations such as in lease terms, huge specific risk associated with investment in direct property) that lead to inefficiencies in the market and create opportunities for investors and property companies and strike a balance between the risk and return for investors with the relatively lower-cost funding for property companies compared to traditional secured debt and equity needs to be examined. The efficient market hypothesis would suggest that if markets are efficient, then there are no opportunities for any abnormal gains. In that context, innovative mechanisms serve to rebalance the risk and return in any transaction or help in addressing sources of inefficiencies in the market, should they exist.

Lease financing

The growth in lease financing instead of financing property ownership by companies has been phenomenal over the last four decades, and this has largely been due to tax shield that lease financing provides. Three arguments that are often put forward in favour of lease financing are that (i) it provides 100% financing of space, (ii) it 'finances' property asset off balance sheet and (iii) it is beneficial from the taxation point of view. Sale and leasebacks are special case of lease financing. With these oft-cited benefits, it is expected that lease financing allows companies to unlock value from property assets. However, this may not always be possible.

The argument that the lease financing provides 100% financing for space required by the company is flawed. While it is true that the capital required for lease transaction is lower than required for ownership, the two transactions are not comparable. Rental payments are fixed only in the short term and at all time have higher claim on the cash flows of the company than some other expenses. This poses a significant risk if the lessee becomes financially constrained. Thus, the liability for rental payment for lessee is equivalent to liability on a bond or debt (Lizieri *et al.*, 2001). Moreover, when an investor buys a property, she acquires working space and an investment in performance of property market relative to her business performance. Besides claim on the future stream of rents, other sources of value accrue to the investor. These additional sources of value arise because property has reversionary value after the expiry of lease term and also has the option to redevelop before completion of lease attached to it (Lizieri *et al.*, 2001). These options have value if the rents and yields are more variable, and these options would rise or fall in value depending on the relative performance of property market relative to tenant's own business performance. However, given the risk of owning a building and its management, non-property occupiers may be less keen to finance the property than specialist property investors.

The second argument that leasing finances property assets off balance sheet needs more investigation. It is right that leasing does not appear on the balance sheet of a company as loan does, but does it have an impact on the value of the company is not clear. From the perspective of financial risk for a company, the higher the gearing (debt), the more is the equity risk. However, if the company replaces debt (for purchase of property) by another expense that is not on the balance sheet and appears only on the profit and loss account (lease payments) but has a higher claim on cash flows, would it lower the risk of equity? A stream of research (see, e.g. Dhaliwal, 1986; Ely, 1995; quoted in Lizieri *et al.*, 2001) has argued it otherwise. These operational leases are sticky and have the same effect as debt on equity risk. In fact, the equity risk is better estimated after taking into account the effect of operating leases, and the underlying market 'true' value of a company does not depend on whether or not the cost of space is disclosed in balance sheet or profit and loss accounts.

The tax advantage associated with leases is only marginally more than debt as the interest payment on debt is also an expense from tax point of view in the profit and loss statement. The level of gearing possible in a purchase of a building would, however, determine the extent to which interest can be claimed as an expense. This advantage loses its value if the company is a tax-exempt entity. There is though a demand side perspective. There are many institutional investors (such as pension funds, insurance companies) who seek asset with long duration of maturities and are constrained from investing in equities or other volatile securities (Lizieri *et al.*, 2001). These investors would constitute the demand side for assets which could be long leased to companies.

If lease financing does not add value *per se*, then any value add from such deals would have to come from mispricing, which then would mean that some would gain and some would lose.

Asset-backed securities

The argument in favour of ABS is that these mechanisms, which are secured by income or value of the underlying portfolio of property assets, can (i) reduce the cost of borrowing for the company issuing these securities compared to secured debt because the rating of securities is on the strength of tenants occupying the property and not the corporate owning the assets, (ii) increase the leverage on property assets than the LTV that lenders would offer, (iii) allow investors to diversify into property without the need for taking full ownership of the property, (iv) offer better returns than an equivalent-rated corporate bond and (v) limit the exposure to single asset or borrower for an investor.

The clear advantage of securitisation is that it permits the risk to be spread over a range of investors, and the relatively low cost of each security permits investors to take exposure to a portfolio of property assets and hold it in their portfolio. Investors who would have faced market barriers in investing in property can gain exposure to property lending market. Since these investors do not face specific risk associated with property, the required return from their investment in these securities is lower. This may put downward pressure on interest rates on ABS.

The advantage to a company that securitisation reduces the weighted average cost of capital as the coupon payment on securities is lower than the interest on a loan is debatable. The aforementioned claim is based on the argument that these securities receive ratings on the strength of tenants which are better than company's itself and hence are rated higher. This reduces the coupon demanded by investors. However, the impact of the price of securities on company's valuation is not that straightforward. Since these securities are traded in the secondary market, their price at any given point in time depends on the risk–return profile perceived by the market for holding these securities, which continually changes. From this perspective, issuing securities exposes the company far more to the scrutiny by the market, which has its own advantages and disadvantages. Moreover, the debt that was secured on the company as a whole is assessed on the basis of the quality of the overall rental cash flow to cover interest payments and on the value of underlying property assets as security in the event of default. However, the creation of security ring fences certain good properties through mortgages and subsidiary structures for asset-backed securitisation, which undermines the quality of remaining cash flow for the company (Lizieri *et al.*, 2001). Hence, the benefits for the company from claimed reduced cost of borrowings are not that straightforward.

On one hand, asset-backed securitisation may lead to financing flexibility; on the other hand, it could lead to inflexibility in occupiers market.

Long leases, upward-only rent reviews as in the United Kingdom, senior claim on company's assets, have has led to superior ratings for a number of issues but this has hampered the development of flexible occupier market with leases that are shorter and have break clauses and innovative rent fixing arrangements. There is a counter view too. In the United States, leases are short, there is flexibility in rent fixation, and leases are tenant favouring, but the growth of asset-based securitisation market is no less. In the United States, it is argued that investors also focus on the quality of buildings besides the strength of the lease.

While securitisation allows property companies to increase their gearing, it comes at a cost. With high leverage, equity investors demand higher returns as their risk increases. Moreover, securitisation poses constraints on company's operations as securitised assets can be disposed off or their uses are changed easily.

Mortgage-backed securitisation

Mortgage-backed securitisation allows originating banks to access new sources of capital. The risks which in traditional debt structure are borne by one lender are spread over a large number of investors. Another source of risk diversification happens due to the pooling of a large number of property loans in a CMBS structure, which reduces the specific risk associated with one property for investors. Investors can gain access to property markets which were previously subject to entry barriers, lack of information, illiquidity and high transaction costs. The rating agencies play the role of market makers as they rate mortgage-backed securities on the same risk parameters as they would for a corporate bond. The behaviour of rating agencies has, however, been criticised heavily after the subprime loan crisis in 2007 discussed in Chapter 6. A number of authors argue that rating agencies did not price the risk appropriately due to moral hazard problems, and others argue that risk was difficult to price as sufficient time series of data covering more than one property cycle was not available.

Given that mortgage-backed securities allow risk diversification, the coupon demanded by investors on these securities is lower than the interest charged on individual loans. Lenders being aware of securitisation would reduce the interest charged to borrowers. Kolari *et al.* (1998) estimate that for every 10% increase in securitisation as a proportion of origination, the spread on home loans declines by 0.2%. In case of CMBS, the spread over risk-free rate had contracted phenomenally until 2007. However, after the 2007 subprime crisis, the spread on CMBS rose sharply and delinquencies have increased substantially (Figure 3.6).

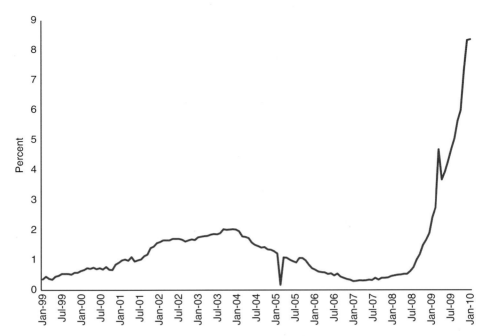

Figure 3.6   US CMBS 2004–2008 vintage delinquencies.
Source: Reproduced by permission of RREEF (2010).

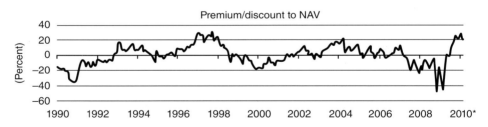

Figure 3.7   REIT premium or discount to NAV in the United States. * indicates estimate.
Source: Reproduced by permission of RREEF (2010).

REITs

REITs have been able to channelise retail funds into property equity (see Appendix 4.1 for a brief description of REITs). The growth and acceptance of REITs worldwide indicates the potential of this mechanism in channelising funds for property investment. Since REITs are traded on public markets, any market information gets quickly reflected in the price of the security. The problem, however, is that the NAV or the underlying portfolio is determined through conventional valuation in the direct property market.

A number of studies indicate that the indirect property market (securities traded on the public markets) leads the direct property market. The result is that REIT securities are traded either at a premium or discount (Figure 3.7). The disagreement on value between the direct and indirect market also offers opportunities for arbitrage.

Impact of new investment mechanisms on business culture and practices

Arms length (market) versus relationship (bank based)

One of the major criticisms of public investment mechanisms is that they are arms-length deals. They shift the responsibility of monitoring and management of asset cash flows to the market. The financing is done by the market, and banks are merely conduits between investors and investees. Investors in the public market have rather short-term perspective than those who invest in direct property. In public markets, credit rating agencies play a crucial role. However, the experience of 2007 subprime crisis indicates that failure could happen on part of credit rating agencies (Chapter 6).

One major risk with property is the large lot size of most commercial property assets, which, along with property heterogeneity, exposes lenders to high level of specific risk. Loan syndication though allows for sharing of risks among lenders, reduced monitoring and due diligence costs but also exposes them to another risk, counterparty risk. This risk arises because of the reduced level of due diligence that banks in a syndicate undertake, each assuming that others would have done detailed loan appraisal and risk analysis. During strong markets, the tendency to do detailed risk analysis by participating banks in a syndicate is far more less.

Caution in lending has led to cyclical trends in property lending. During strong markets, competition among banks leads to compression in interest rates, high LTVs on already inflated valuations and lax due diligence. Precisely, the reverse happens during weak markets.

Cultural impediments   The new market-based mechanisms for investment in property may conflict with the business culture. For example, the first asset securitisation in Japan was in 1994. Three years after, in an attempt to encourage securitisation, regulators in Japan amended trust and special purpose corporation laws that addressed tax and commercial code hurdles. These changes cleared the way for establishment of privately placed bonds backed by property and for debt collateralised by property (Feder and Kim, 2002). Despite these changes, the development of securitisation market in

Japan has been slow. A major reason for slow development of securitisation market is the cultural impediments that prevent financial institutions from fully embracing securitisation. Japanese law requires that obligators be notified of loan assignments (Feder and Kim, 2002). However, financial institutions are unwilling to notify debtors that their loans have been assigned since they believe that this would embarrass their clients and would also damage the banking relationships.

The due diligence process that goes with new mechanisms also faces cultural barriers. Loans and customers verification on phone or face-to-face meetings as in the United States is seen as an invasion of privacy in Japan. Bankruptcy and dealing with it is also viewed differently in Asia (Feder and Kim, 2002). Culturally, Asians view bankruptcy as a personal failure, which causes problems in taking corrective actions. Instead of letting the bankrupt entity fail, governments and courts in Asia have tried to keep them alive, often by asking banks to restructure loans rather than foreclose, at the cost of economic recovery.

Another cultural impediment that comes in the way of mechanisms such as sale and leaseback, particularly in Asia, is that companies are reluctant to sell their property assets as this is viewed as a sign of weakness or even failure.

Valuation practices   Valuation practices prevalent in different markets cause impediments for the development and adoption of new mechanisms. As has been discussed earlier, valuation practices have hindered innovations in lease structures. There are differences across markets as well. For example, while valuers in Western countries value assets on the basis of discounted cash flow method, that is, the return rate generated from properties, the valuation approach used in many Asian markets is very different. In Japan, there is a practice of government notifying official land values, which is used in valuation by banks and landlords (Feder and Kim, 2002). This leads to substantial differences in the valuation arrived at by using discounted cash flow methods and alternate practices used in some markets.

Conclusions

To summarise, the chapter presented a nontechnical overview of the mechanisms through which property is financed. The evolution of these mechanisms, either bank based or market based, depends on the investor requirements as well as the institutional and regulatory framework within which financial systems operate. In any economy, both bank-based and market-based mechanisms are available to channelise funds from investors to property asset class. A range of investors (households, institutional investors, corporations, unregulated investors) through intermediaries (mutual funds, security dealers, banks, ABS, REITs, private equity, sovereign funds) and various investment mechanisms invest in property.

The innovation in property investment has been in the lease financing and development of public markets for property asset through ABS, CMBS and REITs. In addition, property derivatives have also come up recently. The discussion in the chapter suggests that some of the oft-cited advantages of these mechanisms are unfounded. The contribution of these mechanisms though has been in widening the space of investment in property. Advantages to investors associated with innovative mechanisms depend on their individual circumstances.

References

Bhide, A. (1993) The hidden cost of stock market liquidity. Journal of Financial Intermediation, **34**, 1–51.

Brown, D. (2003) Investment fund vehicles for pan-European real estate a technical and commercial review. *Briefings in Real Estate Finance*, **2** (4), 289–301.

Brueggeman, W.B. and Fisher, J.D. (2008) *Real Estate Finance and Investments*, 3rd edn. McGraw-Hill International Edition, Boston.

Dhaliwal, D. (1986) Measurement of financial leverage in the presence of unfunded pension obligations. *The Accounting Review*, **61** (4), 651–661.

Ely, K. (1995) Operating Leases: *The Retail House of Cards*. Kleinwort Benson Research, London.

Fama, E. (1970) Efficient capital markets a review of theory and empirical work. *Journal of Finance*, **25** (2), 383–417.

Feder, P.N. and Kim, L.L. (2002) The state of the North Asian real estate market: the rise in non-performing loans, new investment vehicles and exit strategies and the need for government reforms. *Briefings in Real Estate Finance*, **2** (2), 162–173.

Geltner, D.M., Miller, N.M., Clayton, J. and Eichholtz, P. (2007) *Commercial Real Estate Analysis and Investments*. Thomson South Western, Mason.

Kolari, J.W., Fraser, D.R. and Anari, A. (1998) The effects of securitization on mortgage market yields: a cointegration analysis. *Real Estate Economics*, **26** (4), 677–93.

Langford, G., Garcia, D. and Lerman, A. (2009) *Sovereign Wealth Funds: Real Estate Partners in Growth*. Deloitte.

Larkin, D.E., Babin, M.L. and Rose, C.A. (2003) Structuring European real estate private equity funds. *Briefings in Real Estate Finance*, **3** (3), 229–235.

Levine, R. (2001) Bank based or market based financial system: which is better?. http://www.econ.brown.edu/fac/Ross_Levine/finance/rlevine/Publication/2002_JFI_BB%20vs%20MBFS.pdf (accessed 4 October 2011).

Lizieri, C., Ward, C. and Lee, S. (2001) *Financial Innovation in Property Markets: Implications for the City of London*. The Corporation of London in Association with the RICS Research Foundation, Mimeo.

Rajan, R.G. (1992) Insiders and outsiders: the choice between informed and arms length debt. *Journal of Finance*, **47** (4), 1367–1400.

RREEF (2009) *Global Commercial Real Estate Debt: Deleveraging into Distress*, RREEF Research, London.

RREEF (2010) *Global Real Estate Securities: The Outlook for 2010 and Beyond*, RREEF Research, London.

Shleifer, A. (2000) Inefficient Markets: An Introduction to Behavioral Finance. Oxford University Press, Oxford.

Stiglitz, J.E. (1985) Credit markets and the control of capital. *Journal of Money, Credit and Banking*, **17** (2), 133–152.

Wenger, E. and Kaserer, C. (1998) The German system of corporate governance: a model which should not be imitated. In: *Competition and Convergence in Financial Markets: The German and Anglo-American Models* (ed. W. Stanley). pp. 41–78. North-Holland Press, New York.

4

Property Investors, Investment Vehicles and Strategies

Internationally, commercial property finance has evolved as a sophisticated mechanism to finance an asset which traditionally was private in nature. Over a period of time, property has emerged as a separate asset class and offers a number of direct and indirect investment opportunities. In commensuration with the opportunities, a range of investors have emerged such as private investors, high net worth individuals (HNIs), private equity funds, institutional investors and commercial banks, who through a wide range of investment vehicles invest in property.

The objective of this chapter is to provide an introduction to the types of property investors, their perception about property and their investment mechanisms. A natural starting point for the discussion is to look at the size of investment and its sectoral distribution and global location.

Size of property

According to an estimate by RREEF (2010), of the total US$24.7 trillion global commercial property market in 2009, the value of invested commercial property market is around US$9 trillion. Invested market is that part of the property market where the space is owned by professional property investors, such as money managers, funds, private investment vehicles, listed companies and institutions. This market is about 60% of the investible market, which also includes investment grade space that is owner occupied.

Real Estate Finance in the New Economy, First Edition. Piyush Tiwari and Michael White.
© 2014 John Wiley & Sons, Ltd. Published 2014 by John Wiley & Sons, Ltd.

A large part of the invested stock (about 48%) is located in American continents. North America (largely the United States) accounts for more than almost 90% of the invested stock located in this region. Europe accounts for 36% of total invested stock, of which around 92% is located in Western Europe. The share of Austral-asia in total invested stock is about 16%, dominated largely by Japan and Australia. Going forward, the potential for investment largely exists in Europe and Asia as the share of invested stock in total investible in Western Europe and mature Asia is about 50%. In all regions, as the economies mature, opportunities for investment will increase. RREEF (2010) predicts that the share of emerging Asia (particularly China and India) in global invested commercial property will increase from 5% in 2009 to 15% in 2014.

Besides the volume factor of invested commercial property, their importance can be gauged from the fact that in the United States and United Kingdom, the invested commercial property is about 30% and 25% of GDP, respectively (DB Research, 2010). In Germany, the share is about 25%. In most countries of Western Europe, the share is about 20%, while in countries of Eastern Europe, invested commercial property to GDP ratio is about 10% (DB Research, 2010).

Investment and investors

Globally institutional property industry has transformed substantially over the last five decades. Changing needs of capital users and providers, regulatory shifts, advances in financial engineering and risk management methodologies, new opportunities created by cyclical and secular changes have led to a wide array of investment vehicles and strategies (Conner and Liang, 2003). Institutional investing in property started with mortgages and direct property and then gradually expanded into public securities (like Property Investment Trusts or Real Estate Investment Trusts (REITs) and shares of listed companies) and opportunistic and value-added investments (Conner and Liang, 2003). The developments in risk management tools and sustained performance of property markets have attracted institutional investors to private equity investments in property companies.

Investors have different objectives for investing in assets including property. There are investors who have growth objectives. They have longer time horizon for their investments, and much of their returns come as capital returns when the asset is sold. Then, there are others who have income objectives. Such investors have short-term cash flows as an important determinant for their investment. Some investors have both these objectives for different parts of their wealth. Besides these objectives, investors also face constraints related to risk that they can take, liquidity of

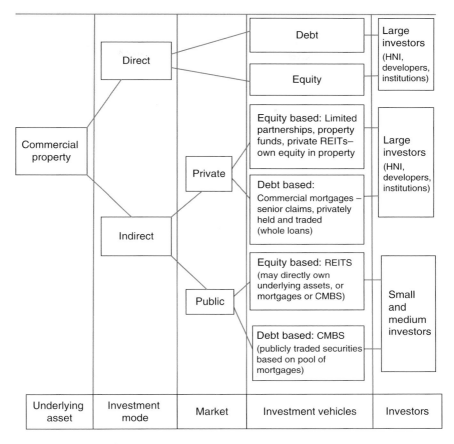

Figure 4.1 Property investment system.

the asset, time horizon of their investment, expertise and management burden involved in managing their assets, size of investor and capital available for investment. The share of invested in total global commercial property market is only 36%, implying that a larger share (64%) of commercial property is held for own use. The trend towards holding property as an investment has been observed during last three decades, a period during which a number of property investment vehicles emerged offering opportunities for private and public investment (Figure 4.1). These vehicles have emerged to suit the level of involvement that investors want. Investors who want to manage their investments actively invest directly in property. However, passive investors want a slice of property asset without actually getting in the day-to-day management of their assets. Typical vehicles for passive private equity investment are limited partnerships (LPs), property funds or real estate funds (REFs) and private Property Investment Trusts (REITs). These vehicles, though not traded on public markets, closely mirror

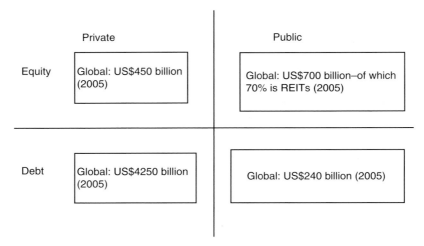

Figure 4.2   Investment in commercial property.
Source: RREEF (2006). Reproduced by permission of RREEF.

corporate stock because they also offer investment ownership interest in property, sometimes leveraged. Another private passive vehicle is commercial debt. There is also public market for equity (REITs) and debt (commercial mortgage-backed securities (CMBS)) vehicles in commercial property (see Appendix 4.1 for a brief description of REITs and CMBS). Though still about 93% of investment made in property is private, the public markets have witnessed phenomenal growth. In some countries like Hong Kong and Australia, about 90% of investment is made through public market vehicles.

The reason for the popularity of public vehicles has been due to their liquidity. These vehicles provide mechanisms to individuals and institutional investors to get exposure to property quickly and in a cost-effective way. Some investors, particularly institutional investors, want their assets to be priced regularly. Public vehicles, since they are traded on stock market which prices the asset on continuous basis, offer that potential.

The share of investment through various vehicles is presented in Figure 4.2. Commercial property investment is highly leveraged. Large share of investment (about 74%) is through private debt.

The extent of debt and equity in different markets differs (Figure 4.3), and the relative share is a function of market cycle and market maturity. For example, public markets in South Korea and China are underdeveloped, and hence, the sources of funds for property investment are private equity and private debt. In Australia, where REIT markets are well developed, public equity becomes the major source for investment. In case of the United States, public debt is the major course, mainly due to the well-developed CMBS market.

As shown in Figure 4.3, the capital structure (proportion of debt and equity in financing property investment) is dependent on market cycle as well. In

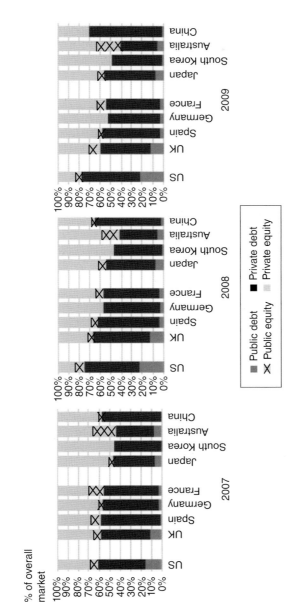

Figure 4.3 Sources of property investment in select markets.
Source: RREEF (2010). Reproduced by permission of RREEF.

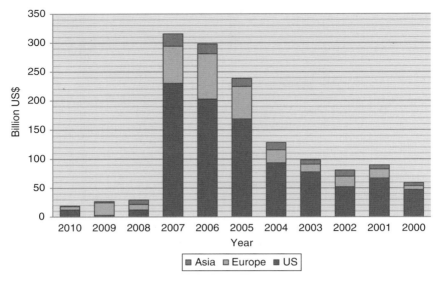

Figure 4.4   Global issuance of CMBS (US$ billions).
Source: RREEF (2010).

the United States, for example, at the peak of the market in 2007, debt accounted for just over 60% of the U.S. property market, but as the financial crisis unwound in 2008 and 2009, this share rose to nearly 80% of the overall market. This contrasts strongly with the United Kingdom and Australia where overall debt shares have fallen as public equity markets have been successfully recapitalised (RREEF, 2010).

As mentioned earlier, the two sources of finance from public markets, REITs and CMBS, have grown substantially over the last two decades (Figure 4.4 and Figure 4.5).

The CMBS market grew from almost negligible in 1990 to about US$ 310 billion in 2007. During 2008–2009, the CMBS market had completely shut down because of the financial crisis that unfolded in 2007. It has been a major source of public debt in the United States and is gaining in importance in Europe and Asia.

The United States is the largest REITs market, and this has grown substantially over the 1972–2010 period (Figure 4.5). The market capitalisation of REITs in the United States is about US$ 780 billion.

Besides institutional investors, two other groups of investors that have been active in the property investment market are Sovereign Wealth Funds (SWFs) and equity-rich individuals (HNIs). SWFs control huge sums of capital and at the moment have low or no allocation to property. However, as reported by RREEF (2008), this is changing and there is a significant potential for a share of these funds to be invested in property. HNIs comprise a diverse

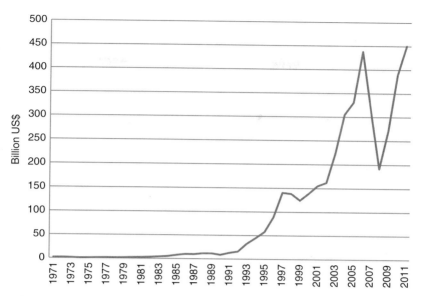

Figure 4.5   Market capitalisation for REITs in the United States (US$ billion).
Source: Based on data from NAREIT (2012).

group – retail-driven investors in German open-end funds and Australian wholesale funds and HNIs from the Middle East, Asia and Eastern Europe. As indicated by Figure 4.6, their allocation for property (an example of asset allocation of Middle Eastern HNIs) had increased during 2004–2007.

With the increasing diversity of investors interested in property, the profile of investors has also changed (Figure 4.7). The change in profile, however, differs from market to market and is a function of local conditions. The New York office market (Figure 4.7) has witnessed an increase in the share of private investors in 2005 compared with 2001. The increased share of private investors has been due to repricing of risk by investors following September 2001, which led to an increase in the share of local buyers, and national buyers such as institutional investors moved to other locations. The London office market witnessed a substantial increase in the share of investment in office stock by foreign investors during 2001–2005. American, Irish, German and Middle Eastern investors have increased their activity in this market. Hong Kong office stock is largely under public ownership. However, the trend indicates that the share of REITs and foreign investor ownership is increasing.

Property investment activity has become global, and the share of cross-border investment has increased more than fourfold during 2001–2007 (Figure 4.8), amounting to nearly 28% of the total investment. Europe witnesses a large share of cross-border investment activity within European Union (EU) countries. The share of cross-border investment activity is also increasing in the United States and Asia-Pacific. In 2007, the share of cross-border investment

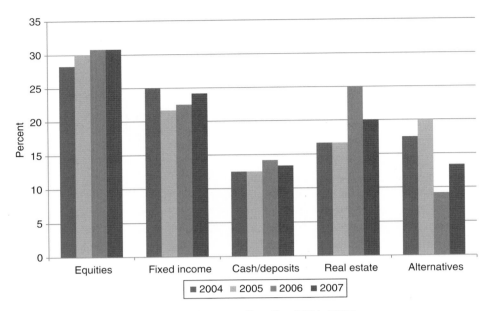

Figure 4.6   Middle Eastern HNWIs asset allocation 2004–2007.
Source: RREEF (2008), global property investment and performance 2007 and 2008.
Reproduced by permission of RREEF.

in the United States was 21% and in Asia-Pacific was 12%. Investment behaviour has changed substantially over the last 10 years. In recent years, due to globalisation of economic activities, convergence of political and economic structures (e.g. due to the enlargement of the EU), convergence in property market practices and increased market transparency, cross-border activity has increased. Capital from the United States and the United Kingdom was at the forefront of cross-border investment in 2007 (RREEF, 2008), amounting to nearly 40% of total global cross-border investment. With better understanding, increased confidence and development of diverse property investment products across the globe, a large proportion of investment has become cross-continental (Table 4.1). The destination of capital flows depends on investors' risk and return preferences. While a large proportion of the American capital has flown into emerging markets, the UK capital has been largely concentrated on mature markets in Asia and Europe.

Property in investment portfolio

Figure 4.9 presents global total returns for various asset classes. During the period 1999–2009, property returns (direct and indirect) have outperformed equity returns for 5-year and 10-year holding period. Property has delivered this higher return than equities at a far lower volatility (Tiwari and White, 2010).

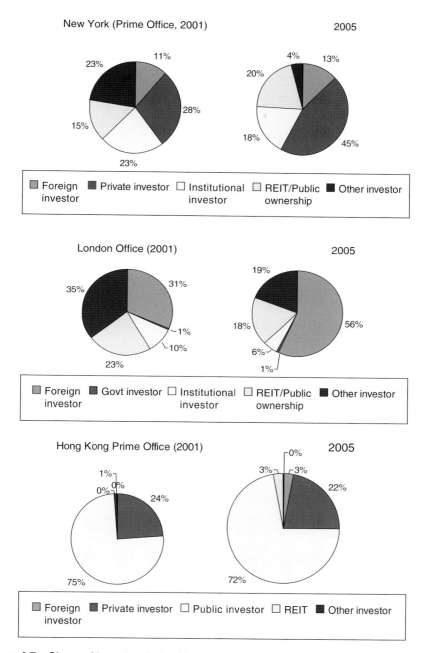

Figure 4.7 Share of investors in total invested stock.
Source: CBRE research, including CBRE (2006). Reproduced by permission of CBRE.

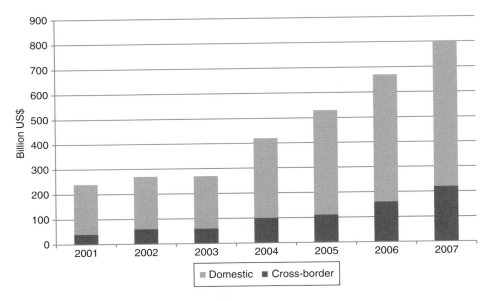

Figure 4.8   Property investment by origin.
Source: RREEF (2008), global property investment and performance 2007 and 2008.
Reproduced by permission of RREEF.

Table 4.1   Cross-continental investment activity 2006 (billion US$).

Sources of capital	Destination of activity		
	America	Europe	Asia-Pacific
America		23.4	4.4
Europe	4.7		0.7
Asia-Pacific	7.1	8.7	
Total cross-regional	11.8	32.1	5.1
Total cross-border	20.0	84.4	11.9
Total transaction	311.0	212.5	63.1

Source: Reproduced by permission of RREEF (2007).

There is huge amount of literature that looks into the question whether property (direct or indirect or both) provides diversification benefits to investors in mixed-asset portfolios comprising stocks, bonds and cash. Mueller *et al.* (1994), for example, looked at the inclusion of REITs in a mixed-asset portfolio and found that while REITs had similar returns to small-cap stocks, the associated risks were one-third that of small-cap stocks. Ibbotson (2001) found that REITs provided positive and significant diversification benefits to a mixed-asset portfolio of stocks and bonds. Ziering and McIntosh (1997) echoed similar results when they studied the benefits of including both REITs and core property in a mixed-asset portfolio of stocks and bonds from 1972 to 1995 for the U.S. markets. Their results showed that core property

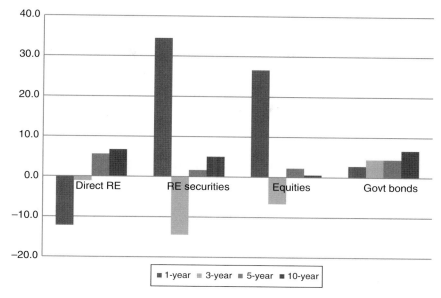

Figure 4.9   Global total returns by asset classes (1999–2009).
Source: RREEF (2010). Reproduced by permission of RREEF.

had low correlations with stocks and bonds and lower volatility. They concluded that property provided diversification benefits, as well as effective inflation-hedging capabilities.

On the question of how much of the wealth should be assigned to property, Feldman (2003) analysed both public and private property in a mixed-asset portfolio with stocks and bonds in the United States. Feldman found that maximum property allocation of 45% was possible during 1987–2001 with 15% allocated to REITs and 30% allocated to direct unleveraged property. Though these studies have suggested that the weight for property in mixed-asset portfolios of investors could be as high as 45%, in actual practice, institutional investors have assigned only 5–15% of their portfolio to property. Mueller and Mueller (2003) list the reasons for low assignment of weight for property in investor portfolio as small market size and illiquidity of property assets. Even indirect property assets like REITs, though liquid, have small market capitalisation.

In order to expand the size of opportunities for investment in property, researchers have looked at whether overseas property investment brings in the diversification benefits to investors' portfolios.

However, with international investment, there are additional risks not encountered in domestic investment portfolios. Exchange rate risk is just one that could affect return performance. Home currency returns fall if the foreign currency depreciates. Interest rate differentials may also play a role.

Lower interest rates in one country may encourage investors in that country to borrow in local currency to increase their investments. Theoretically, we should expect interest rate parity, that is, real interest rates should be equal across countries. While this may be a long-run equilibrium condition, it may not hold in the short run, and arbitrage opportunities will therefore be created.

A number of studies have been undertaken to examine this issue. Key concerns surround whether or not there are international diversification benefits from holding direct property assets and the role of currency fluctuations. The earliest studies date back to the 1980s after the first wave of financial deregulation liberated international financial flows. Marks (1986) examined stock and property returns for six countries from the perspective of investors in each country. For the period 1978–1984, he found that property in the United States outperformed the stock index in other countries, except Japan. He also highlighted the impact of currency fluctuations on investment risks and returns. Webb and Rubens (1989) use data from the United Kingdom and the United States over a long time period, 1926–1986, and compute efficient asset portfolios. They find that international property does not enter an efficient asset portfolio. Giliberto (1990), comparing U.S. and UK property returns, suggests some benefits from overseas diversification, while Ziobrowski and Curcio (1991) find no diversification benefit when examining U.S. and UK property data. Further, Ziobrowski and Boyd (1991) reach the same conclusion when leverage is present and hedging occurs to compensate for currency fluctuations when taking on local currency loans. Worzala (1992) and Worzala and Vandell (1995) examine mean returns and deviations from U.S. and UK property and suggest that there are international diversification benefits from property but less so when currency fluctuations are considered. They also suggest some instability in results over different time periods.

Newell and Webb (1998) examine property returns in the United States, the United Kingdom, Canada, Australia and New Zealand. They consider the possible impact of appraisal smoothing on the risk attached to direct property assets. Their findings are that risk is underestimated both due to smoothing and also when currency fluctuations are ignored. They also suggest some diversification benefits from the inclusion of international property in multi-asset portfolios. Stevenson (1998) examines 18 stock markets, five bond markets, U.S. direct and indirect markets and UK direct and indirect markets. In this research, only non-property international financial assets are held in portfolios. His results suggest keeping property assets in a portfolio with international financial assets. Property is also present in a low-risk/low-return portfolio. Chua (1999) examines the United States, the United Kingdom, France, Germany and Japan. Adjusting for appraisal smoothing, he finds that adding property improves risk-adjusted portfolio return performance in comparison to portfolios excluding property. Cheng *et al.* (1999) use data from the United States, the United Kingdom and Japan. They design efficient portfolios and suggest that currency risk is significant but that international property can be included in portfolios for investors who are not too risk-averse. Hoesli *et al.* (2002) examine the United States, the United Kingdom, Australia, France, the Netherlands, Sweden and Switzerland. They suggest that 15–25% of an efficient portfolio should be devoted to property assets, both national and international. However, there is no analysis of the impact of currency movements.

Literature on international indirect property investment goes back to the early 1990s. Among the earliest of studies is that of Asabere *et al.* (1991), who examine equity returns of international property companies during the 1980s. They analyse returns, standard deviations and betas. They find a negative correlation between international property and U.S. treasury bills and weak positive correlations with long-term government debt. They also find that the global property index outperforms domestic property but not global equities. Barry *et al.* (1996) examine emerging markets and find that risk-adjusted return performance improves as investment allocations to emergent markets increase. Eichholtz (1996), examining nine countries, finds that international property portfolio diversification improves portfolio performance. Mull and Soenen (1997), who adjust for the investor's home currency, argue that the addition of U.S. indirect property provides limited portfolio improvement. Gordon *et al.* (1998) examine 14 countries and construct efficient frontiers. They find that inclusion of international property improves portfolio performance and that, as returns rise, property causes risk to fall.

Gordon and Canter (1999), using the same aforementioned countries, examine correlations between stock markets and property securities. While they find that portfolios including international property assets outperform those that exclude property, they also find that correlations between asset classes vary substantially over time. Stevenson (1999) covers 16 countries and compares stock, bonds and property indices. Looking from the perspective of an Irish investor, he finds that UK property contributes only a small allocation of a mid-level risk/return portfolio. International property comes out of the portfolio when adjustment for currency is made. In a related paper, Stevenson (2000) finds that the diversification benefits of international property investment are eroded when currencies are considered. Interestingly, however, he suggests that strategies for hedging against currency risk could improve diversification benefits. Conover *et al.* (2002) analyse the United Kingdom, the United States, Canada, Hong Kong, Japan and Singapore, constructing efficient frontiers. They suggest that portfolios containing international securitised property outperform those without it.

Guerts and Jaffe (1996) suggest that the removal of market risk as a motivation of international investment is naïve and will not reduce risks sufficiently to encourage international investment. They suggest that investors will exhibit significant home asset bias, which they relate to possible institutional barriers to overseas investment in different countries, the transactions costs which overseas investment can incur and taxation of income from investment assets. Investors may have imperfect information on institutional structure and hence on the behaviour of institutions in other countries. The cost of learning institutional behaviour may outweigh the reduction in unsystematic risk and hence the expected increased return of overseas diversification. Guerts and Jaffe suggest that there are a number of factors that investors must take into consideration. First, they list risk assessment variables, including political, economic and credit risk and financial risk ratings attached to countries. Second are property rights variables, including security, arbitrary expropriation, bribery and corruption, entrepreneurship and innovation and intellectual property rights. Third are sociocultural factors including life expectancy, literacy, quality of life and home ownership. Finally, fourth are foreign investment variables covering the degrees of foreign control and treatment of foreigners. Stable economic policies aid the reduction of credit risk and improve a nation's financial risk rating. These are, furthermore, consistent with political stability, which also respects private property rights. Political instability is often positively correlated with arbitrary expropriation, corruption, lack of security of income streams from investments and violation of intellectual property rights. These factors increase country risks and significantly discourage investment.

The proportion of allocation to property in a portfolio of investment has, however, undergone change. Post 2007 financial crisis, investors became wary of investing in property. Basing on a number of industry surveys, a study by RREEF (2010) reports that investor sentiment towards property has warmed over the course of 2009 (Figure 4.10). In 2003, more than 70% of investors had more than 10% investment allocated to property. This share had reduced to just about 30% in 2008. Beginning 2009, as property markets are recovering, the share allocated to property increased.

Investment strategies

As property markets have matured over the past decade, increasing range of options for investing in property asset class have emerged. These options cater to different risk/return requirements. Based on geography of asset location (domestic or international) cash flows, asset liquidity characteristics

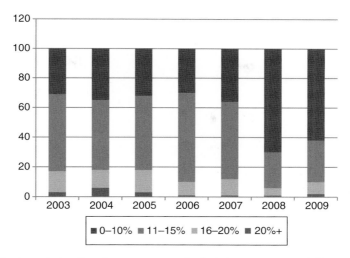

Figure 4.10   Investor's allocation to property in their investment portfolios.
Source: RREEF (2010). Reproduced by permission of RREEF.

and management of asset, RREEF (2010) classifies investment strategies of equity investor in property in four categories: core, opportunistic, value added and listed property stocks.

Core

These strategies are at the lower end of risk/return spectrum. Returns are more focused towards income return, and the focus of core strategy is on more mature, transparent and liquid markets. These strategies are, however, exposed to market movements as there tends to be little scope to manage assets through the cycle. These strategies also tend to be exposed to greater liquidity or redemption risk as many core funds are open ended.

Opportunistic

These strategies are more risky than core-type strategies, and a higher proportion of return comes from value growth. Opportunistic strategy tends to be highly leveraged and usually focuses on more volatile or emerging markets. Though these strategies have more scope to manage their way through market cycles, they suffer from inherent weaknesses (RREEF, 2010). First, they are highly leveraged which can lead to cyclical problems of increased debt costs and reduced availability, which makes it difficult to execute investment programmes or to refinance existing loans. Second, their focus on development or asset-repositioning programmes can require high levels of cash flow.

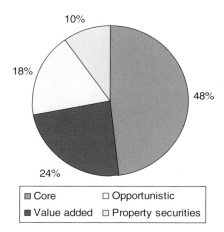

Figure 4.11   Global property investment market.
Source: RREEF (2010). Reproduced by permission of RREEF.

Value added

These strategies fall between core and opportunistic strategies, in terms of return targets, leverage and appetite for risk. Value-added strategies face similar challenges with regard to leverage, but the levels of finance tend to be lower and the income return tends to be higher, thus making refinance somewhat less of hurdle. Value-added strategies also face the challenge of being more exposed to movements in market value, but active management policies make it easier to guide their way through the periods of declining value (RREEF, 2010).

The listed property sector

The listed property sector (REITs or Listed Property Trusts (LPTs) and listed developers) possesses many of the characteristics of property as well as the broader equity markets. Property securities suffer from the volatility that the stock market suffers. Despite this volatility, property securities have advantages such as liquidity and scope for diversification, whether relative to broader equity and property markets, across countries and across portfolios.

RREEF (2010) has estimated the global property investment market by investment strategy. About 48% of the market comprises of core properties, that is, at the lower end of risk/return. Opportunistic properties, which are on the upper end of risk/return, comprise about 18% of the market. Value-added properties are about 24%, and the rest are property securities (Figure 4.11).

Return on investment by investment strategy has varied across geography and over time. Table 4.2 presents returns in different markets by investment

Table 4.2 Return on investment in nominal terms.

	Europe			Americas		Asia		
	United Kingdom (%)	Continental Europe (%)	CEE (%)	North America (%)	Latin America (%)	Japan (%)	Asia ex Japan (%)	Global (%)
Core	7	7	9	7	9	5	6	6.90
Value added	10	9	11	9	11	7	11	9.10
Opportunistic	12	14	16	15	17	12	17	14.80
Property securities	7	10	11	10	13	7	10	9.30
Inflation								

Source: Reproduced by permission of RREEF (2010).

strategy. The hierarchy of return has been consistent with the investment strategy, but they have differed across different regions. It, however, is clear that property has generated attractive returns on nominal (without adjusting for inflation) and real (after adjusting for inflation) terms.

Property investment and leverage

As mentioned earlier, the commercial property investment is highly leveraged, and the leverage has increased substantially during the last 15–20 years. In the United States, banks hold US$1.7 trillion of commercial property loans, roughly half of the loan issued for commercial property in the United States (DB Research, 2010). Table 4.3 presents key ratios that depict the importance of commercial property debt in the economy. Commercial property loans total 24% of all bank loans outstanding. European banks have commercial property loans of about US$2.6 trillion on their books. Total commercial property loans account for about 11% of total bank loans outstanding in Europe (13% in the United Kingdom and 10% in Germany) and 24% in the United States. There are also substantial regional differences in terms of public commercial property loans: the CMBS volume outstanding accounts for 8% of commercial property loans in Europe, while the share in the United States is roughly 25%. A comparison with the residential mortgage market (Table 4.3) highlights that practically all indicators are considerably higher than in the commercial mortgage market.

The financing structure poses considerable risk as the overall debt is quite high as a proportion of nation's GDP. A large part of this debt is securitised as CMBS or RMBS. While securitisation has the advantage of transferring the risk from lending institutions to investors, it also has risks. When a CMBS transaction matures, the loans have to be refinanced, depending on

Table 4.3 Key ratios related to commercial property debt.

Figures and key ratios denoting the economic importance of commercial real estate debt financing (US$ billion)

	US	Europe	UK	DE
Total credit market				
1 Total loans	7058	23700	4325	5368
2 Total securitisations	9579	2619	860	125
3 Total credit market	16637	26319	5185	5493
Residential mortgage market				
4 RMBS volume outstanding	6739	1610	639	24
5 Mortgage loans from banks	3026	6773	1379	1337
6 Mortgage loans from others*	7760	n.a.	n.a.	n.a.
7 Mortgage loans from banks as share of total loans	43%	29%	32%	25%
8 RMBS in relation to mortgage loans	62%	24%	46%	2%
9 RMBS share in total securitisations	70%	61%	74%	19%
10 RMBS share in total credit market	41%	6%	12%	0.4%
Commercial mortgage market				
11 CMBS volume outstanding	855	195	98	24
12 Commercial real estate – invested stock	3987	3308	612	826
13 Commercial real estate loans from banks	1690	2569	557	514
14 Commercial real estate loans from others*	1693	n.a.	n.a.	n.a.
15 Mortgage-backed covered bonds (CBs)/pfandbriefe outstanding	18	2227	275	319
16 of which covered by commercial real estate	n.a.	n.a.	n.a.	128
17 CB/pfandbriefe share in invested stock	0.45%	67%	45%	39%
18 Commercial real estate loans from banks as share of total loans	24%	11%	13%	10%
19 CMBS in relation to commercial real estate loans	25%	8%	18%	5%
20 CMBS share in total securitisations	9%	7%	11%	19%
21 CMBS share in total credit market	5.1%	0.7%	1.9%	0.4%
22 Commercial real estate loan share in invested stock	85%	78%	91%	62%
23 CMBS share in invested stock	21%	6%	16%	3%

* e.g. insurance companies, pension funds, GSEs.
Source: Reproduced by permission of RREEF and DB Research (2010).

how much of the loan has already been amortised. In line with the given structure (interest-only loans, partial interest-only loans, amortising loans), this gives rise to a more or less pronounced refinancing risk for the bank/lender and a 'maturity risk' for the bondholder. Various factors may lead to the failure of a refinancing move: the value or the rating of the collateral may have deteriorated owing to changes in demand, changes in income streams from the property and/or changes in the capital market, meaning that the risk premiums may increase. If there are not enough buffers available, this can make refinancing economically unattractive (DB Research, 2010). The probability of refinancing proving to be more difficult increases if credit standards at the time of issue were laxer, the subordination level of the receivables was lower and/or none or only part of the principal has been redeemed. The share of interest-only loans or partial interest-only loans securitised in CMBS has strongly increased over the past few years. In 2009, it totalled 100% in European CMBS issues (2003: 31%) and 94% in American CMBS issues (2003: 39%) (DB Research, 2010).

Conclusions

Based on the factual evidence, this chapter presented a review of the profile of property investors, investment opportunities, investment vehicles, investment strategies and geography of their investment.

The discussion previously brings out the following trends:

- The profile of property investors has become diverse with institutional investors (such as insurance companies, pension funds), banks, private equity funds and HNIs investing in property.
- A number of vehicles for direct and indirect investment in property have emerged which have helped in the development of property investment market.
- Research has demonstrated diversification benefits in investors' portfolio by inclusion of direct and indirect property both domestic and overseas. However, since the opportunities for investment in domestic property market are rather limited, investors have explored overseas property markets during the last two decades.
- With globalisation, integration of various markets and desire to diversify investment portfolios by including assets overseas, there has been a trend towards cross-border investment in property.
- Various property vehicles offer opportunities for investment according to risk/return requirements of investors. Nearly half of the property investment market is concentrated in low risk/return opportunities. Another important point that has emerged from the discussion earlier is that the

return on investment not only varies by investment strategy but also by geography.

- Finally, the debt in property investment has increased substantially over time.

Three trends that have emerged in the property markets, which are seen as a dominant feature of the new economy, are technology-led growth of investment vehicles such as CMBS and REITs, globalisation and associated investment flows and leverage. Implications of these trends will be explored further in Chapters 6 and 7, when we will discuss property cycles and risks.

Appendix 4.1 In this section, a brief description of CMBS and REITs has been presented. For detailed and technical discussion on these, refer to Geltner *et al.* (2006).

Commercial mortgage-backed securities (CMBS)
Source: **Adapted from *RREEF (2010)***

CMBS are securitised receivable assets using mortgages on commercial property as collateral. Securitisations are of two types: either 'true sale' or synthetic. With true sale securitisation, a bank sells a package of loan receivables to a so-called special purpose vehicle (SPV). Full ownership is transferred to the SPV, meaning that the receivables – including all the related risks (credit risk, interest rate risk, etc.) – are no longer on the bank's balance sheet. The SPV then issues bonds/debt securities (CMBS) on the capital market in order to fund the purchase of the assets. The SPV's receivables are split up in tranches, that is, divided into various risk/reward categories to serve differing investor interests. These tranches are assessed by a rating agency. The so-called senior tranche is the safest investment. By contrast, the junior tranche has to bear the initial losses. Payment defaults and returns are distributed according to the cascade principle, that is, investors holding the junior tranche receive the highest return but are also the first to be affected if defaults occur. After them come the investors who buy the mezzanine tranche, if any, and finally the senior investors. Typically, banks and SPVs are senior tranche investors. The mezzanine tranches are usually purchased by insurance companies, pension funds or other asset managers. The junior tranche is held in most cases by hedge funds, pension funds or other dealers/operators of actively managed funds and in some cases also by issuers to indicate reliability.

The future payments (repayment of principal and/or only interest) do not flow to the bank that issued the loans, but to the CMBS investors. This results in their participating fully in the success or failure of the property deal, depending on the tranche chosen.

With a synthetic securitisation, the loan receivables stay on the books of the lending institution. The credit risk (payment arrears, default – depending on the structure) is transferred to the SPV via credit default swaps. In addition, the investor assumes a counterparty risk since in the case of the bank's insolvency, the insolvency practitioner can take recourse to the receivables on the bank's balance sheet. The funds obtained from CMBS issuance are taken by the SPV and partly invested in the credit derivatives and in lower-risk assets (e.g. sovereign bonds or covered bonds).

The illiquid and long-term nature of the (commercial) property market, combined with high transaction costs, means that if there is a macroeconomic shock, it is not easy for supply to readjust in the short-term and re-establish market equilibrium. In such cases, the role of CMBS is basically to help make the commercial property market more liquid and more transparent. At the same time, CMBS offer improved risk allocation for issuers and investors. This way, more investors can participate in the comparatively illiquid, long-horizon market which would otherwise be the preserve of fewer investors. Moreover, investors can take more targeted action in new markets and thus diversify their investment risks. Risk is spread among a wider investor community. However, this fundamental assessment implicitly requires that all market participants are able to adequately value the risks of a specific transaction *ex ante* and that as a result a particular transaction will fit well in an investor's overall portfolio.

CMBS differ from bonds (such as covered bonds) in terms of the risk to investors. In case of bonds, the investor acquires a claim on the issuer and on the underlying asset (the mortgage loan); this gives it double backing. The CMBS investor, by contrast, only obtains a claim on the pool of receivables and not on the issuer.

Generally, the LTV ratio on bonds is capped by law (LTV on covered bonds in Europe is capped at 60–80%). These standards do not apply to CMBS. The higher CMBS default risk – on the junior tranches in particular – is attributable not least to the missing option of direct action between the investor and the bank.

Majority of CMBS originate in the United States, where the market has been developing since the early 1980s. The first non-U.S. CMBS instruments were issued in 1989 in Europe (in the Netherlands and shortly afterwards in the United Kingdom) and the Caribbean (Dutch Antilles). The share of U.S. issuance in the global CMBS market has declined on the growth of CMBS markets in Europe and Asia (Japan in particular). At the peak of CMBS issuing activity in 2007, the U.S. share was down to 'only' a little less than 73%. The European CMBS market is dominated by the United Kingdom and Ireland. These two countries account for nearly 70% of cumulated CMBS issuance in Europe.

Table A.4.1   Select statistics about REITs.

Country comparison table

Country	Market capitalization US$ millions	Total rate of return – 1 year (%)	Total rate of return – 3 years (%)	Weighted average dividend yield (%)
Australia	70747	10.4	−25.0	9.7
Belgium	6761	17.2	−2.4	1.4
Canada	20610	56.2	−3.3	8.1
France	64526	45.5	−9.6	0.2
Germany	713	45.5	N/A	
Hong Kong	9518	64.5	9.9	8.1
Japan	29432	6.7	−19.4	6.9
Malaysia	1542	38.6	10.2	3.7
Netherlands	11234	40.9	−6.0	
New Zealand	2540	12.7	−4.9	8.4
Singapore	23134	85.6	−4.2	8.9
South Africa	3400	17.5	12.4	8.5
South Korea	132	28.4	12.1	8.4
Turkey	1889	151.3	−1.8	
United Kingdom	37176	14.5	−26.3	4.6
United States	271850	27.9	−14.2	5.6

Source: Ernst and Young (2010).

Real Estate Investment Trusts
Source: **Adapted from http://www.sec.gov/answers/reits.htm**

Real Estate Investment Trusts, known as REITs, are entities that invest in different kinds of property or property-related assets, including shopping centres, office buildings, hotels and mortgages secured by property. There are basically three types of REITs:

- Equity REITs, the most common type of REIT, invest in or own property and make money for investors from the rents they collect.
- Mortgage REITs lend money to owners and developers or invest in financial instruments secured by mortgages on property.
- Hybrid REITs are a combination of equity and mortgage REITs.

REITs are governed by certain regulations related to payout, holding period of an asset, type of investment, etc. For example, in the United States, the REITs must pay 90% of its taxable income to shareholders every year. It must also invest at least 75% of its total assets in property and generate 75% or more of its gross income from investments in or mortgages on real property. Many REITs trade on national exchanges or in the over-the-counter market.

The biggest REIT markets are in the United States and Australia (where they are called LPTs). In Asia (Japan and Singapore) and Europe (United

Kingdom), REITs were introduced during the last 5–10 years, and they have already reached substantial market capitalisation (Table A.4.1).

References

Asabere, P., Kleiman, R. and McGowan, C. (1991) The risk–return attributes of international real estate equities. *Journal of Real Estate Research*, **6** (2), 143–152.

Barry, C., Rodriguez, M. and Lipscomb, J. (1996) Diversification potential from real estate companies in emerging capital markets. *Journal of Real Estate Portfolio Management*, **2** (2), 107–118.

CBRE (2006) *REITS Around Asia*. CBRE Research, December.

Cheng, P., Ziobrowski, A., Caines, R. and Ziobrowski, B. (1999) Uncertainty and foreign real estate. *Journal of Real Estate Research*, **18** (3), 463–80.

Chua, A. (1999) The role of international real estate in global mixed-asset investment portfolios. *Journal of Real Estate Portfolio Management*, **5** (2), 129–137.

Conner, P. and Liang, Y. (2003) *The Expanding Frontier of Institutional Property*. Pramerica Property Investor, Pramerica Financial, May. NJ, US.

Conover, C., Friday, H. and Sirmans, G. (2002) Diversification benefits from foreign real estate investments. *The Journal of Real Estate Portfolio Management*, **8** (1), 17–25.

DB Research (2010) *Commercial Property Loans Facing Refinancing Risks*. Deutsche Bank Research, July. Frankfurt am Main, Germany.

Eichholtz, P. (1996) The stability of the covariance of international property share returns. *Journal of Real Estate Research*, **11** (2), 149–158.

Ernst and Young (2010) *Global Property Investment Trust Report 2010: Against All Odds*. Ernst and Young.

Feldman, B.E. (2003) Investment Policy for Securitized and Direct Real Estate, *Journal of Portfolio Management. Special Real Estate Issue*, 112–121.

Geltner, D.M., Miller, N.G., Clayton, J. and Eichholtz, P. (2006) *Commercial Real Estate Analysis and Investments*, 2nd edn. South-Western, Division of Thomson Learning, Mason.

Giliberto, S. (1990) *Global Real Estate Securities: Index Performance and Diversified Portfolios*. Salomon Brothers, Inc., New York.

Gordon, J. and Canter, T. (1999) International real estate securities a test of capital markets integration. *Journal of Real Estate Portfolio Management*, **5** (2), 161–170.

Gordon, J., Canter, T. and Webb, J. (1998) The effects of international real estate securities on portfolio diversification. *Journal of Real Estate Portfolio Management*, **4** (2), 83–92.

Geurts, T. and Jaffe, A. (1996) Risk and real estate investment: an international perspective. *Journal of Real Estate Research*, **11** (2), 117–130.

Hoesli, M., Lekander, J. and Witkiewitz, W. (2002) International evidence on real estate as a portfolio diversifier. *Working Paper: Research Paper No 70*. FAME. Zurich, Switzerland.

Ibbotson Associates (2001) *Stocks, Bonds, Bills and Inflation, 2001 Yearbook*, Ibbotson Associates Inc., US.

Marks, E. (1986) Real rates of return among foreign investors in US real estate. *Real Estate Finance Journal*, **1** (3), 56–61.

Mueller, A.G. and Mueller, G.R. (2003) Public and Private Real Estate in a Mixed Asset Portfolio. *Journal of Real Estate Portfolio Management*, **9** (3), 193–203.

Mueller, G.R., Pauley, K.R. and Morrill, W.K. Jr. (1994) Should REITs be Included in a Mixed-Asset Portfolio? *Real Estate Finance*, **11**, 23–28.

Mull, S. and Soenen, L. (1997) U.S. REITs as an asset class in international investment portfolios. *Financial Analysts Journal*, **53** (2), 55–61.

NAREIT (2012) *REITWatch, August, National Association of Real Estate Investment Trust*, www.reit.com (accessed 23 August 2012).

Newell, G. and Webb, J. (1998) Real estate performance benchmarks in New Zealand and South Africa. *Journal of Real Estate Literature*, **6** (2), 137–143.

RREEF (2006) Global Insight, August, London.

RREEF (2007) Global Real Estate Investment and Performance, March, London.

RREEF (2008) *Global real estate investment and performance 2007 and 2008*. RREEF Limited, London.

RREEF (2010) *Global Property Insights 2010*. RREEF Research, February, London.

Stevenson, S. (1998) The role of commercial real estate in international multi-asset portfolios. *Working Paper BF No. 98-2*. University College, Dublin.

Stevenson, S. (1999) Real estate's role in an international multi asset portfolio: empirical evidence using Irish data. *Journal of Property Research*, **16** (3), 219–242.

Stevenson, S. (2000) International real estate diversification: empirical tests using hedged indices. *Journal of Real Estate Research*, **19** (1/2), 105–131.

Tiwari, P. and White, M. (2010) *International Real Estate Economics*. Palgrave Macmillan, UK.

Webb, B. and Rubens, J. H. (1989) Diversification gains from including foreign real estate in a mixed asset portfolio. Paper presented at *the American Real Estate Society Meetings*, San Francisco.

Webb, J., Curcio, R. and Rubens, J. (1988) Diversification Gains From Including Real Estate In Mixed-Asset Portfolios. *Decision Sciences*, **19**, 434–452.

Worzala, E. (1992) *International direct real estate investments as alternative portfolio assets for institutional investors: an evaluation*. Unpublished dissertation, University of Wisconsin-Madison.

Worzala, E. and Vandell, K. (1995) International real estate investments as alternative portfolio assets for institutional investors: an evaluation. Paper presented at *the IRES/ERES Meetings*, Stockholm.

Ziering, B., Winograd, B. and McIntosh, W. (1997) The Evolution of Public and Private Market Investing in the New Real Estate Capital Markets. *Real Estate Finance*, **14** (2), 21–29.

Ziobrowski, A. and Boyd, J. (1991) Leverage and foreign investment in US real estate. *Journal of Real Estate Research*, **7** (1), 33–58.

Ziobrowski, A.J. and Curcio, R.J. (1991) Diversification benefits of US real estate to foreign investors. *Journal of Real Estate Research*, **6** (2), 119–142.

5

Financial Markets, the New Economy and the Risk

Introduction

In literature, the 'new economy' is the name given to those industries benefiting directly and indirectly from the latest revolution in information and communication technologies and the extensive use of the latest electronic systems, advanced software, digitalisation and the internet (Chorafas, 2001). The new economy contrasts with the old economy which includes those companies that are still embedded in old business models (characterised by paper-based supply chain management, traditional ways of inventory management, relying on high street financial institutions for credit, little product innovation, etc.) in its creativity, which is the source of growth and wealth in the new economy (Chorafas, 2001).

In this chapter, we will explore the interlinkages between the new economy, real estate and financing of real estate. The real estate industry has undergone transformations during the last quarter of a century. A lot of these transformations, particularly in the nature of space being demanded, its location and the range of indirect investment opportunities that have emerged, are being attributed to the technological advances and availability of information. The availability of information about real estate sector has improved due to widespread use of information and communication technologies.

Real Estate Finance in the New Economy, First Edition. Piyush Tiwari and Michael White.
© 2014 John Wiley & Sons, Ltd. Published 2014 by John Wiley & Sons, Ltd.

Is the new economy a recent phenomenon? This question has been debated in literature. Rowlatt *et al.* (2002) argue that there have always been new economies and the concept is independent of time or technology. Developments such as printing, steam, railways, canal, power and mass media have all fuelled the industrial revolution of the early nineteenth century. However, characteristics of the new economy of the twenty-first century differ from earlier developments in three ways (Rowlatt *et al.*, 2002):

- Information is the key and this has been made possible by the development of infrastructure to assemble, analyse, communicate and manage information in 'computer-mediated networks'.
- The market boundaries have expanded from physical locations to include virtual locations, thereby reducing the transaction cost and expanding the universe of consumers and suppliers of goods and services. The internet has made this possible and penetration of the internet has expanded phenomenally.
- The transfer of information among enterprises or individuals, which adds to value, has dramatically increased.

It is the sheer scale of information processing power that has provided the driving force for the new economy (Dixon and Thompson, 2005). The other forces such as globalisation have provided further impetus to the new economy. Traditional macroeconomic models have considered the role of technology in economic growth of nations (see, e.g. Schumpeter, 1939; Perez, 2002) or at the firm level (Scarbrough and Corbett, 1992). These models argue that technology enhances labour and capital productivity which then contribute to economic growth. There are also studies which have explored the spatial impacts of technology on cities (Berry, 1973; Castells, 1996) and on real estate (Gibson and Lizieri, 2001). On one hand, the impact of technology could lead to clustering of activities. On the other hand, technological and organisational possibilities have the potential for organising social and work practices without physical proximity. Both of these have consequences for the nature of real estate that is occupied, invested and financed.

Over the last two decades, financial industry has undergone substantial transformation – from a traditional high street characterised by institutions offering and advising clients on the various products to finance and invest in assets to a sophisticated system which has developed innovative ways to channelise capital through the use of technology, innovation and product development. The new economy opens up global competition for financial institutions. Even institutions with competitive edge within their local territory might not maintain this edge if they don't think about global competition. Globalisation has eroded traditional geographical boundaries and the whole notion of time zones.

These changes in the financial industry have had profound impact in the way investors invest in real estate and the way real estate is financed. A whole spectrum of new real estate-based products have emerged which allow immense options for investment- and knowledge-based advisory by real estate service providers. Broadly speaking, two types of real estate investment opportunities have existed – direct, investment in traditional brick and mortar type of real estate asset, and indirect, investment in securities of real estate companies and real estate investment trusts. The new economy has expanded this horizon as technology has allowed a number of derivative products to be developed with underlying assets as real estate and globalisation has facilitated investors around the world to these products. Besides traditional sources of finances for real estate (commercial bank loans and investor equity), financing is being done through various new sources of equity and debt – raised internationally through private equity funds, sovereign funds, mortgage-backed securities, index-based derivatives and many more variants.

The new economy, however, is highly leveraged with risks compounded, and this has implications for organisations as they have to carefully balance competing objectives of short-term profits and long-term financial stability. The new economy has faced challenges in recent times – dot-com bubble burst in 2000 which led to major correction of the NASDAQ and of New York Stock Exchanges and subprime mortgage loan crisis of 2007 which caused collapse of financial institutions like Bear Stearns, Lehman Brothers and capitalisation of banks by governments across the globe to save them from collapsing and has led global economy in an unprecedented recession – and many organisations have been scrambling for professional guidance. However, the difficulty is that the financial institutions and technology companies responsible for the changes taking place are themselves struggling to make right guesses on the course they should follow.

The source of growth and wealth creation in the new economy is creativity. However, an important feature of the new economy is risk. Traditional view on financial risk comprising credit risk and market risk is limiting, as recent experience of the 2007 financial crisis demonstrates, and the attention is now also focusing on the operational risk, which covers a whole environment in which the management of credit, market and other risks takes place. These risks facing an institution get amplified because of globalisation, deregulation, innovation and technology (Chorafas, 2001). One of the major assumptions that was part of traditional risk assessment that money will always be available if crisis hits is challenged in the new economy. This assumption came under severe test during the 2007 financial crisis. Some of the large economies like the United States and the United Kingdom channelised large amount of public money to bail out their financial institution, but economies like Greece, Spain, Iceland and Ireland have been badly affected. Liquidity in the financial market completely dried up, and money went out of many assets (including real estate) into safer opportunities (like government bonds). The mortgage-backed securities market had completely shut down globally as the risk exposure of various institutions to these securities was not known.

The objective of this chapter is to theoretically discuss how risks associated with investment and financing of real estate in the new economy change. However, it would be important to start with an understanding of value determinants of real estate in the twenty-first century. Some of these determinants have been facilitated by advances in technology which have improved access to information and reduced transaction costs in particular related to cross-border transactions. This discussion is followed by theorisation of links between real estate and the new economy. The chapter then reviews the developments in real estate investment and finance particularly from the perspective of risk, which is the core of this chapter. Finally, the chapter concludes with a brief discussion on how the risk has changed in the new economy.

Value determinants of real estate in the twenty-first century

Three factors that are contributing to the value of real estate are globalisation, sustainability and innovation. In this section, we explore them further.

Economic globalisation

Let's begin by observing and interpreting recent changes in the global economy. Compared to most of the twentieth century when the world economy was highly polarised towards the United States, Europe and Japan, the twenty-first century appears to be increasingly multipolar. Since the 2008–2009 financial crisis, the clout of emerging economies has grown substantially with global growth becoming more diffused and no one country dominating the global economic scene. Emerging economies have become a powerful force in international production, trade and finance (World Bank, 2011). The share of emerging and developing economies in international trade flows has increased from 26% in 1995 to 42% in 2010, and a large increase in trade is due not to trade between developed and developing nations but among the developing nations (World Bank, 2011). Foreign direct investment (FDI) is also witnessing similar trends. About a third of FDI in developing countries currently originates in other developing countries. The emerging and developing countries hold three-quarters of all official foreign exchange reserves. The risk of investing in emerging economies has also declined. As investors and multinational companies increase their exposure to emerging and developing economies, international demand for real estate in these economies grows. A large part of the global economic growth in next two decades would be generated in emerging economies such as Brazil, China, India, Indonesia, the Republic of Korea and the Russian Federation, and these economies would witness major transformations to their economies, corporate sectors and financial systems.

One of the transformations that are happening in emerging economies is the rise in innovation and innovative capacity of these countries. China and India are investing heavily in R&D. Examples of major technological advancements in emerging economies are siting of major research facility by Microsoft in China; invention of microcar, Nano, by Tata in India; and various aeronautical breakthroughs in Russia (World Bank, 2011). Another transformation in emerging economies is in terms of realignment of growth from external sources to internal demand. There is already a trend towards an increase in domestic demand in East Asia and East Europe. These economies are also witnessing increasing trade flows, in terms of exports and imports. As international trade shares of emerging economies increase, the global wealth and asset holding will shift towards emerging economies with surpluses (World Bank, 2011). International financial landscape already reflects this. In 2010, emerging economies held three times the international reserves held by advanced economies. Of the global cross-border mergers and acquisitions, about a third was by firms based in emerging economies. These commercial interests have reinforced financial globalisation as evidenced by the trend that a growing number of emerging market firms undertake at least one cross-border acquisition within 2 years of accessing international capital markets. As firms in emerging markets play an increasingly important role in the global business, they compete with firms in developed economies for resources, technologies and access to markets. Firms in emerging markets have advantage over firms in developed economies in trawling through difficult policy environment in other developing countries as they have experiences similar to conditions in their home countries (World Bank, 2011).

An implication of these global economic trends is that the commercial activity is organising around the network of gateway cities that form a series of global pathways in developed and emerging markets (ULI, 2011). The list of gateway cities has expanded from London, New York and Tokyo to include Paris; Hong Kong; Washington, DC; Seoul; Singapore; Los Angeles; and Shanghai, which together with the traditional three have become destinations for real estate investment flows. Major international airport and seaport infrastructure allows organisation of commercial activities in a way that allows service and manufacturing sector jobs to low-cost locations.

Sustainability

There is a worldwide movement towards sustainability over the last decade. Though there still is lack of consistency and comparable standards, firms, cities and governments are pursuing strategies that are aligned with efficient energy usage, water conservation and reduced carbon emissions. Governments in some countries have legislated on the sustainability requirements for buildings. Five major cities and two states in the United States have enacted energy performance measurement and disclosure policies to help tenants and investors make better informed decisions (JLL, 2012). Buildings in Europe are required to display energy performance certificates, and Australia is implementing similar measures (JLL, 2012).

There is also a voluntary move by firms towards sustainability performance measurement and disclosure. A global initiative by a nonprofit entity Carbon Disclosure Project (CDP) to collect data on environmental information from firms through voluntary disclosure process has seen more than 3000 firms including 400 Fortune 500 firms reporting their carbon emissions, water management and climate change policies to CDP. In 2012, more than 655 institutional investors representing in excess of US$78 trillion in assets supported CDP in engaging with companies worldwide to disclose and ultimately manage climate change issues. A similar initiative is underway at the city level, and in 2012, CDP is requesting sustainability disclosure from 150 cities from all continents of the world. Sustainability rating systems such as LEED, Energy Star and NABERS are frequently used by owners in rating their buildings as they seek to attract international tenants. There is also a trend towards solar energy. In the United States alone, more than 1 gigawatt of photovoltaic solar energy capacity was installed, and much of these installations were at commercial properties (JLL, 2012). According to ULI (2011), new or retrofitted Grade A buildings with green ratings are securing higher rents and achieving higher values when sold. Developers, owners and investors are realising that investing in available energy- and water-saving technologies can produce low-risk returns, creating more marketable and valuable real estate assets (ULI, 2011).

Innovation and preferences

Two trends are important here: (i) innovations are changing the way local consumer services are demanded, the way goods are supplied and the way activities are managed. There is more information available in the marketplace, more of it on real-time basis and on smartphones that it is changing industries along the way (ULI, 2011); (ii) innovations are also impacting on the global economic order with emerging economies becoming important in global economic growth. To understand the role of innovation in economic growth, let's begin by reviewing key messages from the literature on growth path of nations. The economic growth of nations has path dependency (Blakemore and Herrendorf, 2009). In the pregrowth period, economies remain locked in persistent subsistence living conditions primarily engaged in agricultural activities. The early stage of development is accompanied with labour flows from agriculture into industry and services sectors. In a later stage, the economic structure shifts towards services sector involving labour flows from agriculture and industry to services. As countries progress, they purchase modern capital from the advanced economies and adopt the advanced production techniques appropriate for their level (Blakemore and Herrendorf, 2009). In this phase, countries become competitive relative to leading economies. As this phase ends, innovation becomes important for growth in developed nations as existing industries in developed economies are subjected to global competition particularly from industries in emerging economies that have significant labour cost advantages. Innovation explained relative high growth in developed world (including Japan, which grew phenomenally since the 1950s) compared to emerging markets for most of the twentieth century.

It is, however, important to understand the difference between two concepts of innovations: technological innovation and business innovation. In simple terms, technological innovation is about inventing something by leveraging technology, while business innovation is about inventing a better way to do something by using an innovative and disruptive business model. The second half of the 2000s has seen emerging markets becoming hotbeds of business innovation. They are reinventing systems of production and distribution, and they are experimenting with entirely new business models. These economies which had until recently been associated with cheap labour-led manufacturing are now becoming leaders in innovation. As discussed earlier, local companies in these economies are willing to go global driven by a mixture of pull and push factors, pull factor being ambition to bestride the world stage and push factor being the growth of even cheaper competitors in, say, Vietnam or Cambodia, who are also moving up the value chain. Given that a large proportion of population in emerging economies lives in tier 2 and tier 3 cities, companies from both emerging and developed economies are rethinking their business models from production to distribution systems in order to penetrate this market.

The world's biggest multinationals are locating their research and development activities in emerging markets (*Economist*, 2010). Companies in the *Fortune* 500 list have 98 R&D facilities in China and 63 in India (*Economist*, 2010). These economies are also contributing to the technological innovation increasingly, a trend that has diverged from past where technological breakthrough used to happen in developed economies and then they use to trickle down to other nations. General Electric's health-care arm has built a

R&D centre in Bangalore (India), its biggest anywhere in the world. Cisco has built its second global headquarters – Cisco East – in Bangalore. Microsoft's R&D centre in Beijing is its largest outside its American headquarters. Knowledge-intensive companies such as IT specialists and consultancies have hugely stepped up the number of people they employ in developing countries. For example, a quarter of Accenture's workforce is in India (*Economist*, 2010).

Technological innovations particularly related to information and communication technologies have facilitated business innovations in developed and emerging markets. For example, the impact of e-commerce on retailing has been profound. This is also influencing the way logistics industry operates and inventories are managed. Requirement to hold large inventories has reduced as communication through the supply chain has become quicker due to technological advances. In terms of logistic real estate, these changes may imply that the warehouses are constructed near distribution hubs rather than production hubs. A recent report by ULI (2011) argues that the internet allows work from fringe locations, thereby sustaining demand for second homes in the country and resort locations. Technology also reduces the demand for commercial space, while the use of space becomes more efficient.

Theorising real estate linkages in the new economy

Two main factors that are driving real estate value in the new economy – globalisation and technology – have impacted the use, investment, development and real estate service provision. As discussed earlier, even though the supply of space in the use market is defined by its physical location, the demand drivers are global. Over the last two decades or so, the growth and expansion of transnational enterprises has had profound impact on the nature of space (floor plate, specification and network connectivity requirements) that is demanded. Suppliers of space, though largely local, have responded to the demand factors because international ownership of space is increasing through various indirect investment channels. Most of the new space that is being built in most markets adheres to global standards. Investors in real estate assets, as discussed in Chapter 4, are also becoming global. Local developers are forming joint ventures or strategic alliance with developers overseas to produce new space. Real estate service providers have played an important role in the whole process by aligning their service standards to the requirements of global clients. They have expanded the scope of the services that they provide and have expanded and standardised practices across different markets. Globalisation makes it necessary to account for different cultures, business environments, moral values and

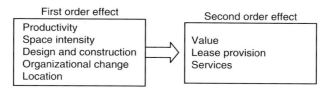

First order effect

| Productivity |
| Space intensity |
| Design and construction |
| Organizational change |
| Location |

Second order effect

| Value |
| Lease provision |
| Services |

Figure 5.1 Technology and real estate impacts. *Source*: Adapted from Dixon and Thompson (2005).

often contradictory regulatory rules and laws. Globalisation also forces working round the clock, moving and trading across time zones and country borders.

Though the impact of globalisation on real estate is now clearly understood (see, e.g. Tiwari and White, 2010), the research on impact of technology (defined here as information and communication technology) on real estate, as discussed earlier, is still in early stages. Many authors (see, e.g. Boulton *et al.* (2000), Borsuk (1999)) were starting to forecast the demise of physical assets in the new economy. They argue that the penetration of technology would enhance productivity and this would reduce the demand for real estate space. However, this initial hype of technology has been misconstrued in the sense that demand for real estate has not reduced but technology has affected the intensity of use of real estate, its configuration/layout and location, the amount procured and the duration over which commercial real estate is procured (Dixon and Thompson, 2005). The impact of technology can be viewed as first-order and second-order impact, as shown in Figure 5.1.

The impact of technology on productivity is extensively debated in literature. Some argue that productivity will increase job losses, while others argue that productivity will lead to decrease in cost of production and hence prices, which in turn will increase the demand for goods and hence employment. Employment has an impact on demand for real estate space. While the impacts on jobs are not very clear, one discerning pattern that is emerging is in space intensity. There is an increasing trend in separation of front and back office works. The back office work is getting located in low-cost areas and often overseas to destinations like India, China, Central Europe and Ireland.

The design and construction of space has also changed. Flexibility, efficiency and effectiveness in design and use are increasingly becoming the defining features (Dixon and Thompson, 2005). In case of office real estate, four themes largely driven by technological and organisational change have emerged in the development as discussed by Myerson and Ross (2003). These are (i) narrative office, where design and layout are used as brand differentiators (examples of such buildings are Asahi Beer building in Tokyo,

Toyota's headquarter in London, Cisco's smart buildings in Silicon Valley); (ii) nodal office, where new ways of working that encourage hot-desking, and hotelling for networking purposes, complement more mobile work methods (example is McKinsey and Co's Amsterdam Harbour complex); (iii) neighbourly office, where design and layout promotes social interaction (example is Cellular Operations centre in Swindon, United Kingdom); and (iv) nomadic office, consisting of a series of geographically distributed spaces for work (example includes work space operated by British Telecom in the United Kingdom).

New organisation/business model in the new economy is highly networked with features such as flat, fast, flexible, process-driven, global and highly interdependent (CORENET, 2004). This has implications for location of work space and type of buildings. The traditional work paradigm, which consisted of permanent employment, standardised working hours (9 AM–5 PM), full-time employment, state-provided social security provisions, workplaces co-located in centralised buildings and strong intra-organisational cooperation based on face-to-face meetings with external contacts limited to certain gateways, is giving way to a new paradigm (Dixon and Thompson, 2005). The twenty-first-century work paradigm is characterised by spatial dislocation, self-employment, diversity and flexibility in working patterns and stronger external boundary cooperation (Dixon and Thompson, 2005). Some of these trends are reflected in 'working from home' or 'outsourcing' of part of the processes of a firm. Work space is becoming far more dispersed and buildings, 'smart'. A smart building is highly networked.

The second-order impact of the preference shift is on value, lease covenants and service provisioning. Traditional leases are incorporating ICT as part of the services provided by landlords. Earlier tenants were reluctant to pay premium for such services, but now, these have become more of a norm. Networked buildings are being valued higher than other buildings, which are slowly getting phased out. Another feature of building that is being co-demanded is energy and water efficiency as occupiers are adapting to principles of sustainability. Technology is providing ways to manage energy and water consumption better.

ICT has also changed the way real estate services are provided. The transformation has happened through the provisioning of online listing services, bundled service provision and shorter leases (Dixon and Thompson, 2005).

Before we discuss risk associated with the new economy, it is imperative to chalk out linkages between the new economy and the real estate based on the aforementioned discussions. Figure 5.2 illustrates how new economy and real estate are connected.

The framework presented in Figure 5.2 is a modified version of research undertaken by Dixon and Thompson (2005). While setting technology and

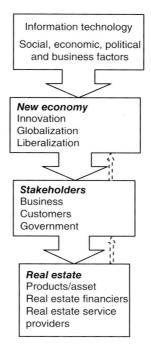

Figure 5.2   New economy and real estate linkages.
Source: Based on Dixon and Thompson (2005).

globalisation (defining features of new economy) as the context, the
framework links the economy, firm and urban- and regional-level impacts
to real estate (Dixon and Thompson, 2005). In this framework, market
barriers that exist in real estate can be examined in the context of broader
political, social and economic factors and how these factors together with
forces of the new economy impact real estate. An important feature of the
linkages presented in Figure 5.2 is that while the new economy impacts real
estate through social, economic, political and business factors with
stakeholders as conduit, the real estate also impacts these factors again
through stakeholders.

   The theoretical framework earlier allows us to take a critical view of new
economy's impact on real estate as it combines technical and social factors
in an integrated framework (Dixon and Thompson, 2005).

Financing of real estate in new economy

The spectrum of property investment and finance has also been enhanced
by the forces of the new economy. The real estate investment space
comprises of direct opportunity, indirect opportunity and synthetic

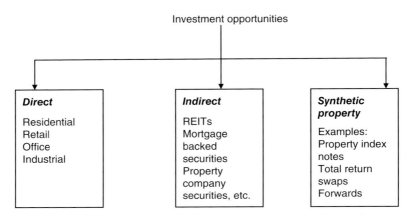

Figure 5.3   Real estate investment space.

opportunities (real estate derivatives) (Figure 5.3). While direct and indirect real estate investment opportunities have existed for quite long, the emergence and penetration of synthetic real estate market has direct relation to the new economy.

The direct real estate investment opportunities comprise of owning residential, retail, office and industrial physical assets. These assets have characteristics such as heterogeneity and spatial fixity and require lumpy investment. Indirect opportunities include real estate investment trusts, mortgage-backed securities (residential, commercial or hybrid) and securities of real estate companies. Synthetic real estate market includes real estate index notes, total return swaps and forwards. Table 5.1 presents key characteristics of various real estate investment opportunities.

What is important in Table 5.1 is the role of technology in different real estate investment opportunities. The traditional investment opportunities such as direct property investment of investment through property funds have had low penetration of technology. Public investment opportunities such as REITs and CMBS did benefit from technology. In fact, the developments in financial engineering, which have benefited from advances in information technology, made it possible for CMBS to evolve and grow. During the last two decades, real estate derivatives have emerged and technology is the backbone of this development as well.

A real estate derivative is a financial derivative whose value is derived from the value of an underlying real estate asset. In practice, real estate asset market is inefficient and it is hard to accurately price real estate asset; real estate derivative contracts are typically written on a real estate index. Real estate index attempts to aggregate real estate market information to provide a more accurate representation of underlying asset performance. Trading or taking positions in real estate derivatives is also known as synthetic real estate.

Table 5.1 Key features of commercial real estate investment opportunities.

	Direct	Indirect						Synthetic
		Open-ended real estate funds	Closed-ended real estate funds	Speciality funds	Private equity and hedge funds	REITs	CMBS	Real estate derivatives
Main investor group	Institutional investors, high net worth private investors	Private investors	High net worth private investors	Institutional investors	Institutional investors, high net worth private investors	Institutional investors	Institutional investors	Institutional investors
Tradability	Poor	Good	Poor	Poor	Poor	Very good	Good	Poor
Transaction costs	Very high	High	Very high	Moderate	High	Low	Low	Low
Correlation with other assets	Low	Moderate	Low	Low	Moderate	Correlated with equities	Low	Low
Transparency	Low	High	Medium	Medium	Low	High	High	High
Risk for investors	Liquidity risk/ concentration risk	Liquidity risk	Liquidity risk	Concentration risk	Liquidity risk/ concentration risk	Stock market liquidity	Stock market liquidity	Liquidity risk
Technology	Low	Low	Low	Low	Low	Medium	Medium	High

Source: Adapted from information in ECB (2008).

Real estate derivatives usually take the form of a total return swap, forward contract or futures or can adopt a funded format where the real estate derivative is embedded into a bond or note structure. Under the total return swap or forward contract, the parties will usually take contrary positions on the price movements of a real estate index.

The most common benchmarks used for writing real estate derivative contracts in the United Kingdom are the various real estate indices published by the Investment Real Estate Databank and FTSE UK Commercial Real Estate Index Series. IPD indices are also used in a number of other countries such as Australia, France, Germany, Italy, Japan and Switzerland as the basis for commercial real estate derivatives. In the United States, commercial real estate utilises the National Council of Real Estate Investment Fiduciaries (NCREIF) real estate index, the NPI. There are two main residential real estate indices in the United States which trade – Radar Logic's RPX and, the main index, S&P/Case–Shiller Home Price Indices (see Case–Shiller index).

The FTSE UK Commercial Real Estate Index Series currently covers £16 billion of prime investible real estate assets directly held in the United Kingdom. The FTSE UK Commercial Real Estate Index Series is valued daily.

Three synthetic real estate products in the United Kingdom are real estate index notes (PIN), total return swaps and forwards. The PINs are essentially bonds. The cash flows of these bonds are structured in a way that is meant to be similar to a transaction in the physical real estate. This means that the PIN pays the capital return on redemption of the bond and it pays a quarterly coupon to investors.

In this way, the seller of the PIN pays the IPD annual or FTSE UK Commercial Real Estate capital growth at redemption and the income return, paid quarterly (IPD) or monthly (FTSE), to the counterparty. This means that the counterparty is, therefore, receiving the total return of the UK commercial real estate market, just as they would with a physical transaction in real estate.

A real estate total return swap is simply an exchange of cash flows. Here, the total return on real estate, as measured by the change in the relevant IPD or FTSE UK Commercial Real Estate Index, is exchanged for the return on cash.

A real estate forward contract is based upon the real estate returns in any annual period – the expected total return, for example, is agreed at trade, and on maturity, the difference between the realised total return and the traded price is exchanged. Forward agreements are over the counter, requiring a counterparty to be found. Risk of default of either party must be considered in the trade.

The financing of real estate investment opportunity happens in the broader financial market – through a combination of debt and equity. Investors, using variety of mechanisms, leverage their equity and invest in real estate. Financial institutions, which are at the centre of financial markets, offer a number of products (such as deposits, loans, securities, investment advice, portfolio management and trading) for their clients. The clients not only shop for financing and execution skills but also for expertise, price and value. Quality of service, which was not important in the past, is changing. Quality has become an important determinant of price. The traditional view that price is determined by own cost of production and distribution at a given point in time is not relevant in the new economy. With deregulation, globalisation, innovation and technology that affect pricing of instruments as well as market sensitivity and subsequent behaviour, uncertainty increases substantially. Price is determined while accounting for the risks that globalisation brings and also through a careful consideration of risks associated with future events that are uncertain.

Leverage and risks

Leverage has become widespread in the new economy. Leverage (also called gearing) means that an individual, a company or a nation spends beyond its means on financing by borrowing. A key feature of financial market is that it matches those who need to borrow with those who have surplus financial resources in a spatial and inter-temporal way. Developments in commercial real estate investment markets indicate that these investments are highly leveraged. This can have important implications for financial stability of an economy via a number of channels (ECB, 2008). First, a significant proportion of many banks' assets are comprised of loans extended for investment in commercial real estate. Second, loans for commercial real estate investment tend to be more volatile than many other types of lending in banks' loan portfolios. Third, adjustments in commercial real estate prices can also indirectly impact on banks' balance sheets in that they have negative implications for the real economy. Fourth, institutional investors, such as insurance companies, pension funds, hedge funds and private equity firms, sometimes have large investments, both directly and indirectly, in commercial real estate markets.

The effects of these channels have been reinforced by a number of other factors (ECB, 2008): (i) financial innovation is playing an ever increasing role in commercial real estate financing, possibly generating risks; (ii) major real estate markets worldwide are increasingly becoming interdependent; and (iii) it has been noted that financial crises in which commercial real estate markets have played a significant role have on several occasions been linked to financial liberalisation, revealing possible shortcomings in public policy initiatives.

Leveraging is done by means of loans and trading: derivative financial instruments are, in principle, geared. Highly geared capital structure and imaginary cash flows are means used for leveraging. Derivative instruments are extensively used for leverage and/or to hide major losses which causes huge amount of risks.

Recent practice in real estate financing has been that many of the investments by entities are highly geared. The more leveraged an entity is, the less likelihood that it can face up to its financial obligations in case of crisis. During the 2007 financial crisis, highly leveraged firms were severely affected. The problem with leverage is that it conjures vast amount of virtual value and results in higher rate of growth in value than could otherwise be possible (Chorafas, 2001). During the period prior to 2007, real estate yields were very close to treasury bond yields, implying that risk for investing in real estate was not getting priced appropriately. Real estate fundamentals did not fully justified the firming of yields, and the large part of capital value appreciation that real estate market was witnessing was due to leverage.

There are two biggest risks for a leveraged entity – one, stable market as in this case customers are less prone to enter into a risky contract and this would affect leveraged entity's growth and, second, high volatility as in this case when adversity hits, leveraged entity leads itself into reverse leverage. Reverse leverage causes a vicious circle of disposing assets at fire-sale prices to face margin calls (Chorafas, 2001). Reverse leverage is dangerous because gearing means debt, which speculators assume to capitalise on projected changed in asset values. When the market falls and reverse leverage happens, it can lead to huge losses to investors and even bankruptcy.

As mentioned earlier and as would be discussed in later chapters, in real estate markets, leverage has substantially increased. One of the major consequences of high leverage is on the volatility. The volatility in real estate markets has increased. Highly geared markets imply that the extreme events increase (Figure 5.4).

Figure 5.4 illustrates the behaviour of a market if the market is low geared versus when the market is high geared. In case of low-geared market, the occurrence of extreme events is rare and fairly spaced out. However, in the presence of high gearing, the frequency and magnitude of rare events multiply. The problem is that in the first case, extreme events are more like outliers but in the second case uncontrollable factors play a key role in the outcome and the process itself and its expected results.

In a seminal contribution to the financial theory, Modigliani and Miller (1958) demonstrated that in a perfect market (where investors are rational

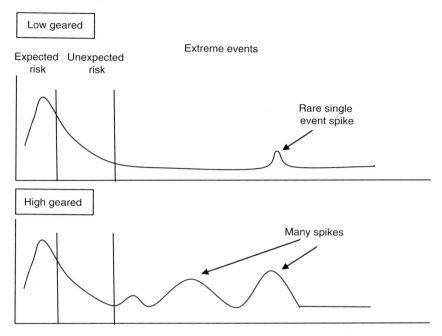

Figure 5.4 Leverage and frequency of extreme events in real estate markets. *Source*: Adapted from Chorafas (2001).

and information is readily and freely available, capital market operates perfectly, all firms in the same sector face similar risks and probability distribution of expected earnings is same as present operating earnings), market value of a company does not depend on its capital structure (i.e. debt and equity). Given the Modigliani and Miller theorem, why do companies gear themselves so heavily? In this situation, the rationale for a company (aka investor) to get geared is to increase its return on equity (MGI, 2010). Increased gearing increases the risk for shareholders, and to compensate for additional risk, shareholders require higher return. Companies in order to show higher profits leverage themselves more, and this further leads shareholders to demand higher return. The vicious cycle continues and all remains well in the good market, but when the economic cycle turns, the risk translates into huge losses.

The assumptions in the Modigliani and Miller hypothesis on capital structure are rarely satisfied, and opportunities exist for optimisation of capital structure through leverage. The task becomes tedious when model includes credit, interest rate, currency, equity and operational risks. Gearing, which is an important feature of the new economy, further complicates the optimal capital structure model, and a number of questions arise (Chorafas, 2001): Is financial leverage advantageous? How much gearing is too high or too low? How much of financial flexibility is lost due to leverage? How much risk of a downturn is increased?

Though there is no clear answer to these questions and a rigorous research is required to understand the implication of gearing, these questions would be central to the discussion on real estate cycles and bubbles in Chapter 6. Two important characteristics of the financial market (real estate market is a part) have emerged. First, as observed during 2007 financial crisis, markets have become much more interlinked, thereby cancelling the diversification benefits. Second, derivatives emerged on the market and became popular because they were thought to offer better risk-adjusted return. However, higher volatility and less than expected diversification benefits has meant that the risks with derivatives are much higher than thought.

Conclusions

In this chapter, we explored how features of the new economy such as innovation and technology complemented by globalisation and sustainability are contributing to the value of real estate. Technology has improved information availability in real estate sector. Globalisation complemented by technology has opened up opportunities for flow of funds for investment in the 'so-called' localised real estate assets or their derivatives. This has been facilitated by the development of a range of indirect real estate investment opportunities particularly real estate derivatives. The feature of the new economy is that it has changed the perception towards risk and investment has become highly leveraged. Though the research on the role of the new economy in changing risk in real estate investment is in early stages, it does appear that leverage and possible mispricing of risk posed challenges for the financial stability of economies as demonstrated during the recent financial crisis of 2007.

References

Berry, B. (1973) The Human Consequences of Urbanization. Macmillan, London.

Blakemore, A. and Herrendorf, B. (2009) *Economic Growth: The Importance of Education and Technological Development. Productivity and Prosperity Project*, W.P. Carey School of Business, Arizona State University.

Borsuk, S. (1999) Nowhere yet everywhere, the space place paper, www.thespaceplace.net (accessed 16 October 2013).

Boulton, R., Libert, B. and Samek, S. (2000) *Cracking the Value Code: How Successful Businesses Are Creating Wealth in the New Economy*. Harper Business, New York.

Castells, M. (1996) T*he Information Age: Economy, Society and Culture, Vol. 1 – The Rise of the Network Society*, 2nd edn. Blackwell, Oxford.

Chorafas, D.N. (2001) The impact of risk and uncertainty on financial institutions. In: *Managing Risk in the New Economy*. New York Institute of Finance/Prentice Hall Press, New York.

CORENET (2004) *Corporate real estate 2010*, CORENET, Atlanta.

Dixon, T. and Thompson, B. (2005) Connectivity, technological change and commercial property in the New Economy a research agenda. Paper presented at *European Real Estate Society Conference 2005*, Dublin, June 2005.

ECB (2008) *Commercial Property Markets*. European Central Bank, Germany.

Economist (2010) *The World Turned Upside Down: A Special Report on Innovation in Emerging Markets*. The Economist, London.

Gibson, V. and Lizieri, C. (2001) Friction and inertia: corporate change, real estate portfolios and the UK office market. *Journal of Real Estate Research*, **21**, 5–79.

JLL (2012) *Perspectives on ESS: Four Sustainability Trends to Watch in 2012*. Jones Lang LaSalle, Chicago.

MGI (2010) *Debt and Deleveraging: The Global Credit Bubble and Its Economic Consequences*. McKinsey Global Institute, New York.

Modigliani, F. and Miller, M.H. (1958) The cost of capital, corporate finance and the theory of investment. *American Economic Review*, **48**, 261–97.

Myerson, J. and Ross, P. (2003) *The 21st Century Office*. Laurence King Publishing, London.

Perez (2002)

Rowatt, A., Clayton, T. and Vaze, P. (2002) Where, and how, to look for the new economy, *Economic Trends*, **580** (March), 29–35.

Scarbrough, H. and Corbett, M.J. (1992) Technology and Organization. Routledge, London/New York.

Schumpeter, J. (1939) *Business Cycles: A Theoretical, Historical and Statistical Analysis of Capitalist Process*. McGraw Hill, New York.

Tiwari, P. and White, M. (2010) *International Real Estate Economics*. Palgrave, New York.

ULI (2011) *What's Next? Real Estate in the New Economy*. Urban Land Institute, Washington, DC.

World Bank (2011) *Global Development Horizons 2011 Multipolarity: The New Global Economy*. World Bank, Washington, DC.

6

Real Estate Asset Bubbles

An introduction to cycles in real estate

A cycle is a sequence of events that repeat (Miller, 1997). In economics, traditional business cycles undergo four stages: expansion, prosperity, contraction and recession. After a recessionary phase, the expansionary phase can start again. In real estate, we talk about a number of phenomena which are cyclical in nature – real estate rental cycle, investment cycle and development cycle. One of the comprehensive definitions of the real estate cycle is offered by the Royal Institution of Chartered Surveyors in its 1994 publication on Understanding the Property Cycle: 'Property cycles are recurrent but irregular fluctuations in the rate of all-property total return, which are also apparent in many other indicators of property activity, but with varying leads and lags against the property cycle' (Pyhrr et al., 1999).

Why do real estate cycles form? A comprehensive framework to explain the formation of real estate cycles is presented by Barras (1994) (see Figure 6.1).

According to Barras (1994), a real estate cycle is linked to economic and credit market cycle. An economic upturn (expansion) is associated with credit expansion. Credit investment is the key cyclical driver of economic growth. Key influence of economic cycle transpires to real estate market through increase in occupation demand. Supply being inelastic does not

Real Estate Finance in the New Economy, First Edition. Piyush Tiwari and Michael White.
© 2014 John Wiley & Sons, Ltd. Published 2014 by John Wiley & Sons, Ltd.

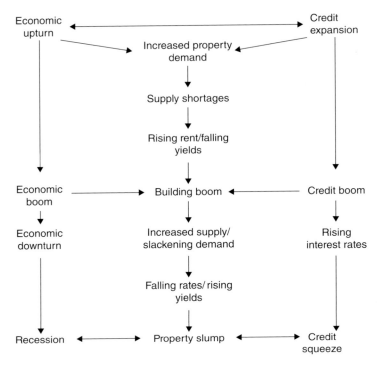

Figure 6.1   Barras (1994) model.
Source: Barras (1994).

quickly adjust to increase in demand. Rents rise, vacancies fall, and yields
fall. Falling yields lead to capital value appreciation. Rising real estate
prices lead to new construction activity. Development activity has lag and
this further amplifies the economic cycle. In fact, building boom coincides
with economic and credit boom. Demand for credit causes interest rates to
rise. On the real side of the economy, there is a build-up in inflation pressures. Increased supply and rising prices cause economy to slow down, and
the period of economic downturn begins. On the financial side of the
economy, increased demand for credit and rising interest rate initiate the
period of credit slowdown. In real estate sector, the new supply comes with
a lag. Increased supply coincides with slackening demand due to slowdown
in the economy. Rents start falling, vacancies rise, and yields rise. This
causes the downturn in the real estate market, leading to slump in real
estate market. The real estate slump coincides with the economic recession
and credit squeeze. This leads to an overhang of distressed assets and
incomplete projects.

The aforementioned framework suggests that there are a number of cycles
that arise in real estate with different lead–lag structures. Real estate

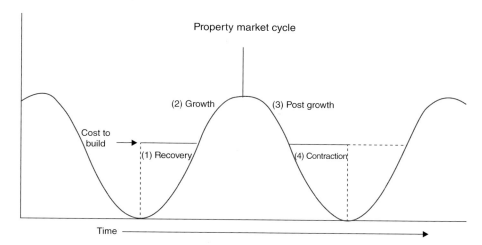

Figure 6.2 Office market rental cycle.
Source: Reproduced by permission of RREEF.

professionals (academics and practitioners) discuss these cycles in real estate use (rental cycle), investment (yield cycle) and development (construction cycle) markets.

Cycles in the use market

The factors causing the cycles in the use market are largely local. These are related to demand and supply for use of space. At a given point in time, different markets face different conditions regarding rental growth. Real estate consultants depict the position of a market using a diagrammatic representation (called the property clock by Jones Lang LaSalle and the property cycle by RREEF) of the markets with an indicative position of the market at a particular point in time. Though these diagrams do not indicate either the level of growth in rental values or the peak and amplitude of the property cycle, these are useful ways of presenting the direction in which future rents are expected to move. Figure 6.2 is the representation of a rental cycle for office market. The general conditions for the recovery phase are high but show declining vacancy rates and stable to rising rents. The growth phase is characterised by low and declining vacancy rates, and rising rents that support construction of new space. The post-growth phase is characterised by low but increasing vacancy rates and rising/flattening rents. The contraction phase witnesses high or increasing vacancy levels and declining rents.

The retail market also has cycles (the underlying driver of retail is consumer demand, which is affected by the economy), but these are not as

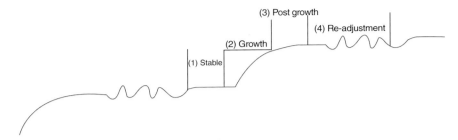

Figure 6.3   Retail property market rental cycle in Europe.
Source: RREEF Real Estate Research. Reproduced by permission of RREEF.

pronounced as the office market cycles. A representation of the retail cycle is shown in Figure 6.3 (RREEF, 2006a). Stage 1 is characterised by stable rents and an upturn in consumer spending. Stage 2 is the growth phase when rents are rising and there is strong consumer spending and/or retailer demand. During Stage 3, rents start to stabilise and consumption growth also slows down. Stage 4 is the readjustment phase. During this stage, rents are stable or start declining. Consumer spending is also slow or declining.

The position of major real estate markets on the office market cycle as of October 2007 is presented in Figure 6.4. The clock indicates the movement of rental values along rental cycle from the fourth quarter of 2009 to fourth quarter of 2010. London (United Kingdom), where the rents had bottomed out by the end of 2009, has witnessed growth in rents during 2010. New York (United States), where rents were falling during 2009, has almost bottomed out by the end of 2010. Tokyo (Japan) is still at the bottom of the clock, though there are some signs of growth in rents. A general trend that can be seen is that from a scenario where rents were falling in most markets during 2009, the rents have started to rise in at least half of the markets.

Cycles in investment market

Capital values undergo cycles as well. The fundamental drivers of capital values are expected rents and yields. The cyclical behaviour of rents (which is also reflected in cyclical behaviour in vacancies) causes capital values to follow cyclical pattern as well. Figure 6.5 shows an office capital value clock at the end of fourth quarter 2009 and fourth quarter 2010.

One observation that could be made by looking at Figure 6.4 and Figure 6.5 is that the position of a market on capital value clock is ahead of rental clock. The reason for such a divergence is due to the fact that capital values are formed based on expectations in rents. Rents are translated into capital values using the present value concept. Relation between rents and capital values is presented in the following:

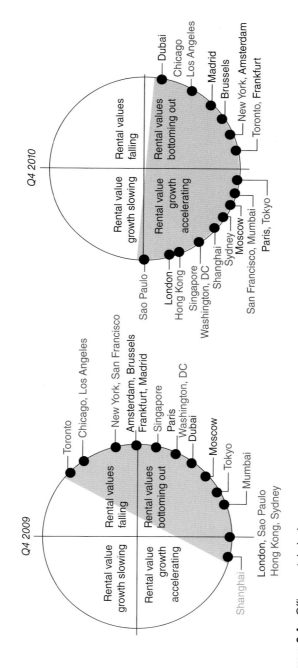

Figure 6.4 Office rental clock.
Source: Reproduced by permission of Jones Lang LaSalle.

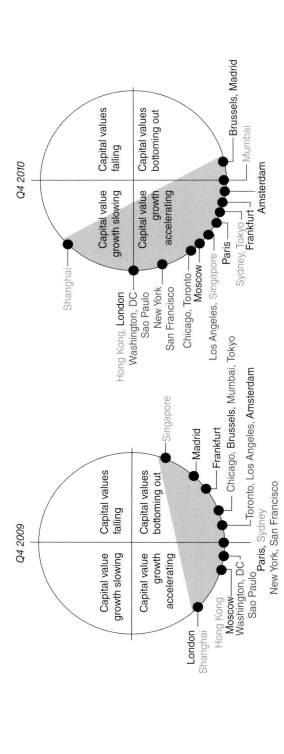

Figure 6.5 Office capital value clock.
Source: Reproduced by permission of Jones Lang LaSalle.

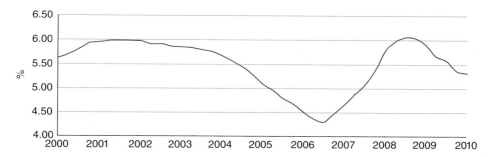

Figure 6.6 Weighted office market yield in Western Europe.
Source: Reproduced by permission of Jones Lang LaSalle.

$$V = \frac{E(R)}{i}$$

where V is the capital value, R is the rent and i is the discount rate.
Assumption here is that R is constant in perpetuity, which is a strong
assumption. If rents are assumed to grow at a rate g, the aforementioned
formula could be modified as

$$V = \frac{E(R)}{i-g} = \frac{E(R)}{y}$$

where y is the initial yield.

In valuation of real estate assets, the 'expectation' is treated rather
cursorily. While current passing rent is taken as $E(R)$, initial yields are
determined based on yields of recently concluded comparable transactions. As shown in Figure 6.6 for Western European office markets, yields
are also cyclical.

Cycles in development market

Development industry is also cyclical in nature as the cues for new development activity to commence are demand outstripping (inelastic) supply
in the occupation market (leading rents to rise and vacancies to fall) and
rising capital values (which means falling yields). Development activity
commences when capital values are greater than the development cost.
However, this may sound easier, but neither the cost nor the capital values
are easy to estimate in advance. For example, delays in planning permissions
or construction hold-ups (perhaps caused by unforeseen environmental and

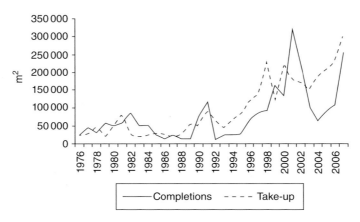

Figure 6.7   Office completions and take-up in Dublin.
Source: McCartney (2007).

geological problems) may cause costs to escalate. Moreover, as discussed earlier, development adds to new stock after a lag. McCartney (2008) presents evidence of development cycles in Dublin office market (Figure 6.7). He finds that there is a lag of 1 year between completions and take-up.

The cyclical behaviour of rents, yields and new supply is a fundamental feature of real estate markets. The lags and leads in these cycles and various exogenous and endogenous factors that cause them are often difficult to anticipate with the consequence that the basis for investors'/valuers'/ developers' 'expectation' about future rents, yields and demand for space becomes immediate past information. As would be discussed later in this chapter, while discussing market efficiency, expectations which are based on past information may lead to overpricing or underpricing of assets as these could be significantly divergent from intrinsic values of assets. If there is substantial divergence from intrinsic values, this may lead to extenuated cycles and very high volatility, often termed as bubbles or boom and busts.

Expectations and bubbles

An economic bubble, sometimes also referred to as a speculative bubble, a market bubble, a price bubble, and a financial bubble, is 'trade in high volumes at prices that are considerably at variance with intrinsic values' (King *et al.*, 1993; Lahart, 2008). A bubble could also be described as a trade in assets with inflated values. Economists have attributed uncertainty (Smith *et al.*, 1988) speculation (Lei *et al.*, 2001), or bounded rationality (Levine *et al.*, 2008), as the causes for bubbles. However, recent evidence suggests that bubbles even happen in the absence of these. It has been suggested that bubbles might ultimately be caused by processes of price coordination or emerging social norms. Since it is often difficult to observe intrinsic values in real-life markets, bubbles are often conclusively identified only in retrospect, when a sudden drop in prices appears. The boom and the bust phases of the bubble are examples of a positive feedback mechanism, in contrast to the negative feedback mechanism that determines the equilibrium price under normal market circumstances. Prices in an economic bubble can fluctuate erratically and become impossible to predict from supply and demand alone.

The focus of this chapter is on real estate asset bubbles. A starting point to understand the bubbles is the financial theory on 'market efficiency'. According to Malkiel (as quoted in Malpezzi, 2004), 'a capital market is said to be efficient if it fully and correctly reflects all relevant information in determining security prices...Formally, the market is said to be efficient with respect to some information set...implies that it is impossible to make economic profits by trading on the basis of [that information set]'.

If the capital markets are efficient, opportunities for excess or abnormal returns do not exist. Since all the information is incorporated into prices, the investor is unable to make profits by trading on the information. The aforementioned definition is a theoretical definition of market efficiency and is seldom satisfied. Based on the information set, three common definitions of market efficiency have been used. The first, known as the weak form efficiency, states that future price movements cannot be predicted based on an information set containing all past price movements (Malpezzi, 2004). The semi-strong form of efficiency states that prices should reflect all publicly available information, which would include not only past price information but also all public financial information and any other information that might affect asset prices. The third variant, the strong form efficiency, says that even material, non-public information is priced asset values.

It's almost impossible to satisfy strong form efficiency criteria. Even the semi-strong definition of market efficiency is difficult to meet. Hence, most economists rely on the weak definition, which implies that future asset prices cannot be predicted based on past price information and consequently historic prices are of no value in forecasting future prices. This leads to the related concept of a 'random walk', in which asset price changes follow a random pattern. If asset price formation follows random walk, it is not possible to earn excess profits, and there is no incentive for speculation.

Investors form expectations regarding asset prices and returns. There are four models on how expectations are formed – myopic expectations, perfect foresight, rational expectation and adaptive expectation (see Malpezzi, 2004, for discussion). Malpezzi (2004) explains that *myopic expectations* models assume that investors are 'flying blind' going forward. At the other extreme, *perfect foresight* assumes that people know the future. *Rational expectations* state that people use all available information to make optimal forecasts about the future. Finally, the *adaptive expectations* model assumes that people are backward looking, which means that we assume the future will be like the (recent) past (Malpezzi, 2004). Rational expectation implies that asset prices will follow random walk as all available information is already factored in price and change in price over time is unpredictable. Adaptive expectations imply that the expected level of prices is based on past values of actual price levels.

The literature demonstrates that real estate cash flow variables (rents, vacancies, yields) are cyclical and real estate performance (rates of return) is cyclical. The problem arises when most investors, valuers and developers incorrectly view such phenomena as 'trends', not cycles, and make their decisions based on these past trends. Herring and Wachter (2002) argue that investors show a particular form of adaptive expectations and myopic pricing behaviour, disaster myopia, due to the low frequency and non-observation of negative events. The ability to estimate a low-frequency event – like a collapse in real estate prices – depends on the frequency with which the shock occurs. Valuers tend to overprice in booms (underprice in downturns). Most investors capitalise the present economic situation into perpetuity when forecasting the future, acting as if the current trends (whatever they are) will continue forever (Roulac, 1996). As a result, most investors do the wrong thing at the wrong time over the cycle, buying high (during the boom) and selling low (a foreclosure sale during the bust), following the 'herd instinct' and doing what the crowd is doing (Roulac, 1996). Despite all the conditions of a downturn, developers attempt to support their decisions based on current values or expected values derived from extrapolating the past trends in prices. The consequence of the behaviour of real estate investors and developers is akin to a Ponzi scheme in that new investors/developers are attracted by the profits made by first investors. History is full of examples where investor assumptions and real estate reality have diverged over the cycle. An example for the U.S. market during the 1980s and 1990s is discussed in Roulac (1996).

Efficient Market Hypothesis of the formation of price expectations requires rational expectations, that is, that expectations of future prices be formed based on how market forces, demand and supply, actually impact market prices; all that are knowable about these forces are incorporated into prices, without estimation bias, so that no one can profit from past (publicly available) information. When the price expectations are built on past performance, random walk does not hold, and it is possible to predict pricing based on past trends, and excess profits could be earned by investors who know this is how other investors will price real estate (Malpezzi, 2004).

If expectations of real estate investors are 'backward looking', that is, they depend on extrapolating past price changes, then real estate prices will not form a 'random walk'. The empirical literature finds considerable evidence for backward-looking expectations in real estate pricing. Research supports the finding that real estate markets often violate the random walk and rational expectations hypotheses (Ott *et al.*, 2008). The conditions prevailing in the real estate markets – infrequent transactions, lack of information about negative events and low frequency of shocks – generate disaster myopia. The underestimation of bad events itself generates bubble (Malpezzi, 2004). Adaptive expectation based on past prices leads to investment decisions. Over time, supply builds up and prices no longer remain sustainable leading bubble to burst. The phenomenon is further aggravated as the optimistic investors are wiped out and they no longer have the capital to continue in real estate markets. Lenders also suffer losses as their real estate portfolios are worth less than their loans. They withdraw from lending for real estate. These conditions further magnify the disaster.

Formation of real estate bubbles and its detection

Camerer (1989) contains a comprehensive review of the literature on asset price bubbles where he divides the theory on such deviation of prices from the fundamentals into three categories: growing bubbles, fads and information bubbles. Growing bubbles are deviations from the fundamental value of an asset in which the bubble component is expected to grow at a certain rate such that it provides a reasonable return for the agents who participate in the bubble. Fads are mean-reverting deviations from intrinsic value caused by social or psychological forces, and information bubbles are due to differences in agents' beliefs about how the economy works. In addition, the category of 'intrinsic bubbles' predicts that stable and highly persistent fundamentals lead to stable and highly persistent under- or overvaluations also. These bubbles can also cause asset prices to overreact to changes in fundamentals (Froot and Obstfeld, 1991).

How real estate bubbles are formed? A number of empirical studies have focused on understanding this question. One of the hypotheses that have been tested is the existence of serial correlation in prices, which is expected to lead to bubbles. For North American real estate markets, Case and Shiller (1989), Hamilton and Schwab (1985) and Malpezzi (1999) find evidence of serial correlation in prices. For Asian markets of Japan and Korea, Kim and Suh (1993) find that while Japanese real estate prices were serially correlated, evidence was weak for Korea.

Causes for bubbles have also been the focus of investigation for many studies. The authors have analysed demand side (Ortalo-Magne and Rady,

2006) and supply side (such as natural constraints and regulatory environment; see Malpezzi (1999)) causes of bubbles. In fact, Malpezzi (2004) argues that whether demand side events result in bubbles will depend on the prevalence of supply side conditions such as excessive and inappropriate regulations and natural topographical constraints. Supply side constraints make supply inelastic. The study also finds that excessive regulation increases the volatility in prices.

There are many instances of boom and bust episodes in real estate markets. Such episodes most often are not justified by changes in fundamentals. However, there is no consensus on whether such steep rise and decline in asset prices contain a bubble component in its price movements. This is due to the fact that econometric detection of its existence cannot be achieved with a satisfactory degree of precision. Testing for bubbles in such boom and bust episodes essentially involves testing whether the standard models of asset pricing fail in such a way that the failure can be attributed to the presence of bubbles. Or in other words, it looks for the rejection of the null hypothesis that there are no bubbles in the prices (Shiller, 1981; Blanchard and Watson, 1982; Diba and Grossman, 1983; Sarno and Taylor, 2003). Rejection of the null hypothesis of no bubbles cannot be attributed solely to bubbles since it could equally well be caused by the misspecification of the model, if the models are false. In such cases, research ought to find apparent evidence of bubbles when models work poorly or when agents expect the future to be somewhat different than history. The current empirical tests for bubbles do not successfully establish the case that bubbles exist in asset prices (Flood and Hodrick, 1990). The literature available on the empirical side is also quite extensive on the econometric testing of such boom and bust episodes to identify whether there is a bubble component in it, and it is not easy to have a holistic sense of where this literature stands (Gurkaynak, 2008).

Key patterns of past real estate bubbles

Three conditions that have been identified whose combination likely generates a financial crisis are speculative asset price inflation, unsustainable debt–income ratios and liquidity shortage (Barras, 2009). Reinhard and Rogoff (2008) compare the U.S. subprime crisis which unfolded in 2007 with 18 post-war financial crises in industrialised countries and observe several commonalities between the historical episodes and the 2007 crisis. The degree of increase in U.S. housing and equity prices prior to the crisis is quite close to the average increases in equity and housing prices recorded previous episodes of such crises. Apart from a bubble-like growth in asset prices mentioned previously, the other commonalities observed are accelerated debt accumulation and a widening current account deficit.

In this section, we review various underlying drivers of two major crises – Asian financial crisis of 1997 and subprime crisis of 2007 – to understand the interplay of various exogenous and endogenous factors that led to these crises. We will also explain the role of behavioural factors that played on the crises.

Asian financial crisis

During the decades immediately preceding the 1990s, East Asian economies (Thailand, Indonesia, Singapore, Hong Kong, Malaysia, the Philippines, Taiwan and South Korea) were experiencing robust economic growth aided by high saving and investment rates and moderate inflation. Such robust economic performance, aided by a stable environment, attracted capital inflows starting in the second half of the 1980s. There was a rapid surge in the flow of foreign debt, especially the short-term variety into the East Asian economies. This surge in debt inflows was accompanied by sharp increases in asset values, notably stock and land prices. Open financial market policy allowed easy access to international investors.

Many Asian currencies were then managed against a basket of currencies, of which, both directly and indirectly, the U.S. dollar is the most significant component, accounting for over 70% of the weightage. Following the 1985 Plaza Accord, which effectively devalued the U.S. dollar by close to 50% against the yen, the export competitiveness of many Asian economies was boosted in the late 1980s (Koh *et al.*, 2005). The surge in capital inflows into East Asia led to speculation in the real estate market which was driven by cheap financing. Loan volumes rose and credit facilities of up to 90% of the collateral value were common for investments in real estate properties (Mera and Renaud, 2000). Easy liquidity caused the asset values to appreciate sharply. Rising values led to inflated collateral value and caused further credit expansion. Banks competed by increasing loan amounts, reducing interest rates for certain customers and even extending renovation loans (Koh *et al.*, 2005). The loan exposure of the real estate sector in Thailand was estimated at 30–40% of total loans with a value of US$160 billion in 1996 (Table 6.1). Other countries also saw a significant build-up. From 1992 to 1996, more than 70% of bank lending in Malaysia was channelled into real estate and stock market investments (Koh *et al.*, 2005). In South Korea, Korean conglomerates invested a substantial amount of real estate, mostly financed with short-term debt (Mera and Renaud, 2000). Barth *et al.* (1998) estimate that expansion in bank credit to the private sector, relative to GDP growth, was 48% in Hong Kong during the 1990–1996 period; the corresponding figures were 62% in Indonesia, 40% in Malaysia, 115% in the Philippines and 70% in Thailand. The rapid

Table 6.1   Exposure of the banking sector to real estate, 1996.

	Real estate, as % of bank loans	Private bank credit (US$ billion)	Average real estate loans (% of total loans*)	Nonperforming real estate loans (% of total loans˙)	Moody's rating of the banking sector
China	35–40	930	9	n.a.	D
Hong Kong	40–55	300	76	3.0	C
Indonesia	25–30	54	7	18.0	–
Malaysia	30–40	120	58	6.0	D+
Philippines	15–25	40	17	8.0	D+
Singapore	30–40	130	30	4.5	C+
South Korea	15–25	440	17	18.0	D
Taiwan	35–45	400	58	5.0	D
Thailand	30–40	160	44	16.0	E+

*Estimates, based on Asian financial markets, 2nd quarter 1998. J.P. Morgan Inc.
Source: Koh *et al*. (2005).

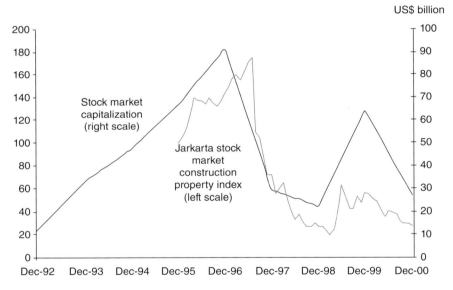

Figure 6.8   Stock market capitalisation and real estate property index – Indonesia.
Source: Koh *et al*. (2005).

expansion in bank credit to the real estate sector continued in 1995 and 1996 even as the ratio of nonperforming real estate loans to total loans rose. As shown in Table 6.1, in 1995, nonperforming loans were 10.4% of all bank loans in Indonesia, 7.7% in Thailand and almost 6% in Malaysia (Koh *et al*., 2005). Ratings for the banking sector in these countries accorded by Moody were very low.

During the 1990s, the stock market and real estate market tracked closely (Figure 6.8, Figure 6.9, Figure 6.10 and Figure 6.11). The asset price inflation

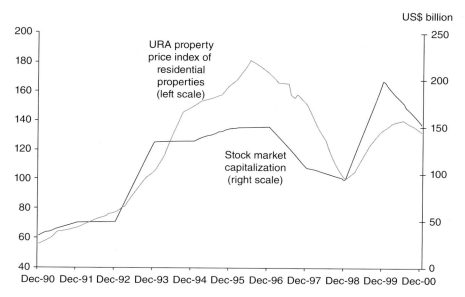

Figure 6.9 Stock market capitalisation and real estate property index – Singapore. *Source*: Koh *et al*. (2005).

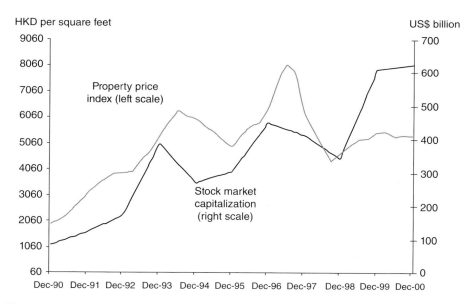

Figure 6.10 Stock market capitalisation and real estate property index – Hong Kong. *Source*: Koh *et al*. (2005).

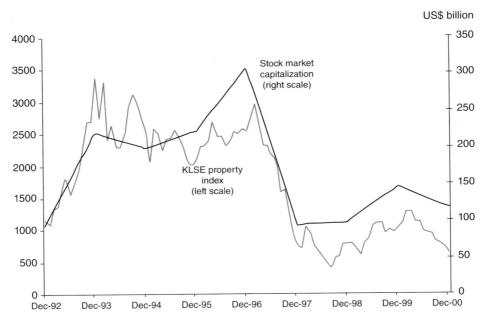

Figure 6.11   Stock market capitalisation and real estate property index – Malaysia.
Source: Koh *et al.* (2005).

for both the asset classes was largely driven by the liquidity and leverage in the market.

In early 1996, interest rates in the United States started to rise, causing appreciation of the U.S. dollar against the Japanese yen. Most domestic borrowers were unhedged against exchange rate risk, making them heavily vulnerable to devaluation in domestic exchange rates. Furthermore, Asian financial institutions had borrowed a significant amount of external liquid liabilities that were not backed by liquid assets, making them vulnerable to panics. Adding to the fragility of the economies were factors like governments' attempts to keep their currencies at artificially high levels, government-directed banking systems and lending decisions, crony capitalism, massive overinvestment by corporations funded by excessive borrowing, the lack of transparency that masked the extent of problems they developed and inadequate financial regulation and supervision.

After the mid-1990s, a series of external shocks (the devaluation of the Chinese renminbi and the Japanese yen and the sharp decline in semiconductor prices) adversely affected export revenues and contributed to slowing economic activity and declining asset prices in a number of Asian economies. During the second half of 1997, currencies and stock markets plunged across East Asia. In Thailand, these events were accompanied by pressures in the foreign exchange market and the collapse of the Thai baht in July 1997. The events in Thailand prompted investors to reassess and test the

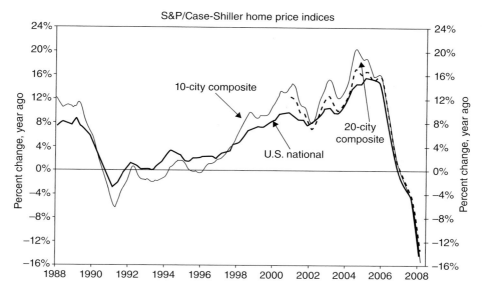

Figure 6.12   House price index in the United States.
Source: Standard & Poor's and Fiserv.

robustness of currency pegs and financial systems in the region. In the year
after the collapse of the baht peg, the value of the most affected East Asian
currencies fell at 35–83% against the U.S. dollar (measured in dollars per
unit of the Asian currency), and the most serious stock declines were as
great as 40–60%. The commercial real estate markets also fell sharply across
Asian cities during 1997–1998. Property prices declined by an average of
40% (Koh *et al.*, 2005).

The U.S. subprime mortgage crisis and the financial crisis of 2008

Housing prices in the United States and many other advanced countries
(such as the United Kingdom) witnessed a secular growth during 1996–2006.
During this period, the nominal house prices in the United States doubled,
and in the United Kingdom, they tripled. The growth in house prices in
the United States and the United Kingdom is shown in Figure 6.12 and
Figure 6.13, respectively.

The rise in prices was also associated with the rise in household mortgage
debt (Figure 6.14). Mortgage debt outstanding as a percent of GDP in the United
States rose from 21% in 1983 to about 76% in 2010. A similar pattern has been
observed in countries like the United Kingdom, Denmark, the Netherlands
and Australia. During this period of rising prices, mortgage banks relaxed their
credit limits and lending standards so much so that even households with
insufficient and poor credit histories were encouraged to borrow heavily at
variable rates of interest to buy into rising market (Barras, 2009). Innovations

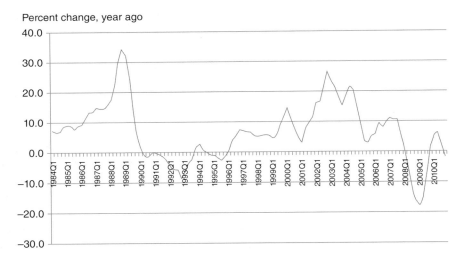

Figure 6.13　House price index in the United Kingdom.
Source: Authors based on house price index data from Halifax (http://www.
lloydsbankinggroup.com/media1/economic_insight/halifax_house_price_index_page.asp)

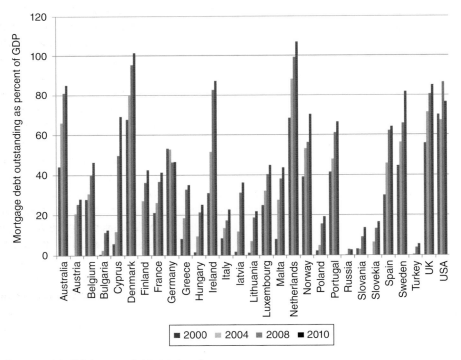

Figure 6.14　Mortgage debt outstanding.
Source: Authors based on data from Hypostat (2011) and Keen (2012).

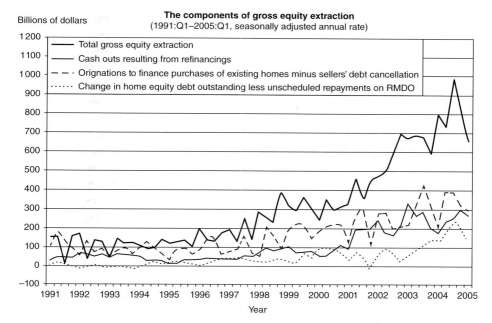

Figure 6.15 Wealth extracted by American households from housing.
Source: Greenspan and Kennedy (2005). Reproduced by permission of Oxford University Press.

in financial markets by means of complex securitised assets such as mortgage-backed securities (MBS), underwritten by complex derivatives such as credit default swaps, allowed banks to lend higher as they thought that these innovations allowed them to hedge lending risk as they could package debt in the form of tradeable securities. Theoretically, these financial instruments are great innovations which, in normal times, could provide more people access to loans, which become cheaper because banks can sell their risks to investors worldwide with varying appetites for different risk-adjusted returns.

The proactive monetary policy in the United States post 2001, together with expansive real estate initiatives, fuelled the house estate price growth shown in Figure 6.13.

The 2003–2006 was also the period that witnessed substantial acceleration in wealth extraction by American households from their housing assets (Greenspan and Kennedy, 2005; as quoted in Sornette and Woodard, 2009), as shown in Figure 6.15, which parallels the accelerated house price appreciation shown in Figure 6.12.

In addition to the run-up that was witnessed in house prices on the direct property side, the indirect property market was also witnessing the price inflation. While financial innovations allowed banks to lend higher, these became the main drivers of price inflation in the indirect property markets.

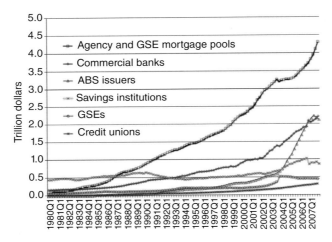

Figure 6.16   U.S. home mortgage assets: flow of funds and investor profile.
Source: Shin (2009).

Particularly, the subprime MBS and complex packages of associated financial derivatives grew substantially. Figure 6.16 shows (i) the total holding of mortgage-related securities of different financial institutions and (ii) the accelerated rate of new issuance of ABS until the peak in March 2007, when the first signs of accelerating loan payment defaults started to be felt on the MBS (Sornette and Woodard, 2009).

The process of formation of MBS bubble and its subsequent bursting points that MBS were 'fragile' as they were linked to two key unstable processes: the value of houses and the loan rates (Sornette and Woodard, 2009). Rising house prices further fuelled investments in MBS, which in turn pushed the demand for and therefore the prices of houses – until the non-sustainability of these mutually reinforcing processes became apparent.

Though theoretically sophisticated instruments, MBS and collaterali-sed debt obligations (CDOs) constituted new types of derivatives. Their complexity together with the lack of historical experience may have led to unrealistic expectations of low risks and large returns. The role of financial derivatives in making markets efficient has been supported by some (most prominent being Alan Greenspan, former U.S. Federal Reserve Bank head) and opposed by others (leading investors like George Soros, Warren Buffet, Felix Rohatyn). While the proponents argue that derivatives allow most states of the world economy to be hedged, thereby bringing in stability, the opponents argue that the risks of these complex instruments are not well understood (one of the reasons being the lack of historical data) to make prognosis of the sort proponents make.

As discussed in Sornette and Woodard (2009), views of opponents have found theoretical support in new out-of-equilibrium models of financial markets in which it is found that while, on one hand, 'the proliferation of financial instruments tends to make the market more complete and efficient by providing more means for risk diversification', on the other hand, 'the proliferation of financial instruments erodes systemic stability as it drives the market to a critical state characterized by large susceptibility, strong fluctuations and, enhanced correlations among risks'.

The housing market and MBS bubbles did not remain confined to these markets but spread to stock market, to commodity market and to the real economy. The stock market in the United States appreciated (as measured by Standard and Poor 500 Index) by about 60% between December 2003 and December 2007. This growth was followed by a sharp decline over the next 1 year.

The growth in housing market, MBS market and stock market led to huge extraction of wealth which led to higher demand for consumption goods. The price of basic commodities rose steeply with characteristics of bubble.

In essence, the features of bubble were seen in all markets. The exuberant price inflation started in the housing and percolated into MBS market, stock market and commodity market. It all tumbled down like house of cards starting 2007.

Explanations in the literature, new economy and role of credit

The literature examining the role of the banking sector in propagating business cycles (see Koh *et al.*, 2005, for a review) demonstrates that the workings of the financial sector can amplify the magnitude of the business cycle as bank credit exposure moves pro-cyclically (also illustrated in Figure 6.1).

Studies that have analysed the causes for Asian financial crisis (see Krugman, 1998; Wade, 1998; Mera and Renaud, 2000; Tan, 2000; Quigley, 2001) have examined the role played by the real estate sector in the crisis. These researchers have argued that real estate markets are vulnerable to waves of optimism and herd behaviour that result in bubbles. In Thailand, for instance, short-term capital inflows found its way into Thailand's real estate market, as banks competed to lend to real estate developers and investors, based on expectations of continued strong economic growth (Tan, 2000).

The pattern of Asian financial crisis (like other financial crises around the world as analysed by Herring and Wachter, 1999) was that East Asian economies first experienced a collapse in real estate prices which led to weakening of banking systems before going on to experience an exchange rate crisis, a banking sector crisis, and a business cycle bust. Koh *et al.* (2005) argue that financial intermediaries' underpriced default option imbedded in the non-recourse mortgage loans as a potential cause for the observed price behaviour in the real estate market. They attribute underpricing to behavioural causes (lender optimism and disaster myopia) and/or rational response of lenders to market incentives (agency conflicts, deposit insurance or limited liability of bank shareholders). A number of researchers (see, e.g. Krugman, 1998; Wade, 1998; Mera and Renaud, 2000; Tan, 2000; Quigley, 2001) argued that lax regulation in the real estate market and lax pricing of risk by banks have been responsible for real estate crises in East Asian countries. These studies argue for reforms in the regulation of the real estate markets and in the treatment of real estate loans by financial institutions in order to prevent the recurrence of asset bubbles.

The pattern of events has not been different for the subprime and the financial crisis of 2008, and a number of explanations have been presented in the literature to explain the crisis. Doms *et al.* (2007) argue that the reason for financial crisis has been the bursting of house price bubble in the United States, the United Kingdom and some other advanced countries. Depreciating house prices led to default on mortgages and depleted the value of MBS. The problem, however, was that the subprime loans were in general risky and the rising house prices hid their riskiness by allowing mortgage terminations to happen through mortgage refinance. Interest rates remained low due to monetary policies in these countries, which made refinancing attractive. When prepayments became expensive, with huge leverage, households found it difficult to refinance and defaults started to happen. Defaults rose sharply in the United States in 2006 and 2007 (Damyanyk *et al.*, 2011).

Another explanation accorded for the crisis is the role that institutional investors and banks played (Sornette and Woodard, 2009). The creation of MBS allowed institutional investors to take large exposure in real estate. The development of MBS and other financial innovations that took place at the time when property prices were rising gave banks the illusion that the default risk could be diversified away. They kept on lending and refinancing (Figure 6.14 shows the growth in mortgage debt as a percentage of GDP), and institutional investors such as pension funds, insurance companies, mutual funds, unit trusts, investment trusts, private banks and commercial banks kept on buying these securities. The size of the MBS held by different institutions (Figure 6.16) explains the amplitude of crisis. Once the mortgage defaults emerged, MBS bubble collapsed. The crisis fed into the financial markets causing liquidity crisis of immense proportion. The penetration of MBS was so deep that banks were not sure how much of these so-called 'toxic' assets were held by whom. The counterparty risk became so high that banks were reluctant to lend even to each other.

Behavioural causes behind the formation of bubble have also been researched. It has been argued that managers' greed and poor corporate governance are some of the key factors that led to the formation of bubbles. Incentive mechanisms have promoted climate of moral hazard where short-term 'irreversible' gains far outweigh long-term prudence (Sornette and Woodard, 2009). Moral hazard factor gets further amplified by herding behaviour. In an industry where performance is commonly assessed against industry average, managers cannot afford to neglect any high-yield investment opportunity even though they may believe that in the long run, these may turn bad. Often, herding is rationalised by concepts like 'new economy', new 'real options'-based valuation and the beliefs that how can everybody be wrong (Sornette and Woodard, 2009).

Another set of research has argued that poor lending standards, deteriorating regulatory environment and supervisions have also been responsible for letting the bubble form. Keys *et al.* (2008) found that the lending standards in the subprime mortgage market did deteriorate and the main determinant for the deterioration was the securitisation of those loans. The regulatory authorities failed to detect, and the reason for that was the growing prevalence of the ethos of deregulation that pervaded the U.S. government (Poser, 2009), which did not allow financial derivatives to be regulated. Internally too, banks faced the problem of bad quantitative risk models which did not allow them to detect the problems. Basel II (Second of Basel Accord, which provides recommendations on banking laws and regulations issued by the Basel Committee on Banking Supervision), which was meant to ensure that capital allocation for various assets is more risk sensitive and the risk is separated between operation risk and credit risk and quantified, was delayed in its implementation as a number of revisions were announced by different financial market regulatory agencies in the United States without any sound reasoning (Cannata and Quagliariello, 2009).

The rating agencies' behaviour has also been questioned in the literature (Sornette and Woodard, 2009), and some have pointed to the moral hazard problems. Rating agencies may have been compelled to deliberately inflate their ratings either to maximise their consulting fees or because issuer could be shopping for highest ratings (Sornette and Woodard, 2009). The problem also arose as the historical data on which the quantitative models for predicting default probabilities could be based was fairly short from 1990 to 2000, a period during which mortgage defaults were low and home prices were rising. The complexity of MBS further introduced a large sensitivity to model errors (Sornette and Woodard, 2009). All in all, the risk was not quantified appropriately and factored in while according ratings to different MBS tranches, a fact later reflected in the actual default rates.

Two features – globalisation and leverage – have been the key features of the two financial crises reviewed previously. These factors were further amplified by a number of market behavioural issues as discussed previously, lax supervision and regulatory environment. An additional cause for the subprime and financial crisis of 2008 was the enormous unregulated growth of MBS market. The development in the financial derivative markets, which allowed pure vanilla, spatially fixed, heterogeneous, illiquid real estate as set to be converted into instruments that could be invested and traded like highly liquid assets on the financial markets, has the characteristics of the new economy. The sophistication in financial modelling was made possible by advances in information technology.

Conclusions

In this chapter, we presented conceptual discussion on real estate cycles, asset bubbles and also underlying causes for the two bubbles which resulted in the financial crises in 1997 and 2008. Real estate cycles arise due to mismatch between demand and supply (caused by various internal and external factors) in the use, investment and development markets. These are phenomena that repeat regularly though for different types of real estate assets and for different markets, frequency and amplitude of cycles varies. Bubbles on the other hand arise due to significant deviation in asset values from their intrinsic values. A number of explanations have been offered for why bubbles form. Economists have argued that the reasons for bubbles to form are uncertainty, speculation, bonded rationality or expectations. Expectations or belief that asset prices will continue to rise as something new in the economy has happened leads to investment in high volumes in highly inflated assets. Various explanations for this behaviour have been discussed in this chapter. The two financial crises which occurred almost 10 years apart indicate that fundamental causes for the crises – real estate asset and stock price inflation caused by easy liquidity, high leverage and globalisation of investors – have remained same. Behaviour of agents (investors, bankers, regulatory and supervision agencies) has also been similar. In case of financial crisis of 2008, the role of MBS has also been discussed.

References

Barras, R. (1994) Property and the economic cycle: building cycles revisited, *Journal of Property Research*, **11** (3), 183–197.

Barras, R. (2009) Property Cycles in Global Investment Markets In: *Building Cycles: Growth & Instability*. Wiley-Blackwell, Oxford, UK.

Barth, J.R., Dan Brumbaugh, R., Ramesh, L. and Yago, G. (1998) Governments vs. markets. *Jobs and Capital*, **VII** (3/4), 28–41.

Blanchard, O.J. and Watson, M.W. (1982) Bubbles, rational expectations and financial markets. *NBER Working Paper No 945*, Cambridge.

Camerer, C. (1989) Bubbles and fads in asset prices. *Journal of Economic Surveys*, **3**, 3–38.

Cannata, F. Quagliariello, M. (2009) The role of basel II in the subprime financial crisis: guilty or not guilty? *CAREFIN Research Paper No. 3/09*, Universita Bocconi, Italy.

Case, K.E. and Shiller, R.J. (1989) The efficiency of the market for single family homes. *American Economic Review*, **79** (1), 125–137.

Damyanyk, Y. and van Hemert, O. (2011) Understanding the subprime crisis. *Review of Financial Studies*, **24** (6), 1848–1880.

Diba, B.T. and Grossman, H.I. (1983) Rational asset price bubbles. *NBER Working Paper No 1059*, Cambridge.

Doms, M., Furlong, F. and Krainer, J. (2007) Subprime mortgage delinquency rates. Working Paper Series 2007–33, Federal Reserve Bank of San Francisco. http://www.frbsf.org/publications/economics/papers/2007/wp07-33bk.pdf (accessed 16 October 2013).

Flood, R.P. and Hodrick, R.J. (1990) On testing for speculative bubbles. *Journal of Economic Perspectives*, **81** (4), 85–101.

Froot, K.A. and Obstfeld, M. (1991) Intrinsic bubbles: the case of stock prices. *The American Economic Review*, **22** (81), 1189–1214.

Garber, P. (2001) *Famous First Bubbles: The Fundamentals of Early Manias*. MIT Press, Cambridge.

Greenspan, A. and Kennedy, J. (2008) Sources and uses of equity extracted from homes. *Oxford Review of Economic Policy*, **24** (1), 120–144.

Gurkaynak, R.S. (2008) Econometric tests of asset price bubbles: taking stock. *Journal of Economic Surveys*, **22**, 166–186.

Hamilton, B. and Schwab, R. (1985) Expected appreciation in urban housing markets. *Journal of Urban Economics*, **18** (1), 103–118.

Herring Richard, J. and Susan Grossman. (1983) Real Estate Booms and Banking Busts: An International Perspective. *Occasional Papers*, No. 58, Group of Thirty.

Herring, R.J. and Wachter, S. (2002) Real estate bubbles. In: *Asset Price Bubbles: Implications for Monetary, Regulatory and International Policies* (ed G. Kaufman). MIT Press, Cambridge.

Hommes, C., Sonnemans, J., Tuinstra, J. and Velden, H., van de (2005) Coordination of expectations in asset pricing experiments. *Review of Financial Studies*, **18**, 955–980.

Hypostat (2011) Hypostat 2010 A review of Europe's mortgage and housing markets, European Mortgage Federation, Brussels.

Jones Lang, LaSalle (2011) Hot spots emerging in global office markets. http://www.joneslanglasalle.co.in/Pages/Global-Office-Outlook-March-2011.aspx (accessed 4 October 2013).

Keen, S. (2012) Australian house prices, Update June 2012, http://www.debtdeflation.com/blogs/2012/08/02/australian-house-prices-update-june-2012/ (accessed 27 July 2007).

Keys, B.J., Mukherjee, T., Seru, A. and Vig, V. (2008) Did securitization lead to lax screening? Evidence from subprime loans. *Athens Meetings Paper*, European Finance Association, December 2008, Athens.

Kim, K-H and Suh, S-H (1993) Speculation and house price bubbles in the Korean and Japanese real estate markets. *Journal of Real Estate Finance and Economics*, **6** (1), 73–88.

King, R.R., Smith, V.L., Williams, A.W. and van Boening, M.V. (1993) The robustness of bubbles and crashes in experimental stock markets. In: *Nonlinear Dynamics and Evolutionary Economics* (eds R.H. Day and P. Chen). Oxford University Press, New York.

Koh, W.T.H., Mariano, R.S., Pavlov, A., Phang, S.Y., Tan, A.H.H. and Wachter, S.M. (2005) Bank Lending and Real Estate in Asia: Market Optimism and Asset Bubbles. *Journal of Asian Economics*, **15**, 110–62.

Krugman, P. (1998) What happened to Asia, Mimeo. http://web.mit.edu/krugman/www/DISINTER.html

Lahart, J. (2008) Bernanke's bubble laboratory, Princeton protégés of Fed chief study the economics of manias. *The Wall Street Journal*, May 16 A1.

Lei, V., Noussair, C.N. and Plott, C.R. (2001) Nonspeculative bubbles in experimental asset markets: lack of common knowledge of rationality vs. actual irrationality. *Econometrica*, **69**, 831.

Levine, S.S. and Zajac E.J. (2007) *The Institutional Nature of Price Bubbles*. http://www.usc.edu/schools/business/FBE/seminars/papers/MOR_9-14-07_Levine.pdf (accessed 4 October 2013).

Levine, S.S. and Zajac E.J. (2008) *When and Where Can Institutionalization Occur? The Case of Price Bubbles in Financial Markets*. Best Paper Proceedings (2008) Academy of Management, Anaheim, California.

Malpezzi, S. (1999) A simple error-correction model of housing prices. *Journal of Housing Economics*, **8**, 27–62.

Malpezzi, S. and Watcher, S. (2004) The role of speculation in real estate cycles, mimeo, http://www.capitalmarketsgroupaz.com/pdf/The%20Role%20of%20Speculation%20in%20Real%20Estate%20Cycles.pdf (accessed 4 October 2013).

McCartney, J. (2008) An empirical analysis of development cycles in the Dublin office market 1972–2008, in *Quarterly Economic Commentary*, Winter, ESRI, Dublin.

Mera, K. and Renaud, B. (2000) *Asia's Financial Crisis and the Role of Real Estate*. M.E. Sharpe, Armonk, New York.

Miller, M.K. (1997) Cycles and timing. *Exploring*, **21** (1).

Ortalo-Magne, F. and Rady, S. (2006) Housing market dynamics: on the contribution of income shocks and credit constraints. *Review of Economic Studies*, **73** (2), 459–485.

Ott, S.H., Riddiough, T.J., Yi, H.-C. and Yoshida, J. (2008) On demand: cross-country evidence from commercial real estate markets. *International Real Estate Review*, **11** (1), 1–37.

Poser, N.S. (2009) Why the SEC Failed: Regulators Against Regulation. In: *Brooklyn Journal of Corporate, Financial & Commercial Law*, Vol. **3**. Brooklyn Law School, Brooklyn.

Pyhrr, S.A., Roulac, S.E. and Born, W.L. (1999) Real estate cycles and their strategic implications for investors and portfolio managers in global economy. *Journal of Real Estate Research*, **18** (1), 7–68.

Quigley, J.M. (2001) Real estate and the Asian crisis. *Journal of Housing Economics*, **10**, 129–161.

Reinhard, C.M. and Rogoff, K.S. (2008) Is the 2007 US sub-prime financial crisis so different? An international historical comparison. University of Maryland, Mimeo.

Roulac, S.E. (1996) Real estate market cycles, transformation forces and systems change. *Journal of Real Estate Portfolio Management*, **2** (1), 1–17.

Royal Institution of Chartered Surveyors (RICS) (1994) Understanding the property cycles. In: *Main Report: Economic Cycles and Property Cycles*. RICS, London.

RREEF (2006a) Asia Pacific property cycle monitor, Nov 2006, RREEF Limited, London.

RREEF (2006b) European property cycle monitor, December, RREEF Limited, London.

Sarno, L. and Taylor, M.P. (2003) An empirical investigation of asset price bubbles in Latin American emerging financial markets. *Applied Financial Economics*, **13** (13), 635–643.

Shiller, R.J. (1981) Do stock prices move too much to be justified by subsequent changes in dividends? *American Economic Review*, Vol. **71** (3), 421–436.

Shin, H.S. (2009) Securitization and financial stability. *The Economic Journal*, **119** (March), 309–332.

Smith, V.L., Suchanek, G.L. and Williams, A.W. (1988) Bubbles, crashes, and endogenous expectations in experimental spot asset markets. *Econometrica*, **56** (5), 1119–1151.

Sornette, D. and Woodard, R. (2009) Financial bubbles, real estate bubbles, derivative bubbles, and the financial and economic crisis. *Swiss Finance Institute Research Paper No 09-15*, Zurich.

Tan, A.H.H. (2000) Sources of the Asian Currency Crisis: Internal and External. Published in ASEAN University Network & The Korean Association of Southeast Asian Studies, Economic Crisis in Southeast Asia and Korea, pp. 306–316.

Wade, R. (1998) The Asian debt-and-development crisis of 1997: causes and consequences. *World Development*, **26** (8), 1535–1553.

7

International Capital Flows in Property: Portfolio Diversification or Return Chasing

Introduction

The total invested direct property stock is about US$11.3 trillion (RREEF, 2011), and according to Jones Lang LaSalle (2012), about US$418 billion has been invested in direct property during 2011. Figure 7.1 presents the quarterly trends in direct property investment. More than 40% of the flows in 2011 were cross-border.

Though the U.S. investors would continue to account for a quarter of investment, investors from other countries such as the United Kingdom, Singapore, China, Japan, Brazil and France are also becoming active in direct property markets. With globalisation of economies and surge in number of global funds, an increasing share of this investment is targeted towards cross-border property assets. According to JLL (2012), during 2011, in the Americas and Europe, listed Real Estate Investment Trusts (REITs) have been net acquirers, while in Asia-Pacific institutional investors were the dominant players. In Asia-Pacific, corporate were net buyers of property for their own use. While in Europe and Americas, the trend was opposite as a number of sale and leaseback-type deals took place. Unlisted funds were large net acquirers of property in Europe but were net divestors in other regions.

Real Estate Finance in the New Economy, First Edition. Piyush Tiwari and Michael White.
© 2014 John Wiley & Sons, Ltd. Published 2014 by John Wiley & Sons, Ltd.

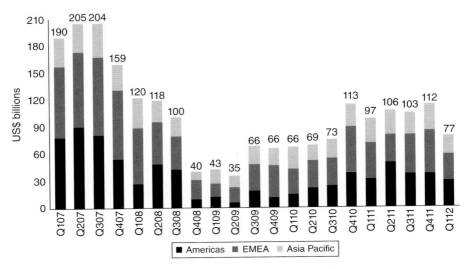

Figure 7.1 Direct commercial real estate volumes (billion US$).
Source: Reproduced by permission of Jones Lang LaSalle.

The top ten investment markets in 2011 were London; New York; Tokyo; Paris; Hong Kong; Washington, DC; Seoul; Singapore; Los Angeles; and Shanghai – they accounted for 32% of total global investment volumes. Various factors affect decisions to invest in property – macroeconomic environment; risk associated with property asset class, depth, liquidity and transparency of property markets; availability of debt and equity capital from banks and/or capital markets; and property investment vehicles and their objectives and regulatory regime within which investors, property markets, capital markets and banks operate.

A large part of investment advice in the practitioner world over the last decade has been to construct global portfolios to benefit from diversification though research conducted in the academia has so far been inconclusive on the diversification benefits from global portfolios that include property.

In the last two decades, though, global investment has become easier with globalisation of economies, dismantling of trade barriers in goods and services, transparency of property markets and demand on investors to look outwards as their domestic markets saturate. In their global property investment advice, RREEF (2011) suggests that global investors should look to allocate significant capital in core property assets across three regions – Americas, Europe and Asia-Pacific. The correlation in total property returns across regions would guide the fund allocations by investors.

While referring to global investors, usually, the reference is made to institutional investors. Institutional investors are large organisations with considerable investible cash reserves. Examples of these investors are

Table 7.1 Asset allocation of institutional investors (% of total assets).

	Bonds		Equities		Mutual funds		Deposits and loans		Other	
	1995	2005	1995	2005	1995	2005	1995	2005	1995	2005
Insurance companies										
Australia	41	30	41	53			13	11	4	6
Canada	53	51	13	26			29	15	5	7
Euro area	44	46	14	23	7.9	17.8	25	17	11	8
Japan	32	52	21	24	1	2	40	20	7	3
Korea	14	46	14	4	3	6	61	24	9	20
Mexico	n.a.	69		1				2		28
Singapore	27	55	31	32			40	12	2	1
Sweden	n.a.	49		46				4		1
Switzerland	n.a.	43		28				29		
UK	30	41	53	33	8	10	8	11	2	6
US	62	56	16	24	1	2	14	12	7	6
Pension funds										
Australia	17	13	44	56			10	11	29	20
Canada	46	36	48	55			4	3	2	6
Euro area	42	34	9	15	29	56	26	20	15	16
Japan	46	30	8	59	0	1	12	8	3	2
Korea	18	80	8	7	10	2	62	10	3	2
Mexico		97		1				0		2
Singapore		92		6		2		0		0
Sweden	87	30	9	42			4	3	0	24
Switzerland		35		22.7				19		23
UK	15	21	69	42	10	28	4	3	2	7
US	26	19	47	47	9	20	6	5	12	8

Source: BIS (2007).

insurance companies, pension funds and investment companies such as mutual funds, investment trusts, hedge funds and private equity funds. In terms of financial assets, institutional investors are as large as the banks. Insurance companies and pension funds are the largest institutional investors with total assets amounting to US$30 trillion in 2005 (BIS, 2007). The asset allocation of insurance companies and pension funds in select countries is presented in Table 7.1.

The asset category 'other' comprises of alternative investments such as hedge funds, commodities, real estate, infrastructure, emerging market assets and private equity. Institutional investors invest in alternative assets to enhance returns, for obtaining better diversification of their investment portfolios and/or to hedge against inflation (BIS, 2007).

According to a market survey of 327 large institutional investors in Australia, Europe, Japan and North America conducted by Russell Investment Group (2006), on average, the aggregate strategic allocation to private equity, hedge funds and property ranges from 14% of total assets in Japan to 21% in Australia and North America in 2005.

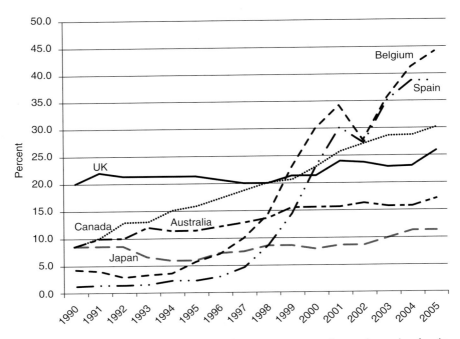

Figure 7.2   Holding of foreign securities by insurance companies and pension funds.

Over the last few years, institutional investors have diversified their portfolios by investing in assets overseas. Though availability of dis-aggregated data by type of investment is a problem for most asset classes, the intent for international diversification can be seen from Figure 7.2. The figure shows the allocation of portfolio investment in foreign securities. While investors in countries on the left panel in Figure 7.2 have built their international portfolios gradually over time, investors in countries on the right have increased their allocation substantially after the adoption of euro.

In this chapter, we examine the role of international property investment in portfolio diversification for investors. The foci of the discussion are insti-tutional investors. These investors invest in direct and indirect property. Since these are large investors, the other issue that has been discussed in this chapter is whether capital flows from institutional investors affect returns in the property market (as is commonly believed).

As a starting point, we briefly outline the Modern Portfolio Theory and the Capital Asset Pricing Model. We then proceed to review research on whether or not investors create well-diversified global property portfolios while investing in property and whether international diversification bene-fits significantly outweigh the added costs attached to internationalisation. There are two opposing schools of thoughts – one that says that significant benefits can be had by holding property assets across different countries and the other that questions the risk reduction benefits associated with diverse international holdings of property assets, arguing that the benefits achieved from international diversification are not significantly more than what can be achieved from other financial instruments (Wilson and Zurbruegg, 2003). After this, we examine research that focuses on real estate investment for both direct and indirect property assets and their potential role in both property-only and multi-asset portfolios. Finally, we discuss whether there is a relation between capital flows from institutional investor and property returns.

Theoretical considerations in portfolio investment

Investors are usually concerned with the risk and return combinations that their portfolio provides. In considering how much property, if any, to hold, we follow the work by Markowitz (1952, 1959), who laid the foundations for capital market theory. He developed the Modern Portfolio Theory (MPT), which considers how investors trade off risk and expected return from their investments. The theory considers the correlation in performance between assets held in a portfolio. Specifically, assets in a portfolio should at most have low correlations between them in terms of performance. This enables the investor to diversify away the risk attached to holding the assets. Essentially, MPT argues that risk and returns on individual assets are not important in themselves, but only as they contribute to the risk and return of the portfolio. The approach by Markowitz identifies the optimal proportion of a portfolio that should be allocated to a given asset. While it has traditionally been applied to the equity market, it can logically be extended to any risky asset class. Optimum combinations of risk and return produce an efficient frontier along which a higher expected return is associated with a greater risk. This is illustrated in Figure 7.3. To find the risk and return trade-off an investor will choose, his preferences for risk and return must be considered. Some investors may be classed as risk-averse and will only accept greater risk for a significantly greater expected return. Alternatively, a risk-taking investor may be prepared to take on a lot more risk for a small increase in expected return.

The investor's preferences for risk and expected return are illustrated on her indifference curve. Along this curve, she is indifferent between different combinations of risk and expected return, thus having constant utility. She would prefer higher expected returns for any given risk level and would therefore prefer to be on indifference curve. Consequently, indifference curves following this one provide less utility. Given the portfolio of assets, the investor will be on the efficient frontier,

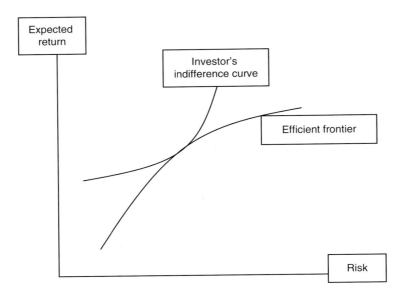

Figure 7.3   Efficient frontier.
Source: Tiwari and White (2010).

and her optimal combination of risk and expected return occurs where this frontier is tangential to the indifference curve.

In practice, calculating the components of MPT makes its application very difficult as means, variances and covariance terms between pairs of assets have to be calculated. These terms increase exponentially when more assets are added to the portfolio. In addition, investors are concerned with expectations of future asset performance, and data on historic returns will provide incomplete information upon which to base expectations (Tiwari and White, 2010).

However, if asset returns could be influenced by some common variable or variables, developing expectations would be easier. Sharpe (1964) developed what is termed the 'market model', which suggested that asset performance could be related to an index of business performance. This is the basis for the Capital Asset Pricing Model (CAPM), in which asset or portfolio returns are determined by random factors and a common market index.

The assumptions upon which CAPM is built are developed from those for MPT and additionally assume the existence of a risk-free asset and free information and that risk expectations are the same across investors. Investors can combine their optimal portfolio of assets with the risk-free asset. Key to CAPM, however, is that investors would be better off if they combined the risk-free asset with the market portfolio. 'The line which joins the risk-free rate to the market portfolio is known as the Capital Market Line (CML)' (Hoesli and MacGregor, 2000, p. 135), Figure 7.4.

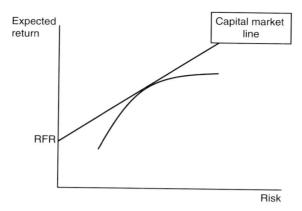

Figure 7.4 Capital market line.
Source: Tiwari and White (2010).

In the aforementioned graph, the optimal position occurs where the efficient frontier is tangent to the capital market line at the market portfolio where risky assets are combined with the risk-free asset. If we only used the risk-free asset, we would earn the risk-free return (RFR). The riskiness of the asset itself has two components: first, market (or systematic or non-diversifiable) risk and, second, specific (or nonmarket or diversifiable) risk. Market risk cannot be removed from assets in a given market, and the market element will impose some degree of correlation across the assets. Specific risks relate to an asset and can be reduced by portfolio diversification, holding assets that have low correlations in performance.

In a direct property portfolio, investors would need to hold a number of properties before experiencing significant reductions in specific risk. This can be an expensive strategy given the high unit value of direct property investments. A potential benefit of international investment is that it reduces market risk, since different countries have different economic circumstances and often have different currencies. Hence, adding overseas assets to a portfolio will reduce portfolio risk, since the correlations between assets in different countries will be lower than the correlation between assets within one country. Investors will therefore be able to achieve a better risk-adjusted return on their portfolio. It may also be the case that substantially higher returns can be earned in overseas markets than would be available in the domestic market.

However, there are additional risks not encountered in domestic investment portfolios. Exchange rate risk is just one that could affect return performance. Home currency returns fall if the foreign currency depreciates. Interest rate differentials may also play a role. Lower interest rates in one country may encourage investors in that country to borrow in local currency to increase their investments. Theoretically, we should expect interest rate parity, that is, real interest rates should be equal across countries. While this may be a long-run equilibrium condition, it may not hold in the short run and arbitrage opportunities will therefore be created.

Geurts and Jaffe (1996) suggest that the removal of market risk as a motivation of international investment is naïve and will not reduce risks sufficiently to encourage international investment. They suggest that investors will exhibit significant home asset bias, which they relate to possible institutional barriers to overseas investment in different countries, the transactions costs which overseas investment can incur and taxation of income from investment assets. Investors may have imperfect information on institutional structure and hence on the behaviour of institutions in other countries. The cost of learning institutional behaviour may outweigh the reduction in unsystematic risk and hence the expected increased return of overseas diversification. Moreover, with globalisation, as more markets are integrated, the less benefit from diversification will be realised as the same economic and financial drivers will affect these markets.

Direct property in multi-asset portfolios

A number of studies have been undertaken to examine the diversification potential of direct property in multi-asset portfolios. Key concerns surround whether or not there are international diversification benefits from holding direct property assets and the role of currency fluctuations. Literature has been inconclusive on the benefits of international diversification.

Webb and Rubens (1989) use data from the United Kingdom and the United States over a long time period, 1926–1986, and compute efficient asset portfolios. They find that international real estate does not enter an efficient asset portfolio. Giliberto (1989), comparing U.S. and U.K. real estate returns, suggests some benefits from overseas diversification. Worzala (1992) and Worzala and Vandell (1995) examine mean returns and deviations from U.S. and U.K. real estate and suggest that there are international diversification benefits from real estate but less so when currency fluctuations are considered. They also suggest some instability in results over different time periods.

Newell and Webb (1998) examine real estate returns in the United States, the United Kingdom, Canada, Australia and New Zealand. They consider the possible impact of appraisal smoothing on the risk attached to real estate assets. Their finding is that risk is underestimated both due to smoothing and also when currency fluctuations are ignored. They also suggest some diversification benefits from the inclusion of international real estate in multi-asset portfolios. Stevenson (1998) examines 18 stock markets, five bond markets, U.S. direct and indirect markets and U.K. direct and indirect markets. In this research, only non-property international financial assets are held in portfolios. His results suggest keeping real estate assets in a portfolio with international financial assets. Real estate is also present in a low-risk/return portfolio. McAllister (1999) conducted a survey of British investing institutions during the 1980s and 1990s to analyse trends in direct property investment. He finds that direct property was more segregated internationally than other asset classes. An implication of low integration levels is the potential existence of international diversification benefits. Chua (1999) examines the United States, the United Kingdom, France, Germany and Japan. Adjusting for appraisal smoothing, he finds that adding real estate improves risk-adjusted portfolio return performance in comparison to portfolios excluding real estate. The optimal allocations to property varied from 4% to 21% depending on the risk tolerance of the investors. Cheng *et al.* (1999) use data from the United States, the United Kingdom and Japan. They design efficient portfolios and suggest that currency risk is significant but that international real estate can be included in portfolios for investors who are not too risk-averse. Hoesli *et al.* (2002) examine the United States, the United Kingdom, Australia, France, the Netherlands, Sweden and Switzerland. They suggest that 15–25% of an efficient portfolio should be devoted to real estate assets, both national and international. However, there is no analysis of the impact of currency movements.

There are an equal number of studies which conclude that including international property has no diversification benefit in mixed-asset portfolios. Ziobrowski and Curcio (1991) find no diversification benefit when the U.S. property was added to the portfolios of British and Japanese investors. Authors generated a number of efficient frontiers for a variety of asset combinations and cross-country combinations. They conclude that any benefits that may exist from international diversification in non-exchange adjusted terms get offset by exchange rate volatility. Further, Ziobrowski and Boyd (1991) reach the same conclusion when leverage is present and hedging occurs to compensate for currency fluctuations when taking on local currency loans. Ziobrowski and Ziobrowski (1995) further examined the diversification of properties across countries by increasing the number of assets under consideration and the time period. The finding from their study suggests that the common stock (not property or bonds) may be the most appropriate foreign asset to hold from the perspective of effective diversification as stocks are less prone to exchange rate volatility than other types of assets. Even after accounting for differentiation in taxation across countries, currency fluctuations and de-smoothing appraisal-based property returns for international investors investing in U.S. property, Ziobrowski *et al.* (1996) find no diversification benefits for British or Japanese investors.

They conclude that 'foreign investors in US real estate may be legitimately buying US real estate for many logical reasons, but rational diversification for the sole purpose of improving portfolio performance does not appear to be one of them'.

Quan and Titman (1997, 1999) find that the reasoning behind weak diversification benefits from inclusion of property in mixed asset portfolios in Asia-Pacific and many countries in Europe is significant positive correlation between property capital value changes and stock market returns as both are driven by common economic fundamentals. A study by Case *et al.* (2000) using appraisal-based property data for 22 markets for the period 1987–1997 provided strong evidence to support globalisation of property markets. Their analysis suggested that one of the reasons why property markets were interlinked was due to common exposure to world economic conditions.

Direct property in property-only portfolios

A number of studies over the last two decades have analysed diversification benefits from international property portfolios.

Sweeney (1989) and Reid (1989) use rental data for office markets and find that there are diversification benefits from international real estate. Gordon (1991), using real estate indices in the United States and the United Kingdom, also finds concurring results. Worzala (1992) though finds results consistent with the ones earlier but when considering currency fluctuations finds that diversification benefits are reduced.

Eichholtz *et al.* (1995) employ U.S. and U.K. direct property indices and find that location has a greater impact than property type upon diversification benefits. They also suggest that the benefits of diversification will vary by country as well as by property type and region. Pagliani *et al.* (1997) analysed the benefits from diversification for different sectors (office, retail, warehouse) from the standpoint of U.S. investor diversifying in property across the United States, the United Kingdom, Canada and Australia over the period 1985–1995. They found that while the international diversification benefits differed across the sectors, they were generally held to be favourable to the U.S. investor.

Goetzmann and Wachter (1995) examine return performance for office markets in 21 countries using asking rent data. They find a strong correlation with global economic cycles and office market performance and therefore suggest that the diversification benefit of international real estate investment will be small. D'Arcy and Lee (1998) examine nine European countries covering industrial, office and retail sectors. They also examine markets in cities within these countries. Their findings suggest that a country's economic policy has the biggest impact on diversification benefits, followed by city-level effects. Some countries were more highly correlated in terms of performance than others.

Addae-Dapaah and Yong (1998) examined countries in Southeast Asia, including Australia and New Zealand. Office rents and capital value data were used. Their findings, however, suggest low cross-country correlations and only small increases in risk due to currency fluctuations. Case *et al.* (1999) cover 22 markets and 21 countries and suggest that property type is important when considering international diversification strategies in real estate. They find that office property offers the least, and industrial the greatest, diversification benefits. Henderson Investors (2000) found that an international property portfolio would provide higher risk-adjusted returns than property from an individual country. Whitaker (2001) examined IPD indices for the United Kingdom and Ireland and the NCREIF series for the United States. Portfolio benefits were found to exist for the U.S.-based investor.

Indirect property investment in multi-asset portfolios

Literature on international securitised property investment goes back to the early 1990s. Among the earliest of studies is that of Asabere *et al.* (1991), who examine equity returns of international real estate companies during the 1980s. They analyse returns, standard deviations and betas. They find a negative correlation between international real estate and U.S. treasury bills and weak positive correlations with long-term government debt. They also find that the global real estate index outperforms domestic real estate but not global equities. Barry *et al.* (1996) examine emerging markets and find that risk-adjusted return performance improves as investment allocations to emergent markets increase. Eichholtz (1996), examining nine countries, finds lower cross-country correlations for property than for either common stock or bond returns. Eichholtz concludes that international real estate portfolio diversification improves portfolio performance. In a study of 19 countries, Eichholtz (1997) finds that the correlation between property and common stock returns varied across countries. European countries have fairly low correlation between property and stock returns, while the United States, the United Kingdom and Canada have fairly high correlations. Far East countries such as Hong Kong have very high correlation. Market maturity is one of the reasons suggested for observed differences in correlations. Mull and Soenen (1997), who adjust for the investor's home currency, argue that the addition of U.S. indirect property provides limited portfolio improvement. Gordon *et al.* (1998) examine 14 countries and construct efficient frontiers. They find that inclusion of international property improves portfolio performance and that, as returns rise, property causes risk to fall.

In their study across six countries, Liu and Mei (1998) find that diversification benefits are driven by unanticipated returns that is partially driven by changes in exchange rate risk. Gordon and Canter (1999), using the data for 14 countries, examine correlations between stock markets and property securities. While they find that portfolios including international property assets outperform those that exclude property, they also find that correlations between asset classes vary substantially over time. Stevenson (1999) covers 16 countries and compares stock, bonds and real estate indices. Looking from the perspective of an Irish investor, he finds that U.K. real estate contributes only a small allocation of a mid-level risk/return portfolio. International real estate comes out of the portfolio when adjustment for currency is made. In a related paper, Stevenson (2000) finds that the diversification benefits of international real estate investment are eroded when currencies are considered. Interestingly, however, he suggests that strategies for hedging against currency risk could improve diversification benefits. Conover *et al.* (2002) analyse the United Kingdom, the United States, Canada, Hong Kong, Japan and Singapore, constructing efficient frontiers. They suggest that portfolios containing international securitised real estate outperform those without it.

Indirect real estate investment in real estate-only portfolios

One of the earliest papers is that of Giliberto (1990), examining data from the 1980s across 11 countries. He computes portfolios where half is invested in the home country. He suggests that Western European property investments dominate the low risk/return portfolios and Japan dominates in portfolios with higher risk/return combinations. Asabere *et al.* (1991) found low positive correlations between U.S. REITs and international property equities, suggesting that the addition of international property should improve portfolio performance. International property equities offered higher exchange rate adjusted returns with greater volatility than U.S. REITs. Hudson-Wilson and Stimpson (1996) found that Canadian investors would have benefited by including U.S securitised property in their property portfolios. Addae-Dapaah and Boon Kion (1996) examine seven countries, including the United Kingdom, Canada, Japan, Australia, Hong Kong and Singapore, looking at mean returns and correlations. They find that correlations change over time and that diversification benefits are improved when currency adjustment is taken into consideration.

Wilson and Okunev (1996) examine the United Kingdom, the United States and Australia. They apply co-integration analysis and construct efficient frontiers. They find that international investment is present in real estate-only efficient frontiers, although not at the highest risk/return levels.

Pierzak (2001) examined 21 countries using mean returns and deviations. His findings suggest that there are diversification benefits from international indirect property investment. Bigman (2002) covers Europe, the United States, Japan and Southeast Asia and finds that international diversification outperforms domestic-only portfolios.

Eichholtz *et al.* (1993) examine 12 countries across three continents. Using principal components analysis, they find a continental factor affecting performance and suggest that in order to achieve diversification benefits, investment should be across the continents. Eichholtz *et al.* (1997) examine 30 countries and create domestic and international indices from their data. They suggest that domestic portfolios are preferred to international portfolios having preferable risk/return characteristics. Interestingly, they note a firm size effect that is also identified by Conover *et al.* (1998). Larger firms perform better than smaller firms.

Wilson and Okunev (1999) examine cycles in equity and real estate markets. They find weak co-movements that suggest there is room for diversification benefits with the inclusion of indirect property in portfolios. The size of the property market and market liquidity also plays an important role in determining international diversification. Analysing property securities in six major property markets, Eichholtz *et al.* (1999) find that the global securitised property markets are very small in comparison to the direct property market. The implication for institutional investors with large capital and very specific asset allocation strategies is that they are forced to use direct and indirect property markets for diversification. While the direct property is illiquid during bear phase of the market, the indirect property maintains high degree of liquidity during bull and bear runs.

Contradictions in research on diversification benefits from international property investment

The aforementioned research highlights some contradictions in findings and sensitivity of results to time period covered, currency risk factors, firm size and ability to provide diversification benefits. Forbes and Rigobon (2002) show that the conventional cross-correlation coefficients of several markets can be biased upwards during periods of increased volatility. Implication of temporal instability of correlation coefficients is that a well-diversified portfolio constituted in one period may not remain so in another period, leading to less diversification benefits than originally anticipated. D'Arcy and Lee (1998) also provide evidence on temporal instability of correlation coefficients. Lu and Mei (1999) find that there was asymmetry in the correlations between better times and worse times. During better times, the correlations were low, while during worse times, these were high. This prompted them to conclude that '...when you need diversification, you don't have it, and you get it when you don't need it'. These results were also confirmed by Conover *et al.* (2002) by their finding that the correlation between U.S. stock and foreign real estate ranged from high at the time of the 1987 crash to low during 1993, when economic conditions were good.

Bond *et al.* (2003) examine the risk and return characteristics of real estate shares from 14 countries from 1990 to 2001. They explore whether country-specific market risks are related to fundamental factors (such as book-to-market value, firm size) or economic risk factors (such as inflation rates, interest rates and default rates). They find variation in mean returns and standard deviations and that there is a global market risk component. However, country-specific market risk is still found to be significant, particularly in the Asia-Pacific region. They find that there are benefits from international real estate diversification, but these follow a more complex pattern than previously understood.

Glascock and Kelly (2007) examine the diversification benefits of international portfolio diversification. They use monthly data from January 1990 to July 2005 and separate out the influences of country and property type. Diversification across property types is found to account for only a small proportion of return variance, while country diversification produces significantly larger performance variation. This finding contrasts with studies examining diversification within countries, where property-type diversification is often more important than diversifying across regions (Miles and McCue, 1982, 1984). However, Glascock and Kelly also suggest that the relative importance of individual country impacts is diminishing. Their findings are consistent with those of Eichholtz (1997). They also show that correlations are higher between property types than between countries.

Capital flows and property returns

Many institutional investors have a large capital for investment in various assets including property. Do capital flows from institutional investors in property affect price of the asset, as was argued over the last decade or so prior to financial market crash of 2007 when property prices were rising fast? In classical finance theory, which is based on the assumptions such as investor rationality and costless arbitrage, capital flows or trading activity do not affect asset prices. However, the recent literature on behavioural finance is critical of these assumptions, and they argue (both theoretically and empirically) that besides market fundamentals, investor sentiments, capital flows and trading volume affect asset prices (Fisher *et al.* 2008).

The relation between capital flows and property returns has been a topic of recent research. Ling and Naranjo (2003, 2006) analyse the influence of equity flows into REITs sector on REIT prices and returns. Fisher *et al.* (2008) investigate the relation between institutional capital flows and returns in private property market. Property practitioners have believed that capital flows affect property returns and capital values. In fact, a large part of yield compression during 2001–2007 was attributed to surge in capital flows in property (Downs, 2007).

A number of possible causal relationships between capital flows and asset price returns have been suggested in literature. These include a price pressure effect, implying that changes in fund flows affect future returns; return chasing behaviour, meaning that returns affect future fund flows; and joint dependency of returns and capital flows due to common exogenous factors driving both and the presence of self-reinforcing feedback relationships between flows and returns (Ling *et al.*, 2009).

According to Ling and Naranjo (2006), changes in economic fundamentals and risk factors produce changes in property-level cash flows or required rate of return for investing in property, which may lead to surge in property values as well as lead to an increase in capital flows in property. A counter-argument would be that property markets, particularly direct property markets, are highly segmented with limited investment options and few information signals for an investor to rely on. In such markets, transactions provide a price revealing function (Ling *et al.*, 2009). The more thinly traded a market is, the more likely it is that the price information provided by transactions will affect subsequent returns (Ling *et al.*, 2009). The market segmentation may also cause capital flows to affect property valuations. In addition, shifting capital values may also affect investor expectations about future cash flows, and they may lower their required rate of return. Segmentation in the market and investor expectation may lead to rise in property values during rising market and may cause precisely the reverse during falling market. Often, the sentiments in the market are driven by irrational investors or noise traders (Lin *et al.* 2009).

Fisher *et al.* (2008) find that the capital flows from institutional investors impact property returns for the office and apartment sectors, while no such effect occurs for retail and industrial property sectors. The effect is far more pronounced in the core business districts where institutional investors are active. Lin *et al.* (2009) find that in indirect property markets, investor sentiments affect returns. When 'investors are optimistic (pessimistic), REIT returns become higher (lower)' (Lin *et al.*, 2009). They also find that even institutional traders, who are considered as informed traders, cannot arbitrage away noise trader risk except in the case of small REITs.

Another question that has been tested is whether institutional investors chase returns or capital flows of other institutional investors while investing in property, a phenomenon more common in equity markets (Ling *et al.*, 2009). Ling and Naranjo (2003) find that U.S. REIT equity flows are positively related to prior returns with two quarter lag. However, they did not find any evidence for capital flows affecting the REIT returns. Further Ling and Naranjo (2006) examined the relationship between capital flows to REIT mutual funds and aggregate REIT returns. Consistent with their earlier study, they found that REIT mutual fund flows exhibit return chasing behaviour. In another study which looks at the determination of capitalisation rate, Hendershott and MacGregor (2005) include trading volume and fund flows as explanatory variables. They find that the share of property in institutional portfolio is negatively associated with capitalisation rates, implying that fund flows from institutional investors are associated with increased capital returns.

Fisher *et al.* (2008) do not find evidence to support that institutional investors systematically chase returns or the capital flows of other institutional investors. In a study for the U.K. property market, Ling *et al.* (2009) find that capital appreciation is positively correlated with capital flows, asset turnover and economic growth. They also find that the capital appreciation is also correlated to lagged capital flows and asset turnover, implying that capital flows affect returns. The authors also find evidence for return chasing behaviour on the part of investors in private property markets.

Conclusions

This chapter discusses what could be the investors' motivations behind international capital flows in direct and indirect property whether it is portfolio diversification or return chasing based on available literature. There are equal numbers of studies that find benefits from international portfolio diversification as those that don't. This raises a question whether international diversification in property can lead to benefits for investors that are more than what can be achieved by including other financial instruments in the portfolio and requires further research. The discussion proceeds to discuss the behaviour of investors while investing in property, focusing on recent literature that analyses if investors chase returns and if capital flows affect returns. The reviewed literature presents mixed evidence and this is an area for further research. With growing international capital flows in property, the motivations for investors to invest overseas need to be analysed further using theories of behavioural finance.

References

Addae-Dapaah, K. and Kion, C. (1996) International diversification of property stock a Singaporean investor's viewpoint. *The Real Estate Finance Journal*, **13** (3), 54–66.

Addae-Dapaah, K. and Yong, G. (1998) Currency risk and office investment in Asia Pacific. *Real Estate Finance*, **5** (1), 67–85.

Asabere, P., Kleiman, R. and McGowan, C. (1991) The risk–return attributes of international real estate equities. *Journal of Real Estate Research*, **6** (2), 143–152.

Barry, C., Rodriguez, M. and Lipscomb, J. (1996) Diversification potential from real estate companies in emerging capital markets. *Journal of Real Estate Portfolio Management*, **2** (2), 107–118.

Bigman, T. (2002) Investing in international listed property companies, *PREA Quarterly*, Winter, **53**–61.

BIS (2007) Institutional investors, global savings and asset allocation. *CGFS Paper No 27*, Bank for International Settlement. Basel, Switzerland.

Bond, S.A., Karolyi, G.A. and Sanders, A.B. (2003) International real estate returns: a multifactor, multicountry approach. *Real Estate Economics*, **31** (3), 481–500.

Case, B., Goetzmann, W. and Rouwenhorst, K.G. (1999) Global real estate markets, cycles and fundamentals, *Working Paper No. 99-03*, Yale International Center for Finance. New Haven, CT.

Cheng, P., Ziobrowski, A., Caines, R. and Ziobrowski, B. (1999) Uncertainty and foreign real estate. *Journal of Real Estate Research*, **18** (3), 463–480.

Chua, A. (1999) The role of international real estate in global mixed-asset investment portfolios. *Journal of Real Estate Portfolio Management*, **5** (2), 129–137.

Conover, M., Friday, H. and Howton, S. (1998) The relationship between size and return for foreign real estate investments. *Journal of Real Estate Portfolio Management*, **4** (2), 107–112.

Conover, M.C., Friday, S.H. and Sirmans, S.G. (2002) Diversification benefits from foreign real estate investments. *Journal of Real Estate Portfolio Management*, **8** (1), 17–25.

D'Arcy, E. and Lee, S. (1998) A real estate portfolio strategy for Europe a review of the options. *Journal of Real Estate Portfolio Management*, **4** (2), 113–123.

Downs, A. (2007) *Niagara of Capital: How Global Capital Has Transformed Housing and Real Estate Markets*. The Urban Land Institute, Washington, DC.

Eichholtz, P. (1996) The stability of the covariance of international property share returns. *Journal of Real Estate Research*, **11** (2), 149–158.

Eichholtz, P. (1997) Real estate securities and common stocks a first international look. *Real Estate Finance*, **14** (1), 70–74.

Eichholtz, P., Koedijk, K. and Schweitzer, M. (1997) Testing international real estate investment strategies, paper presented to the Real Estate Research Institute Annual Seminar, Chicago.

Eichholtz, P., Mahieu, R. and Schotman, P. (1993) Real estate diversification: by country or by continent? *Working Paper*, Limburg University, Maastricht.

Eichholtz, P., Hoesli, M., MacGregor, B. and Nanthakumaran, N. (1995) Real estate portfolio diversification by property type and region. *Journal of Property Finance*, **6** (3), 39–59.

Eichholtz, P., Op't Veld, H. and Vestbirk, S. (1999) Going international: liquidity and pricing in the largest public property markets. *Real Estate Finance*, **16** (3), 74–81.

Fisher, J., Ling, D.C. and Naranjo, A. (2008) Institutional capital flows and return dynamics in private commercial real estate markets. http://kelley.iu.edu/bcres/files/research/FisherLingNaranjo.pdf (accessed 6 December 2011).

Forbes, K.J. and Rigobon, R. (2002) No contagion, only interdependence: measuring stock market co-movements. *Journal of Finance*, **57** (2), 2223–2261.

Geurts, T. and Jaffe, A. (1996) Risk and real estate investment: an international perspective. *Journal of Real Estate Research*, **11** (2), 117–130.

Giliberto, S. (1989) *Real Estate vs. Financial Assets: An Updated Comparison of Returns in the United States and the United Kingdom*, New York: Salomon Brothers, Inc.

Giliberto, S. (1990) *Global Real Estate Securities: Index Performance and Diversified Portfolios*. New York: Salomon Brothers, Inc.

Glascock, J.L. and Kelly, L.J. (2007) The relative effect of property type and country factors in reduction of risk of internationally diversified real estate portfolios. *Journal of Real Estate Finance and Economics*, **34**, 369–384.

Goetzmann, W. and Wachter, S. (1995) The global real estate crash: evidence from an international database. In: *Proceedings of the International Congress on Real Estate*, Vol. 3 (unpaginated). AREUEA, Singapore.

Gordon, J. (1991) The diversification potential of international property investments. *Real Estate Finance Journal*, **7** (2), 42–48.

Gordon, J., Canter, T. and Webb, J. (1998) The effects of international real estate securities on portfolio diversification. *Journal of Real Estate Portfolio Management*, **4** (2), 83–92.

Gordon, J. and Canter, T. (1999) International real estate securities a test of capital markets integration. *Journal of Real Estate Portfolio Management*, **5** (2), 161–170.

Hendershott, P. and MacGregor, B. (2005) Investor rationality: evidence from UK capitalization rates. *Real Estate Economics*, **33**, 299–322.

Henderson Investors/AMP (2000) *The Case of Global Property Investment*. Henderson Investors Ltd., London.

Hoesli, M. and MacGregor, B. (2000) *Property Investment. Principles and Practice of Portfolio Management*. Harlow: Pearson Education Ltd.

Hoesli, M., Lekander, J. and Witkiewitz, W. (2002) International evidence on real estate as a portfolio diversifier. *Working Paper*.

Hudson-Wilson, S. and Stimpson, J. (1996) Adding US real estate to a Canadian portfolio. *Real Estate Finance*, **12** (Winter), 82–92.

Jones Lang LaSalle (2012) *Global Capital Flows 2012*. Quarter 1, Jones Lang LaSalle.

Jones Lang LaSalle (2012) Global Market Perspective, Second Quarter 2012.

Lin, C.Y., Rahman, H. and Yung, K. (2009) Investor sentiment and REIT returns. *Journal of Real Estate Finance and Economics*, **39** (3), 450–471.

Ling, D.C. and Naranjo, A. (2003) The dynamics of REIT capital flows and returns. *Real Estate Economics*, **31** (3), 405–434.

Ling, D.C. and Naranjo, A. (2006) Dedicated REIT mutual fund flows and REIT performance. *Journal of Real Estate Finance and Economics*, 32 (4), 409–433.

Ling, D.C., Marcato, G. and McAllister, P. (2009) Dynamics of asset prices and transaction activity in illiquid markets: the case of private commercial real estate. *Journal of Real Estate Finance and Economics*, **39** (3), 359–383.

Liu, C.H. and Mei, J. (1998) The predictability of international real estate markets, exchange rate risks and diversification consequences. *Real Estate Economics*, **26**, 3–39.

Lu, K.W. and Mei, J.P. (1999) The return distributions of property shares in emerging markets. *Journal of Real Estate Portfolio Management*, **5** (2), 145–160.

Markowitz, H.M. (1952) Portfolio selection. *Journal of Finance*, **7** (1), 77–91.

Markowitz, H.M. (1959) *Portfolio Selection: Efficient Diversification of Investments*. New York: John Wiley & Sons.

McAllister, P. (1999) Globalization, integration and commercial property: evidence from the UK. *Journal of Property Investment and Finance*, **17** (1), 55–61.

Miles, M. and McCue, T. (1982) Historic returns and institutional real estate portfolios. *AREUEA Journal*, **10**, 184–199.

Miles, M. and McCue, T. (1984) Commercial real estate returns. *AREUEA Journal*, **12**, 355–377.

Mull, S. and Soenen, L. (1997) U.S. REITs as an asset class in international investment portfolios. *Financial Analysts Journal*, **53** (2), 55–61.

Newell, G. and Webb, J. (1998) Real estate performance benchmarks in New Zealand and South Africa. *Journal of Real Estate Literature*, **6** (2), 137–143.

Pagliani, J.L., Jr, Webb, J.R., Canter, T.A. and Lieblich, F. (1997) A fundamental comparison of international real estate returns. *The Journal of Real Estate Research*, **13** (3), 317–347.

Pierzak, E. (2001) *Exploring International Property Securities for US Investors*. Henderson Global Investors Property Economics & Research, London.

Quan, D.C. and Titman, S. (1997) Commercial real estate prices and stock market returns: an international analysis. *Financial Analyst Journal*, **53** (3), 21–34.

Quan, D.C. and Titman, S. (1999) Do real estate prices and stock prices move together? An international analysis. *Real Estate Economics*, **27** (2), 183–207.

Reid, I. (1989) Creating a global real estate investment strategy. *Money Management Forum*, 101–104.

RREEF (2011) *RREEF Global Real Estate Investment Outlook and Market Perspective 2011*. RREEF Research. Frankfurt, Germany.

Russell Investment Group (2006) *The 2005–2006 Russell Investment Survey on Alternative Investing a Survey of Organizations in North America, Europe, Australia and Japan*. Russell Investment Group, Washington, US.

Sharpe, W.F. (1964) Capital asset prices a theory of market equilibrium under conditions of risk. *Journal of Finance*, **19** (3), 425–442.

Stevenson, S. (1998) The role of commercial real estate in international multi-asset portfolios. *Working Paper BF No. 98-2*, University College, Dublin.

Stevenson, S. (1999) Real estate's role in an international multi asset portfolio: empirical evidence using Irish data. *Journal of Property Research*, **16** (3), 219–242.

Stevenson, S. (2000) International real estate diversification: empirical tests using hedged indices. *Journal of Real Estate Research*, **19** (1/2), 105–131.

Sweeney, F. (1989) Investment strategy a property market without frontiers, *Estates Gazette*, **89**(35), 20–30.

Tiwari, P. and White, M. (2010) *International Real Estate Economics*. New York: Palgrave, Hampshire, UK.

Webb, B. and Rubens, J. H. (1989) Diversification gains from including foreign real estate in a mixed asset portfolio. Paper presented at the *American Real Estate Society Meetings*, San Francisco.

Whitaker, B. (2001) *Why Should Investors Consider International Real Estate Investment?*, Vol. June. pp. 2–15. Global Real Estate Perspective.

Wilson, P. and Okunev, J. (1996) Evidence of segmentation in domestic and international property markets. *The Journal of Property Finance*, 7 (4), 78–97.

Wilson, P. and Okunev, J. (1999) Special analysis of real estate and financial assets markets. *Journal of Property Investment and Finance*, **17** (1), 61–74.

Wilson, P. and Zurbruegg (2003) Does it pay to diversify real estate assets: a literary perspective. Discussion Paper, No. 0313, University of Adelaide, Adelaide.

Worzala, E. (1992) *International direct real estate investments as alternative portfolio assets for institutional investors: an evaluation*. Unpublished dissertation, University of Wisconsin-Madison.

Worzala, E. and Vandell, K. (1995) International real estate investments as alternative portfolio assets for institutional investors: an evaluation. Paper presented at the *IRES/ERES Meetings*, Stockholm.

Ziobrowski, A.J. and Boyd, J.W. (1991) Bond, leverage and foreign investment in U.S. real estate. *Journal of Real Estate Research*, 7 (1), 33–58.

Ziobrowski, A.J. and Curcio, R.J. (1991) Diversification benefits of U.S. real estate to foreign investors. *Journal of Real Estate Research*, **6** (2), 119–142.

Ziobrowski, B.J. and Ziobrowski, A.J. (1995) Exchange rate risk and internationally diversified portfolios. *Journal of International Money and Finance*, **14** (1), 65–81.

Ziobrowski, A.J., McAlum, H. and Ziobrowski, B.J. (1996) Taxes and foreign real estate investment. *Journal of Real Estate Research*, **11** (2), 197–213.

8

International Financial Innovation, Real Estate and the Macroeconomy

Introduction

This chapter will examine historic changes that have occurred in the financial sector and how they have impacted on the real estate market. The interaction between the macroeconomy and the real estate sector will also be highlighted as financial change has strengthened the link between them. We begin by examining real estate and macroeconomic cycles and discuss the role that financing has played. We also consider whether information asymmetry in the real estate market has had a bearing on pricing decisions and thus on the measurement of risk. Falling yields during the boom period leading up to 2007 suggest that risk may have been underestimated and values inflated. The subsequent increase in yields and the widening yield gap between primary and secondary property suggest repricing but perhaps also an overestimation of risk in the post-financial crisis market.

Real estate and macroeconomic interactions: Cycles and trends

Real estate markets are characterised by periods of significant cyclical volatility. Rent and capital value change can significantly exceed that of the

Real Estate Finance in the New Economy, First Edition. Piyush Tiwari and Michael White.
© 2014 John Wiley & Sons, Ltd. Published 2014 by John Wiley & Sons, Ltd.

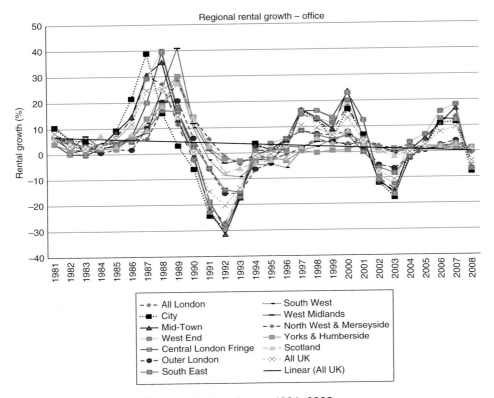

Figure 8.1 Regional office rental value change 1981–2008.

macroeconomy itself. Such volatility is experienced internationally across real estate markets in different cities. London is a relatively highly volatile commercial office market in comparison to other cities in the United Kingdom. New York, Melbourne and Shanghai have all exhibited significant changes in rents and capital values.

The volatility in the London office market has been examined by Barras (1994). Barras (2005) constructs a multi-equation model of the office market that shares similarities with work by Wheaton *et al.* (1997) and Hendershott *et al.* (1999). Rental value cyclical peaks in the London office market have been identified as occurring in 1973–1974, in 1988–1989 and in 2001 (Barras, 2005). Figure 8.1 later shows real rental value change for London office sub-markets and regions in Great Britain from 1981 to 2008.

There is significant rental volatility in 1988–1989 with a deep trough reached in 1992. The next cyclical peak in 2000/2001 is not as high as in the later 1980s; however, a clear cyclical pattern still emerges. Towards the end of the time period, we begin to see the impact of the 'credit crunch' as rental change goes negative. Not only are the cycles global phenomena, but their timing has been becoming increasingly synchronous although the amplitude of fluctuation still varies. Following the cycles that have been experienced, Barras (2005) highlights the questions that tend to arise, 'why did it go wrong? and how can we avoid it happening again?' (p. 63).

Explanations for real estate market cycles are often couched in terms of stock heterogeneity leading to information asymmetry, constraints imposed on market adjustment processes by long leases and construction lags and the speculative nature of development. These factors tend to be endogenous to the property market, and while all of these have a role, it is also important to consider exogenous factors such as the interaction with the macroeconomy and the role of finance.

In addition to considering the role played by exogenous variables, any discussion of cycles also needs to consider the long-run trend, or equilibrium, the path towards which the market should be adjusting. This view of market analysis has led to the development of an increasing body of literature especially since the late 1990s onwards that explicitly models market adjustment processes (see, e.g. Wheaton *et al.*, 1997; Hendershott *et al.*, 1999, 2002a, b; Mouzakis and Richards, 2007; Ke and White, 2009).

Interactions with the UK macroeconomy in 1973 and in the later 1980s and early 1990s tended to exacerbate the property cycles that were experienced. The stimulatory fiscal and monetary policies in 1973, the lowering of interest rates in late 1987 and subsequent tax reductions contributed to the boom conditions on the demand side of the property market in both time periods. Interestingly, both boom periods occurred after financial reforms of the early 1970s (The Competition and Credit Control Act, 1971) and the deregulation of the early 1980s. Hence, both occupier and investment markets would have been stimulated because of these exogenous influences that would have been additional to endogenous factors.

Barras (1994) shows that 'changes in property yields and hence capital values are an integral part of the adjustment process' (Dunse *et al.*, 2007, p. 4). Many authors have identified links between property yields and the stock or bond markets (Hetherington, 1988; Evans, 1990; Ambrose and Nourse, 1993; Key *et al.*, 1994; Viezer, 1999).

McGough and Tsolacos (2001) relate yields to rental growth, gilt yields and the all-share index and estimate three different models including a vector error correction mechanism (VECM), an autoregressive integrated moving average (ARIMA) model and a regression of yields on lagged rents and an autoregressive component. They find that no single model outperforms the others over the time periods tested and therefore suggest that careful attention needs to be given to the determinants of yields.

If prices can differ from their long-run equilibrium values, then it would be reasonable to apply an adjustment procedure such as an error correction mechanism (ECM). Hendershott and MacGregor (2005) adopt this approach arguing that price deviations from long-run values could arise because of transactions costs or non-systematic errors in expectations setting by economic actors. They proceed to model yields using an ECM and include explanatory variables such as expected real rental change and the stock market. Their results suggested that yields were negatively related to real rental growth but were not affected by stock market dividend growth.

While yield movements display relatively low volatility in comparison to rent and capital value changes, they tend to predict future rental movements. As they reflect financial factors more strongly, they may be able to change first, or new information is first embodied into yields before it affects rents or capital values. Henneberry (1999) suggested that in the cycle of the late 1980s and early 1990s, yields moved first before rental values began to change. He also stated that at a regional disaggregation, yields moved across regions at the same point in time, while rents changed first in London before changing in the regions. The time lag between yield changes and rental change was shortest in London but much longer outside London and further north. Henneberry (1999) concludes that as a result of imperfections in the property market, yields are driven by national factors, and local/regional rental trends/cycles are ignored.

Thus, local property cycles are distorted, and external investors influence the timing, amplitude and duration of urban development cycles. 'However, there is a continuing debate about property market efficiency (Evans, 1995; Sivitanides *et al.*, 2001; Ball, 2002; Chen *et al.*, 2004; Hendershott and MacGregor, 2005a, b). Logically, yields are a function of the required rate of return for property and expected rental growth. While yield movements should anticipate rental movements by a substantial margin, in reality many of these studies find that they are very much influenced by current returns from property. The result is that, in practice, the actual lead between national yield movements and urban rental movements is less than an expectations model would predict' (Dunse *et al.*, 2007, p. 5).

Sivitanidou and Sivitanides (1999) tested national and local influences on local capitalisation rates and modelled U.S. office capitalisation rates at a metropolitan level over the period 1985–1995. They found that capitalisation rates incorporated both a local fixed component and time-variant component that exhibited differential persistence across markets. Their analysis of the determinants of capitalisation rates suggested that local office market traits (vacancy rates, absorption and past rental growth) were more important than the national influences, defined as expected inflation and stock returns.

Property yields can also be affected by exogenous changes to property investment sentiment. This reflects the relative performance of the stock and property markets (Barras, 1994; Hendershott and MacGregor, 2005a). Higher levels of funds into property is an indicator of positive sentiment

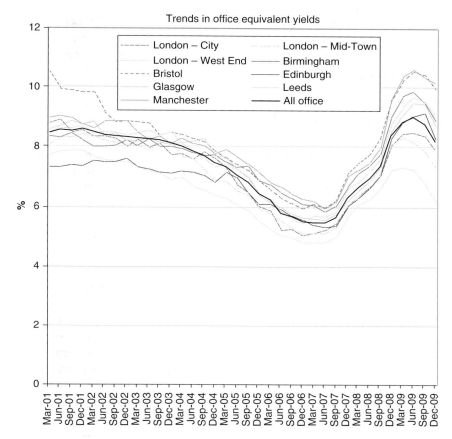

Figure 8.2 Trend in office equivalent yields.
Source: Scottish Widows Investment Partnership.

towards risks in property investment and leads to lower property investment yields and a narrower absolute spatial spectrum of yields. However,
this argument can be extended, and it is hypothesised that the impact of
property investment sentiment stretches beyond the general range of property yields between cities to perceptions about the risk (premium) associated
with individual cities and hence the required yields. Positive and negative
local property investment sentiment, as reflected in the level of investment
funds placed in a particular city, it is argued, will have implications for relative yields/risk premiums between cities (Dunse *et al.*, 2007).

Figure 8.2 later shows equivalent yields for London (City and West End)
and regional office markets from 2001 to the end of 2009. The yields display
a generally falling trend from 2001 until 2006/2007. In fact, the City of
London yields begin to increase before the others and also show an increase
before the financial crisis. Also of note is the narrowing of the gap in yields

between different locations prior to 2007/2008. After this period, not only do we see yield increases until June 2009 but the difference in yields between locations widens. As yields fall towards the end of 2009, the yield gap across locations does not narrow.

It might be reasonable to assume locational risk premiums. Some markets may be perceived as being more or less risky than others. Smaller, less liquid markets may have fewer transactions and less market information on comparables to aid pricing and therefore may be expected to have higher risks attached to them. This would imply that larger markets with more transactions and thus greater liquidity would have lower yields (like London). However, this contrasts with findings that in the long-term London investment, returns have underperformed relative to other smaller regional UK city markets.

Very little research has been undertaken on risk premiums for individual property investments, although Hutchison *et al.* (2007) propose that risk premiums should be applied to valuations depending on the covenant strength or status of tenants, but find no market evidence. Gunnelin *et al.* (2004) discuss the potential existence of risk premiums caused by smaller markets being thinner, having lesser diversified demand and being therefore riskier. The same logic applies to particular properties, and they show, using cross-sectional individual real estate valuation data for offices in Sweden, that standardised discount rates do differ by property type, location and lease. In particular, they estimate different standardised discount rates for Stockholm, Malmö and Göteborg (Gothenburg).

Variations in local market conditions can reasonably be expected to affect yields and pricing decisions. Given the existence of local cycles/trends, it is possible to postulate that there are individual city investment risk premiums perceived by national investors. These premiums could be linked, for example, to the perceived level of risk between cities because of the variation in the amplitudes of local rent cycles or the factors identified by Gunnelin (2004).

Changes to property investment sentiment are also an exogenous influence that is reflected in the level of property yields (relative to shares and bonds). This in turn is a reflection of the relative performance of the stock and property markets (Barras, 1994; Hendershott and MacGregor, 2005a). Higher levels of funds into property as an indicator of positive sentiment towards risks in property investment lead to lower property investment yields and a narrower absolute spatial spectrum of yields. However, this argument can be extended, and it is hypothesised that the impact of property investment sentiment stretches beyond the general range of property yields between cities to perceptions about the risk (premium) associated with individual cities and hence the required yields. Positive and negative local property investment sentiment, as reflected in the level of investment funds placed in a particular city, it is argued, will have implications for relative yields/risk premiums between cities.

Yields have obvious implications for pricing. Falling (rising) yields imply higher (lower) prices or capital values. Clearly from the figure, prices were increasing until 2006/2007 and then saw significant falls until 2009. This leads to the question as to whether prices were too high in 2006 and too low in 2009 or where these prices correct. These questions can only be addressed by considering whether the market is efficient; in other words, does it accurately price assets?

Fama (1970) postulated the Efficient Market Hypothesis (EMH) in which he classified markets into different levels of efficiency. In summary, in weak-form efficient markets, current prices of assets fully reflected past prices. In semi-strong-form efficient markets, prices fully reflect all available information. In strong-form efficient markets, prices fully reflect all information. In weak-form efficient markets, incorporation of new information is gradual, and it takes time therefore to adjust towards equilibrium. Real estate markets are often characterised as weak-form efficient. Information asymmetry, the absence of a central trading place or exchange, contributes to inefficiency. This in turn has an impact on pricing.

A key issue in relation to this is the accuracy of valuations, defined by Crosby (2000) as the ability of a valuation to correctly identify the 'target', where the target is usually taken to be the subsequent sale price or market rent. From a legal perspective, valuation is a subjective process and a matter of opinion and is therefore not an exact science. Pinpoint accuracy is not expected but the valuer has to approach his/her task with professional care. Crosby (2000) notes that legal judgments have accepted a range of potential answers that can be professionally valid provided valuers can demonstrate their calculations and have followed a prudent process. Crosby further argues that this legal requirement to follow due process within guidelines laid down by the RICS (at least in the United Kingdom) creates a defined framework within which surveyors have to operate. This means that comparables are the cornerstone of the valuation process.

Ball *et al.* (1998) argue that the limited range of comparable transactions and the subjective adjustment of yields are the reasons why a wide range of estimates of the most likely selling price can be produced by valuers in the same local market.

There have been a series of annual reports for the RICS by IPD that have monitored the relationship between capital valuations and actual values in the United Kingdom and latterly in Europe (including IPD, 2003, 2004, 2006, 2007, 2008, 2009). This analysis compares sales prices with immediately preceding valuations and in general finds valuations to be conservative, that is, lower than the actual selling prices. Overall, these studies find that valuations have become more accurate since the 1980s, but there are cyclical influences with valuations, for example, becoming more inaccurate in booms. Larger properties are generally more accurately valued.

Average price differences identified across Europe in 2005 (2008) were 21.3% (13.3%) in France, 13.1% (14.2%) in Germany, 13.0% (12%) in the Netherlands and 10.3% (11.8%) in the United Kingdom (IPD, 2009). The breakdown by use reveals only minor differences. A more detailed analysis of the United Kingdom over the period 1998–2008 finds on average just over 60% of valuations each year to be accurate to within 10% of the sale price. The most accurate valuations are for shopping centres with an average mean deviation from sale price of less than 10% in all but 1 year. Valuations of offices are consistently the least accurate in London year on year compared with offices in the rest of the South East of England and the remainder of the United Kingdom (IPD, 2009).

The use of comparative approach to valuation entails a review of the market incorporating a mixture of the recent past and the present. They are backward looking and do not explicitly link values to the capital markets (e.g. investors' target return linked to gilt yields) or the wider economy (e.g. rental income forecasts). The optimal updating rule for the valuation of property would be to form a weighted average of comparable transaction data and the last property valuation. The problem is explained by Quan and Quigley (1989): 'When an appraiser who pursues an optimal updating strategy is faced with uncertainty about the nature of the most recently observed transaction, it is reasonable to "discount" that transaction and to rely more heavily on information acquired in previous periods'. Where transaction data are few and far between, or non-reliable, the valuer is obliged according to RICS guidance to use previous valuations as the basis for current valuations. This introduces a moving average process to the pattern of rental and capital value time series that tends to smooth rental movements and may therefore underestimate the volatility in the market.

It would be reasonable to expect that in booming markets with more transactions, there would be less emphasis placed on historic values than in thinner markets with fewer comparable transaction values.

However, in general, there may be a systematic difference between the true selling price and the average valuation as a consequence of valuation inaccuracy. Valuation accuracy is a function of the information available. Baum *et al.* (1996) argue that valuations may cause mis-pricing in the sense that they can bias the market price because they are used by a potential buyer or seller to establish a likely market price. The greater the cyclical variation, the more valuations will be inaccurate. The scope for inaccuracy is also increased by the higher degree of heterogeneity within an individual property sector.

The question of property market inefficiency does not simply rest on the characteristics of the property market and valuations. Developers instigate development on the basis of expected profitability. The evidence suggests that in undertaking their own calculations, developers use current values or expected values derived from extrapolating the past. In a boom, it is this dominant ethos that unrealistically bids up land and property values. If you do not accept this industry view, then you will be outbid by the others and forced out of the market. The consequences are that construction/development activity is too 'high' and unsustainable, and this in turn means that the downturn, or more likely slump, is greater.

Similarly, banks use valuations and development appraisals presented to them to assess loans, but it is irrational to use these without caution. In property market booms, financial institutions display little caution. Successive deregulations of the financial system are likely to have been a contributing factor. As a consequence, there was greater pressure on staff to make loans in order for the banks to maintain market share and staff do not suffer any losses personally. And as most banks were involved, the losses are shared across the board. There is arguably a collective under-pricing of risk in a market boom, but this is then followed by over-pricing of risk in the subsequent downturn.

In booming markets, many transactions increase the number of comparables. However, if expectations are wrong about future price performance, then too much may be paid if prices are expected to rise further than what actually happens. In these circumstances, the market has underestimated the risk of a particular direction of price movement. Conversely in the bust, lenders may be too cautious, overestimating market risks attached to investment decisions, and subsequently, prices may be too low. This would in turn increase the amplitude of short-run cycles.

Inaccuracies in expectations imply inaccuracies in pricing and reflect inefficiencies in the property market. Barkham and Geltner (1994) have determined that property markets lack informational efficiency. They base this conclusion on a study of desmoothing of direct property returns focusing on capital returns. They desmooth a valuation-based index by attempting to model valuer behaviour. Thus, they implicitly assume inefficiency in the market. Their view is that given the heterogeneity and limited information, valuers do the best they can in the face of what is essentially a signal extraction problem.

Following Quan and Quigley (1989), they argue that valuations follow an autoregressive relationship in which decreasing weights are attached to historic valuations. The current valuation is therefore a weighting of current market evidence and past period valuations, but after desmoothing the returns series, Barkham and Geltner find that there is more volatility in the series. They also find that first-order autocorrelation is absent, as would be expected for an efficient market.

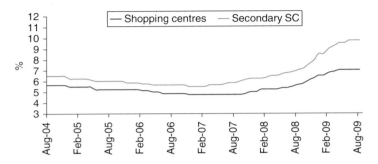

Figure 8.3 Yields on prime and secondary shopping centres.
Source: Reproduced by permission of CBRE.

Brown and Matysiak (2000) contest this view and argue that UK real estate markets may even be semi-strong based on the argument that if they were not, then investors would be encouraged by the consistent abnormal profits and switch their capital from other types of investments. Yet, they acknowledge that market agents can earn abnormal profits from private information.

Prior to the financial crisis and the performance of alternative assets such as government debt and stocks, real estate attracted significant investment. However, information asymmetry and non-rational expectations may have both contributed to investors underestimating risk and paying too much for real estate assets.

The issues with pricing are further revealed by a comparison between yields on prime- and secondary-grade stock. Prime and secondary stock yields for shopping centres are shown in Figure 8.3 in the succeeding text. From 2004 to 2009, yields on secondary stock are always above prime yields; however, the yield gap varies. At the peak of the market just before the financial crisis, the yield gap is 75 basis points in early 2007. By August 2009, the yield gap had increased to 350 basis points. Yields increase on both prime and secondary shopping centres during 2008, but the more significant increase is in the yield on secondary stock. Previously, it has been argued that the amount of money chasing real estate investment opportunities had pushed investors into secondary stock as prime stock was unavailable. Since the financial crisis ensued, repricing has been considerable, particularly in the secondary market.

Figure 8.4 examines yield spreads across Europe. Yields for shops, warehouses and offices are compared against the yield on 10-year German government bonds which represents the closest there is to a risk-free rate in Europe. In the middle of 2007, there is a negative yield gap of 21 basis points for offices and 47 basis points for unit shops in comparison to the less risky German bond yield. This suggests that market expectations for offices and

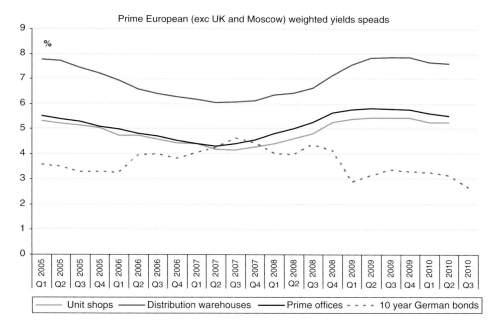

Figure 8.4   Yield spreads: Europe.
Source: Jones Lang LaSalle and Scottish Widows Investment Partnership.

shops were too optimistic during this time period. Distribution warehouses however had a yield 146 basis points above German bonds, reflecting more realistic pricing.

Yields on each real estate sector then increase during 2008, level off during 2009 and fall slightly during the first half of 2010. However, all property sectors have positive and increased yield gaps with German bonds by the end of the time period. Distribution warehouses, for example, are 450 basis points above bonds. However, if shops and offices were overpriced in 2007, the yield shift by 2010 may imply that they were then underpriced as market expectations may have become too negative.

Figure 8.5 compares property yields against UK government 10-year bonds. Running from 1990, the graph picks up the last major cycle, the recession of the early 1990s, the smaller property market cycle peak in 2001, the flow of funds into real estate and the market peak in 2007 before the financial crisis.

The yield gap is approximately 0 in 2007, implying that risky real estate may be overpriced relative to (almost) riskless bonds. This implies that prices for real estate assets may have been too high and expectations too positive. The yield gap in early 2009 is the highest in 20 years. As with the earlier graph for Europe, the implication is that expectations may have become too pessimistic.

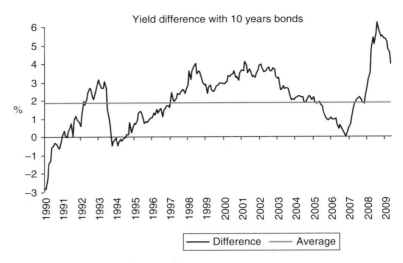

Figure 8.5 The UK real estate yields and government bonds.
Source: Datastream, IPD.

Hendershott (2000) suggests that if investors do not recognise that property markets are mean reverting, then they will not incorporate this into forecasts of market asset values and hence can pay too much or too little for real estate.

Hendershott examines the Sydney office market, and while his research took place before the financial crisis, issues of expectations formation are crucial to pricing decisions and perceptions of market risk. He points to 'profligate lending' as a factor affecting the previous market cycle in different countries. He also argues that investors did not understand the behaviour of the property market. 'Given the incentives of developers to build when value rises substantially above replacement cost and not to build when value is low relative to replacement cost, the property market has to be mean reverting' (Hendershott, 2000, p. 68). If this is ignored by investors, 'they will overvalue properties when prices are already high and undervalue properties when prices are low, exaggerating the cyclical swings in office values and thus in office construction and vacancies' (Hendershott, 2000, p. 68).

A different literature has emphasised flows of capital in the dynamic of property cycles. This is exemplified by the research of Dehesh and Pugh (1999, 2000, 2001) of the Japanese property cycle during the economic 'bubble' years of the late 1980s. It is instructive to follow through the basic rudiments of their thesis that begins in the United States and with capital flows between the two countries. In the early 1980s, there was an economic boom in the United States which was combined with high interest rates. This led to a large inflow of international capital into the United States and hence a high exchange rate for the dollar. This was combined with a current account deficit as demand for imports increased as a result of the high dollar and the economic/consumer boom.

The implications for Japan were:

- The rise in the dollar boosted exports and created a current account surplus.
- The outflow of capital funds pushed up interest rates.
- High interest rates reinforced the state of a weak internal economy suffering from lack of demand.
- The weak domestic economy meant that there was a shortage of investment opportunities, while the high interest rates in the United States provided investment outlets.

The dollar continued to rise against the yen until 1985. The Plaza Accord of the G7 countries in 1985 planned to readjust it downwards. For Japan, the plan included lowering interest rates and the deregulation of finance markets to stimulate domestic demand. At this point, the Japanese property market was already in an upswing of a cycle.

The fall in Japanese interest rates combined with the fall in the dollar stimulated the Japanese economy and the exchange rate. Domestic investment increased, and the net outflow of capital fell from 1986 onwards. However, much of the increased domestic investment went into land and property in Japan because property was seen as secure collateral. The share of total bank loans to the property sector rose from 7% in 1985 to 17% in 1990. The consequences were a continuing increase in land and property values, increases which reached unsustainable levels. The collapse came in 1990 with a rise in interest rates. Real estate values in Tokyo, Osaka and Nagoya fell by 40–60% below the peaks achieved in 1989–1990.

Excess price volatility can be found also in stock markets. Of course, the financial crisis has raised the issue of bubbles more generally in asset markets, particularly the housing market in the United Kingdom and other countries. This issue is discussed more fully in the following section.

Market cycles, risk and regional offices[1]

In this section, we draw together some of the issues raised earlier in an application to regional city office markets in Britain. In volatile markets, there are potentially higher returns to be generated by entering and leaving the market in the trough and peak, respectively. If the timing can be accurately identified, one question that arises is, would this compensate for transactions costs incurred if the holding period was relatively short?

It would be useful to identify risk/expected return combinations across regional cities, perhaps relative to London, and establish their positions on or in relation to an indifference curve of risk/expected return combinations and the efficient frontier for different asset portfolios (e.g. all property or mixed portfolios).

This could then be used to develop a model looking at whether there is under- or overinvestment in particular regional markets and sectors. It is possible to identify markets down to local authority (municipality) disaggregations although it must be borne in mind that some of these would be extremely small from an investment perspective and that such a disaggregation itself might lead to findings of mispricing that reflect the small market size in addition to any other source of market inefficiency.

The movements of yields between 2006 and the summer of 2009 were upwards and across regional centres; the dispersion also increased (see Figure 8.2 in the preceding text). Risk perception has changed which has pricing implications. If yields fell too far in the boom and have increased too far in the slump, the values have been overestimated and underestimated, respectively. Underpricing may therefore be even more of an issue in regional markets that have experienced the greatest yield changes.

These issues, in turn, relate to risk scoring and benchmarking for investment purposes. They have implications for portfolio construction. However, if the risk and return estimates upon which decisions are based turn out to be inaccurate, there is an opportunity to identify a more accurate investment strategy that should have a more optional (on a higher indifference curve) risk/expected return combination.

Risk as measured by the variance is the unconditional variance. If however there is a pattern in risk movements, the variance may itself be an underestimate of the true risk. Correctly understanding the volatility of returns is essential for portfolio management. Volatility clustering or autoregressive conditional heteroscedasticity (ARCH) has been identified in other asset markets. An ARCH process has a conditional volatility significantly in excess of the unconditional variance. Thus, there is a much higher risk of making losses for a process with ARCH during periods of market volatility than the standard mean–variance analysis would indicate.

Variations on ARCH models exist. One important issue is whether the conditional variance affects expected mean returns. This can be determined by employing the ARCH-in-mean or ARCH-M specification. Furthermore, it is possible that negative shocks have a different impact on conditional variance than positive shocks. This asymmetry to negative or positive shocks in markets can be captured by a threshold ARCH (TARCH) or threshold generalised ARCH (T-GARCH) model.

The investment applications outlined previously (see Dunse et al., 2012) lead to a number of specific research tasks to be considered that will help to better understand the office market. These tasks are:

(1) Construction and estimation of a market model that can identify long-term trend and, furthermore, predict market cyclical turning points.
(2) Development and application of a modern portfolio approach to examine risk and expected returns across different city markets.
(3) From these tasks, it will be possible to identify if investment is above or below the level it should be.
(4) Identification of ARCH processes and subsequent extension of analysis to test for ARCH-M and TARCH/T-GARCH processes.

The first task can be tackled in different ways. Either a reduced-form model could be constructed which is the more standard approach given data availability or a structural multi-equation approach if more data were available with a specific element linking into financial markets taking liquidity issues/constraints into consideration. This latter is innovate in real estate as changes in behaviour due to changes in access to finance have not previously been formally considered.

Task two requires identification of utility constant risk and expected return trade-offs captured on indifference curves. The optimality position would require constructing efficient frontiers drawing upon production possibility frontier analyses and superimposing these on the investors' preference sets as reflected by their indifference curves. Regional cities can then be examined to identify their combinations of risk/expected return by commercial property sector.

The third task would enable us to examine whether investment is too high or too low. Given that this would be based upon the construction of long- and short-run models that would have identified market fundamentals, the measurement of whether investment is too high or low would be held against current fundamentals during all time periods of the data analysed. Hence, fundamentals are not held constant, thus avoiding spurious comparisons. The trend itself essentially would be time-varying.

Task four specifically focuses on whether the unconditional risk measure is sufficient to capture volatility in asset markets. If ARCH processes exist, then this would mean that standard risk measures are insufficient to capture market volatility. This would then be examined to evaluate the impact on return performance and symmetry or, otherwise, of response to exogenous shocks.

Research on market models

Rent models are estimated based upon the approach adopted by Hendershott *et al.* (2002) and subsequently followed by many other authors. The approach hinges on capturing rental adjustment which following Hendershott (1996) takes the following form:

$$\frac{R_t - R_{t-1}}{R_{t-1}} = \lambda\left(v^* - v_{t-1}\right) + \beta\left(R_t^* R - R_{t-1}\right) \tag{8.1}$$

where the change in rent from period $t-1$ to period t is a function of the difference between the equilibrium and actual vacancy rate last period and the difference between the equilibrium and actual rent last period, where equilibrium rents depend on real interest rates through a user cost relationship.

Given the short time series or unavailability of vacancy rate data, the aforementioned rental adjustment is usually estimated as an error correction in a reduced-form framework. Consider demand for property as a function of rent and economic activity:

$$D = \lambda_0 R^{\lambda_1} EA^{\lambda_2} \tag{8.2}$$

where D is demand, R is rent, EA is economic activity, $\lambda_1 < 0$ is the 'price' elasticity and $\lambda_2 > 0$ is the 'income' elasticity. By definition, this demand equals the supply of occupied space $(1 - v)SU$, where SU is supply and v is the vacancy rate. Equating demand and occupied supply, taking logs and solving for $\ln R$ gives

$$\ln R = -\gamma_2 \ln \lambda_0 + \gamma_1 \ln EA + \gamma_2 \ln SU + \gamma_2 \ln(1 - v) \tag{8.3a}$$

where $\gamma_1 = -\lambda_2/\lambda_1 > 0$ and $\gamma_2 = 1/\lambda_1 < 0$.

If vacancy rate data are generally not available, then to account for the normal vacancies that would exist in equilibrium, we add and subtract $\gamma_2 \ln(1 - v^*)$ from the right side of Equation (8.3) and treat v^* as a constant, obtaining

$$\ln R = -\gamma_0 + \gamma_1 \ln EA + \gamma_2 \ln SU + err \tag{8.3b}$$

where $\gamma_0 = \gamma_2[\ln(1 - v^*) - \ln \lambda_0]$ and $err = \gamma_2[\ln(1 - v) - \ln(1 - v^*)]$. Lacking data on v, its impact is embedded in the error term.

The reduced-form rent equation can be set within an ECM framework and estimated using a panel approach. The residual from the estimated long-run relationship, Equation (8.3b), is

$$u_t = \ln R_t - \hat{\gamma}_0 - \hat{\gamma}_1 \ln EA_t - \hat{\gamma}_2 \ln SU_t \qquad (8.4)$$

which is the difference between the observed and estimated long-run log rental values. If these variables are co-integrated, this error is stationary and can be used in short-run dynamic model as an adjustment process.[2]

The short-run model is the first difference of Equation (8.3b) with the addition of the error correction term. To this basic model, we also add the lagged value of real rental change because the rent series are autoregressive:

$$r_t = \alpha_0 + \alpha_1 EA_t + \alpha_2 SU_t + \alpha_3 u_{t-1} + \varphi r_{t-1} \qquad (8.5)$$

where lower case letters, except u, represent log differences. Thus, real rent adjusts to short-run changes in the causal variables and also to lagged market imbalances as measured in Equation (8.4). In the estimations, it is expected that α_0 will be approximately 0, α_1 will be positive, α_2 and α_3 will be negative, and φ will be between 0 and 1. $\alpha_3 = 0$ means no adjustment, $0 > \alpha_3 > -1$ means partial adjustment, $\alpha_3 = -1$ means full adjustment and $\alpha_3 < -1$ means over-adjustment.

Comparing Equations (8.3b) and (8.4), the residual in Equation (8.4) is almost certainly dominated by the missing $\gamma_2[\ln(1-v)-\ln(1-v^*)]$ term in Equation (8.3b). Because $\ln(1-v)$ approximates $-v$ for small values of v, the *lagged* residual in our EC model is, in effect, a proxy for $-\gamma_2(v^* - v_{-1})$. (Recall that γ_2 is negative.)

However, it is also possible to estimate versions of Equations (8.3b) and (8.5) where a vacancy rate term is included separately in the model. Ke and White (2013) estimate such a model for Shanghai offices.

Individual long-run models are estimated for each city in Table 8.1. The dataset is annual and runs from 1980 to 2009. In most cases, the demand

Table 8.1 Long-run model estimates for regional city office markets (*following* Equation (8.3b) earlier).

	City of London	Birmingham	Edinburgh	Glasgow	Leeds	Manchester
Constant	49.325	−8.218	27.427	10.713	2.166	16.805
	(9.219)	(−1.417)	(4.009)	(7.486)	(1.247)	(3.915)
Demand*	0.402	−0.741	1.738	0.255	0.599	0.118
	(2.466)	(−2.139)	(3.224)	(2.668)	(−3.217)	(1.439)
Supply	−4.537	2.108	−4.173	−0.417	−0.838	−1.388
	(−7.329)	(2.296)	(−3.308)	(−2.095)	(−2.412)	(−2.818)
Adjusted R^2	0.783	0.116	0.265	0.599	0.308	0.193
DW	0.509	0.478	0.541	0.281	0.388	0.345
F(prob)	0.000	0.093	0.011	0.000	0.006	0.033

*Demand variable is finance and business services employment, supply is floor space stock, and *t*-statistics is in parentheses.

Table 8.2　Offices: short-run model (*following* Equation 8.5 earlier).*

	City of London	Edinburgh	Glasgow	Leeds	Manchester
Constant	−0.042	0.000	0.005	0.005	0.001
	(−1.278)	(0.020)	(0.417)	(0.317)	(0.088)
Change in demand	0.813	0.319	−0.202	−0.188	−0.021
	(1.479)	(1.000)	(−1.327)	(−1.088)	(−0.092)
Change in supply	−1.160	−0.665	−0.322	0.063	−0.367
	(−1.722)	(−1.128)	(−0.784)	(0.162)	(−1.036)
Error correction term	−0.398	−0.298	−0.224	−0.305	−0.305
	(−3.417)	(−3.243)	(−2.629)	(−3.807)	(−2.981)
Lagged dep var	0.331	0.629	0.711	0.877	0.802
	(3.071)	(4.778)	(4.778)	(6.274)	(5.528)
Adjusted R^2	0.816	0.626	0.508	0.636	0.604
DW	1.911	1.932	1.416	1.724	2.133
F(prob)	0.000	0.000	0.001	0.000	0.000

* No short-run model is estimated for Birmingham as the long-run relationship was not significant.

and supply variables are significant and correctly signed. In the case of Birmingham, the model is statistically insignificant (the probability of the F-statistic exceeds 0.05). In Manchester, the demand variable is also statistically insignificant. Short-run models are presented later in Table 8.2.

Table 8.2 shows that the error correction term is correctly signed and significant in each city. The coefficients on the error correction term are all statistically 'close' with the City of London showing perhaps some faster adjustment speeds.

Rental change has witnessed significant cyclical volatility with respect to peak-to-trough movements. The question is, can the aforementioned models provide an accurate prediction of rental movements? As an example, we use the Edinburgh office market as the model to predict rental values from 1992 until 2009. The graph in Figure 8.6 later shows the results.

The black line (ROR_EDIFS) shows the predicted (real logged) rental value, and the gray line (ROR_EDI) is the actual rental value. If we run the prediction from 2000, the forecast values are shown in Figure 8.7 later.

The predicted value is in gray after 2000, and the actual in black.

The forecast accuracy of the model varies considerably depending upon the starting point for the prediction (Figure 8.8). The forecast from 1992 is much more inaccurate, and in 14 out of 18 years, the forecast is inaccurate by more than ±5%. In the case of the prediction from 2000, the forecast is within ±5% for 5 of 10 years predicted. Turning points are 1 year out with the 1992 forecast, and the final one at the end of the dataset is in the wrong direction. The 2000 forecast gets the first turning point correct but wrongly predicts the direction of the final movement in rents. The forecasts essentially miss

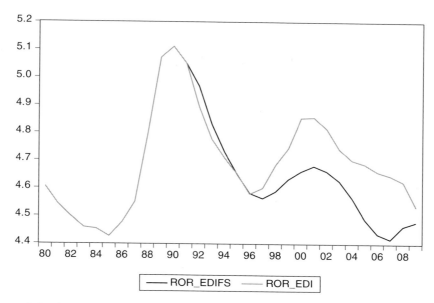

Figure 8.6   Actual and predicted Edinburgh office rents (prediction from 1992).

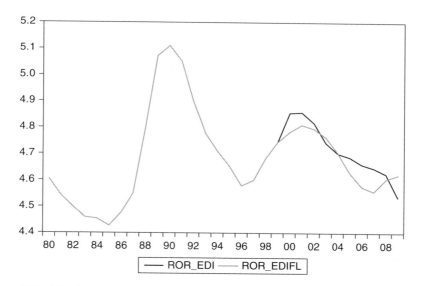

Figure 8.7   Actual and predicted Edinburgh office rents (prediction from 2000).

any structural change in movements in both demand and supply that take place after the start date for the forecast. Similar results appear for other cities. For example, the City of London forecast is described later (Figure 8.9).

Prediction is in gray after 2000 and actual in black. While it forecast tracks the cycle, it under- and over-predicts rental movements. In both Edinburgh

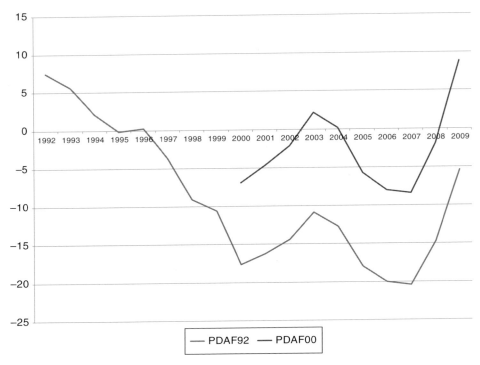

Figure 8.8   Percentage difference between actual and forecast Edinburgh office rents.

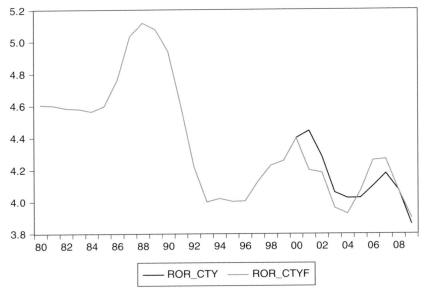

Figure 8.9   Actual and predicted City of London office rents (prediction from 2000).

and the City of London, the predictive inaccuracies seem to be non-random and suggest an autoregressive pattern to forecast errors, implying that not all information has been captured by the exogenous variables used to model rental movements.

Risk and expected return

We apply modern portfolio theory to construct efficient frontiers for offices and, as a comparison, retail across the different city markets. The expected return on a portfolio is a weighted average of the expected returns on individual assets. Thus,

$$E(R_P) = \sum_{i=1}^{n} w_i E(R_i) \tag{8.6}$$

where $E(R_P)$ is the expected portfolio return, w_i is the proportion of the portfolio on asset i and $E(R_i)$ is the expected return on asset i. The risk on the portfolio is

$$\sigma_P = \sqrt{\sum_{i=1}^{n}\sum_{j=1}^{n} w_i w_j \sigma_i \sigma_j \rho_{ij}} \tag{8.7}$$

where σ_P is the portfolio risk, σ_i and σ_j are the individual asset risks and ρ_{ij} is the correlation between i and j.

We examined office markets and then retail markets in the key regional cities. Using 'Solver', the optimal risk-adjusted return was calculated and the weightings across cities were identified.

Weights and allocations for offices are presented in Table 8.3. The risk-adjusted return is maximised by allocating between offices in Edinburgh and Glasgow. The maximum portfolio return is 8% with a weighting towards Glasgow. The model does not choose any weighting in English regional cities.

Allocations for retail are presented in Table 8.4. Initially, weightings are in Birmingham and Edinburgh. However, higher returns can be generated by moving out of Edinburgh and into Birmingham. The highest returns move retail out of Birmingham and concentrate in Leeds. There are no retail allocations to Glasgow or Manchester.

Efficient frontiers for retail and offices are drawn in Figure 8.10 and Figure 8.11, respectively. The efficient frontier for retail is longer and shallower than that for offices, and the latter lying almost entirely above (to the northwest of) the retail frontier. For a given level of risk, offices deliver a higher expected return. In addition, the efficient frontier for offices is clearly shorter than that for offices in addition to being steeper.

Table 8.3   Office portfolio allocations.

Weights for offices						Risk	
Birmingham (%)	Edinburgh (%)	Glasgow (%)	Leeds (%)	Manchester (%)	Max pf rtn (%)	Port var	Port SD
0.00	100.00	0.00	0.00	0.00	5.77	0.011	0.104
0.00	98.58	1.42	0.00	0.00	5.80	0.011	0.104
0.00	94.12	5.88	0.00	0.00	5.90	0.011	0.105
0.00	89.67	10.33	0.00	0.00	6.00	0.011	0.105
0.00	85.21	14.79	0.00	0.00	6.10	0.011	0.106
0.00	80.76	19.24	0.00	0.00	6.20	0.011	0.106
0.00	76.30	23.70	0.00	0.00	6.30	0.011	0.107
0.00	71.85	28.15	0.00	0.00	6.40	0.012	0.107
0.00	67.39	32.61	0.00	0.00	6.50	0.012	0.108
0.00	62.94	37.06	0.00	0.00	6.60	0.012	0.108
0.00	58.48	41.52	0.00	0.00	6.70	0.012	0.109
0.00	54.03	45.97	0.00	0.00	6.80	0.012	0.110
0.00	49.57	50.43	0.00	0.00	6.90	0.012	0.110
0.00	45.12	54.88	0.00	0.00	7.00	0.012	0.111
0.00	40.66	59.34	0.00	0.00	7.10	0.012	0.111
0.00	36.21	63.79	0.00	0.00	7.20	0.013	0.112
0.00	31.75	68.25	0.00	0.00	7.30	0.013	0.112
0.00	27.30	72.70	0.00	0.00	7.40	0.013	0.113
0.00	22.84	77.16	0.00	0.00	7.50	0.013	0.114
0.00	18.39	81.61	0.00	0.00	7.60	0.013	0.114
0.00	13.93	86.07	0.00	0.00	7.70	0.013	0.115
0.00	9.48	90.52	0.00	0.00	7.80	0.013	0.116
0.00	5.02	94.98	0.00	0.00	7.90	0.014	0.116
0.00	0.57	99.43	0.00	0.00	8.00	0.014	0.117

From the efficient frontiers calculated across the cities, the office market may provide optimal allocations for more risk-averse investors than retail since in the case of the former, indifference curves would possibly be steeper, indicating that investors require a larger expected return increase for a given increase in risk. Tangency positions (indicating optimality) would be more likely for risk-averse investors given the relative slopes of the efficient frontier for offices and their indifference curves.

Conditional volatility

The inefficiency of the property market and associated information problems could imply that 'large and small forecast errors [would] appear to occur in clusters, suggesting a form of heteroscedasticity in which the variance of the forecast error depends on the size of the preceding disturbance' (Greene, 1993, pp. 438–439). Hence, we examine ARCH models. If ARCH effects exist, then the conditional variance will be larger than the unconditional variance for certain time periods and risk will be higher than that indicated by the unconditional variance alone (see Miles, 2008). In addition to temporal

Table 8.4   Retail portfolio allocations.

Weighting for retail						Risk	
Birmingham (%)	Edinburgh (%)	Glasgow (%)	Leeds (%)	Manchester (%)	Max pf rtn (%)	Port var	Port SD
0.00	100.00	0.00	0.00	0.00	4.50	0.012	0.112
10.02	89.98	0.00	0.00	0.00	4.60	0.012	0.110
20.13	79.87	0.00	0.00	0.00	4.70	0.012	0.108
30.24	69.76	0.00	0.00	0.00	4.80	0.011	0.106
40.35	59.65	0.00	0.00	0.00	4.90	0.011	0.105
50.46	49.54	0.00	0.00	0.00	5.00	0.011	0.104
60.57	39.43	0.00	0.00	0.00	5.10	0.011	0.103
70.68	29.32	0.00	0.00	0.00	5.20	0.010	0.102
80.78	19.22	0.00	0.00	0.00	5.30	0.010	0.102
90.89	9.11	0.00	0.00	0.00	5.40	0.010	0.102
99.61	0.00	0.00	0.39	0.00	5.50	0.010	0.102
95.68	0.00	0.00	4.32	0.00	5.60	0.011	0.103
91.75	0.00	0.00	8.25	0.00	5.70	0.011	0.105
87.81	0.00	0.00	12.19	0.00	5.80	0.011	0.106
83.88	0.00	0.00	16.12	0.00	5.90	0.012	0.108
76.02	0.00	0.00	23.98	0.00	6.10	0.012	0.111
72.08	0.00	0.00	27.92	0.00	6.20	0.013	0.112
68.15	0.00	0.00	31.85	0.00	6.30	0.013	0.114
64.22	0.00	0.00	35.78	0.00	6.40	0.013	0.115
60.29	0.00	0.00	39.71	0.00	6.50	0.014	0.117
56.35	0.00	0.00	43.65	0.00	6.60	0.014	0.118
52.42	0.00	0.00	47.58	0.00	6.70	0.014	0.120
48.49	0.00	0.00	51.51	0.00	6.80	0.015	0.121
44.56	0.00	0.00	55.44	0.00	6.90	0.015	0.123
40.62	0.00	0.00	59.38	0.00	7.00	0.015	0.124
36.69	0.00	0.00	63.31	0.00	7.10	0.016	0.126
32.76	0.00	0.00	67.24	0.00	7.20	0.016	0.128
28.83	0.00	0.00	71.17	0.00	7.30	0.017	0.129
24.89	0.00	0.00	75.11	0.00	7.40	0.017	0.131
20.96	0.00	0.00	79.04	0.00	7.50	0.018	0.133
17.03	0.00	0.00	82.97	0.00	7.60	0.018	0.134
13.10	0.00	0.00	86.90	0.00	7.70	0.018	0.136
9.16	0.00	0.00	90.84	0.00	7.80	0.019	0.138
5.23	0.00	0.00	94.77	0.00	7.90	0.019	0.139
1.30	0.00	0.00	98.70	0.00	8.00	0.020	0.141
0.00	0.00	0.00	100.00	0.00	8.03	0.020	0.141

clustering of volatility, some cities may display more rental volatility than others. Data suggest that rent variance differs across different cities significantly. Highest unconditional volatility was found in the City of London and then the West End, Bristol and Edinburgh, respectively. Glasgow, Leeds and Manchester show lower standard deviations, less than half of London.

The unconditional variance is much lower than the conditional variance during volatile periods, and ARCH models essentially try to capture the higher volatility missed by the standard mean–variance approach.

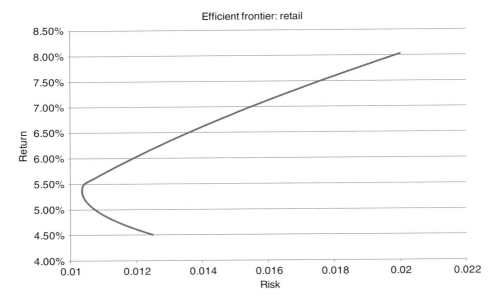

Figure 8.10   Retail.

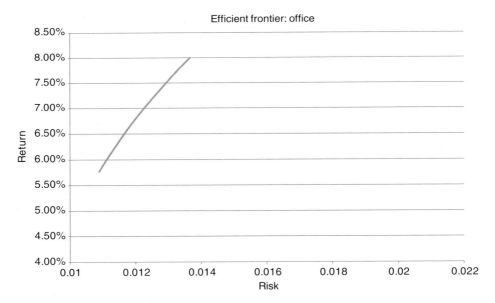

Figure 8.11   Offices.

An ARCH model can be written as an autoregressive moving average (ARMA) (p, q) process. Hence,

$$x_t = \sum_{i=1}^{p} \varphi_i x_{t-i} + \sum_{i=1}^{q} \theta_i \varepsilon_{t-i} \tag{8.8}$$

If the disturbances had constant variance, as assumed by the classical model, the unconditional variance would be constant over time. However, many series display volatility clustering such that they are more volatile in some consecutive time periods than in others. The error variance is therefore time-varying and can be written as a function of its lagged values. Thus,

$$\varepsilon_t^2 = \alpha_0 + \sum_{i=1}^{q} \alpha_i \varepsilon_{t-i}^2 + \mu_t \qquad (8.9)$$

where ε^2 is the variance of the error term and μ is a stochastic disturbance. A generalised autoregressive conditional heteroscedasticity (GARCH) model begins by estimating conditional variance from an ARMA model as in Equation (8.8) and then is specified as

$$\varepsilon_t = \alpha_0 + \sum_{i=1}^{q} \alpha_i \varepsilon_{t-i}^2 + \sum_{i=1}^{p} \gamma_i \varepsilon_{t-i} \qquad (8.10)$$

The coefficient α (commonly known as the ARCH effect) captures the tendency for the conditional variance to cluster, while the γ (commonly known as the GARCH effect) captures the tendency for shocks to have a persistent influence on the conditional variance. In addition, the conditional variance might also influence mean rental growth. This can be tested using an ARCH-M specification:

$$y_t = \sum_{i=1}^{p} \alpha_i y_{t-i} + \sum_{i=0}^{q} \beta_i \varepsilon_{t-i} + \lambda \sigma_t^2 \qquad (8.11)$$

where σ_t^2 is the conditional variance of the ARCH or GARCH process.

Positive and negative price shocks might have a different impact on volatility. Impacts exist in asset markets where negative shocks raise leverage of firms and lead to greater volatility than positive shocks. To address this, T-GARCH models have been developed by Glosten *et al.* (1993) to allow for this asymmetry.

To examine whether ARCH processes exist, we begin by examining ARMA processes with lags added until autocorrelation of residuals is removed. Following this, an LM test for ARCH effects is conducted, and subsequently a GARCH model is estimated if the null of a constant variance is rejected. The GARCH-M model is estimated to discover whether the conditional variance affects the mean office rent change.

Table 8.5   ARCH identification.

City	London	Birmingham	Bristol	Leeds	Manchester	Glasgow	Edinburgh
ARMA	(3,2)	(1,1)	(2,1)	(3,2)	(2,2)	(2,2)	(3,0)
ARCH LM *p*-value	0.007	0.048	0.036	0.093	0.087	0.063	0.049

Table 8.6   GARCH-M analysis.

City	London	Birmingham	Bristol	Edinburgh
Estimated λ	0.0343	−0.0431	0.0559	0.0366
p-value	0.4375	0.0322	0.0451	0.2128

Table 8.5 in the preceding text shows the initial stages of estimation to identify if conditional volatility is present. The dark gray box (for London) shows significant ARCH effects at the 1% level. The light gray boxes (for Birmingham, Bristol and Edinburgh) show significant ARCH effects at the 5% level. For Leeds, Manchester and Glasgow, ARCH effects are not statistically significant at the 5% level.

For those cities were ARCH effects are significant, ARCH-M tests are conducted. The results are presented later in Table 8.6.

The results suggest that increases in conditional variance in London and Edinburgh have no impact on mean rental performance. For Birmingham, there is a decrease in mean rents from an increase in conditional variance. In Bristol, there is an increase in mean rents from an increase in conditional variance. It is possible that in Birmingham and Bristol, periods of volatility are correlated with some other structural changes that impact on the future path of rents.

Conditional variance may be affected differently by negative or positive shocks. The T-GARCH model has been developed to allow for this possibility. It takes the following form:

$$h_t = \alpha_0 + \sum_{i=1}^{q} \alpha_i \varepsilon_{t-i}^2 + \gamma \varepsilon_{t-i}^2 d_{t-1} + \sum_{i=1}^{p} \beta h_{i-1} \tag{8.12}$$

where the term $\gamma \varepsilon_{t-i}^2 d_{t-1}$ is the asymmetric portion of the conditional variance. The dummy variable (d_{t-1}) will be equal to one if the error ε_{t-1} is negative. Applying this to the city markets, the results are presented later in Table 8.7.

In this table, only Birmingham has a statistically significant TARCH effect (London is marginally insignificant at the 5% level). Volatility is increased by negative shocks in the Birmingham market.

Table 8.7 TARCH model results.

City	London	Birmingham	Bristol	Edinburgh
Threshold coefficient	−0.1227	0.3081	0.0344	−0.0306
p-value	0.0511	0.0056	0.1273	0.0682

The next step is to consider exogenous drivers to ARIMA models before testing for the presence for ARCH effects. Adding exogenous variables creates the ARIMAX model where the 'X' refers to the exogenous variable added to the ARMA model components based upon the dependent variable's own values and time series history. Variables such as finance and business services output and local GDP were added to the ARIMA models. While these variables were found to be significant, they did not improve forecast performance over the error correction models presented previously. ARIMA is often used as a data-generating technique for out of sample forecasting; however, the research undertaken here would suggest that such forecasts should be used only with considerable caution. Our results indicate that while the error correction models were often incorrect, the ARIMA and ARIMAX models provided lower-quality forecasts, often missing cyclical turning points.

Bubbles, over- and underpricing: Too much or too little investment?

Kindleberger (1987) defines a bubble as 'a sharp rise in price of an asset or a range of assets in a continuous process, with the initial rise generating expectations of further rises and attracting new buyers – generally speculators interested in profits from trading in the asset rather than its use or earning capacity. The rise is usually followed by a reversal of expectations and a sharp decline in price often resulting in financial crisis'. While this may be tautologically correct, it implies that bubbles can only be identified after they have occurred (Hendershott *et al.*, 2003). Hendershott *et al.* then define a bubble as 'a sharp, temporary price increase that cannot be plausibly explained by changes in fundamental value drivers' (p. 993).

Smith and Smith (2006) define a bubble as 'a situation in which the market prices of certain assets (such as stocks or real estate) rise far above the present value of the anticipated cash flow from the asset' (p. 3). The rapid price rise brings speculative activity on expectations of future price increases rather than focusing on the asset's cash flow or fundamental factors driving the market. 'What truly defines a bubble is that market prices are not justified by the asset's anticipated cash flow' (Smith and Smith, 2006, p. 3).

In practice, it may prove difficult to identify bubbles. Protagonists of bubbles implicitly assume that prices were equal to fundamental values historically before a period of rapid asset price inflation. Opponents argue that observed prices may have been too low and that increasing prices may have (at least in part) reflected an adjustment process towards long-run equilibrium values.

The existence of bubbles is supported by papers such as Hendershott (2000) and Wheaton *et al.* (2001). These authors argue that at the peak of the market, real estate assets are overpriced. They argue that this is because investors do not recognise the mean reversion tendency of markets in general. They argue this because the peak prices observed deviate from their long-run equilibrium values. Investors make the mistake of interpreting the observed 'short-run' prices as equilibrium values and/or that the long-run trend has changed. The investor is unable to evaluate the fundamental long-run equilibrium value of the asset. This is exacerbated in markets where there is limited and asymmetric information. In this situation, it is easier to make mistakes about pricing and expectations about the trajectory of future price movements.

Himmelberg *et al.* (2005) examine the possibility of bubbles in housing markets. They adopt a 'user cost' approach to 'calculate…the financial return associated with an owner-occupied property [compared with] the value of living in that property for a year – the "imputed rent", or what it would have cost to rent an equivalent property – with the lost income that one would have received if the owner had invested the capital in an alternative investment – the opportunity cost of capital' (Himmelberg *et al.*, 2005, p. 74). This approach is then used to discover whether property is over- or undervalued.

This approach can be applied to commercial property. Essentially, the user cost is a function of the risk-free rate, expected capital value change (and income growth for commercial property) plus a risk premium. Property taxes and any elements of tax deductibility on maintenance would also be relevant.

In long-run equilibrium, the capital value-to-income ratio should equal the inverse of the user cost. Thus, the user cost should be equal to the initial yield. Björklund and Söderberg (1999) examine speculative bubbles in real estate markets in Sweden. They suggest that the price boom of the late 1980s was partly due to a speculative bubble driving the market.

Black *et al.* (2006) examine house prices relative to fundamental values using UK data. They estimate a relationship examining a price – income ratio as a function of lagged changes in income, return variance and the coefficient of relative risk aversion. The authors separate the influence of change in exogenous variables from within market factors. They use real disposable income as the exogenous variable in their estimation. They find that towards the end of their period of observation (2005), house prices were overvalued and that this overvaluation was split evenly between 'intrinsic and price dynamics components. The latter component [was] found to be driven by momentum behaviour' (Black *et al.*, 2006, p. 1553).

User costs can change due to changes in exogenous variables that impact on the real estate market in addition to financial variables. These changes will cause the equilibrium user cost to change and hence need to be modelled if we are to avoid assuming a bubble when none is present.

Expectations of future price rises embodied in investors' information sets will lead to speculative bubbles being generated. With rational expectations, we would have

$$E_t\left(V_{t+1}^a \mid \Phi_t\right) = V_{t+1}^a + \varepsilon_{t+1} \tag{8.13}$$

where E is the rational expectations operator, V_{t+1}^a is the value (V) of asset a in the next time period and Φ is the information set available at period t upon which market agents base their expectations. With rational expectations, economic actors get their expectations correct, on average, except for a random error, ε_{t+1}, which has a zero mean and constant variance.

In a bubble scenario, the information set Φ_t will include expected future prices rises of the asset in question. As this causes prices to diverge from fundamental values, then the expected future value of the asset will be systematically above its true fundamental value. In this case, the error term will no longer be random, and systematic errors (mistakes) will be made in asset pricing. As Brooks *et al.* (2001) point out, '...when a speculative bubble is present, the bubble component is larger than the linear combination of [the fundamental price's] future elements. This in fact means that the bubble is actually bigger than the present value of its expected future price' (p. 342).

Detection of bubbles is crucial to discover whether rising values imply that fundamentals have changed, and hence, models of factors that drive fundamental values have been developed in the literature. Research in real estate has tended to focus on housing markets, an early exception being the Hendershott (2000) analysis of the Sydney office market.

Early studies on bubbles in property markets were not consistent with those used in economics or finance. In addition, since identification of fundamental values is necessary to show if deviation from such values has occurred, the next question is whether models for fundamentals accurately identify such values.

Testing for the presence of speculative bubbles has taken different forms, and developments in econometric methodology have also had an influence. The variance of actual prices and the variance of fundamental prices have been compared in the variance bounds test to examine excess volatility. However, fundamental prices have often been calculated *ex post*. Investors, however, will only have an expectation of the future; however well informed (or rational) their expectations, the actual future prices would only be one set of a range of potential future prices that might reasonably be present in their information sets when forming future predictions.

Diba and Grossman (1988a, b) examine bubbles in stock prices. They suggest that if dividends and prices are co-integrated, then it is not possible to reject the null hypothesis of no bubble. Thus, testing for bubbles requires testing for co-integration between the price and dividend time series variables. If the null of co-integration cannot be rejected, then there is a long-run relationship between the two series, and there is no speculative asset price bubble. However, 'the lack of cointegration is not a sufficient condition to prove the existence of bubbles since the model might exclude significant variables that affect stock prices and that are not stationary' (Brooks *et al.*, 2001, p. 346). Diba and Grossman (1988) subsequently found that using dividend and price time series from the S&P 500 index, these series were stationary in first differences. They reject the null hypothesis of no co-integration and thus reject the idea of bubbles in the time series they examined.

Fama and French (1988) and Summers (1986) raise the issue of how to detect bubbles in long time series. This is related to bubbles that collapse and regenerate within a long-run time series. Summers suggests that 'expectations, or bubbles that are based on expectations, might cause a significant temporary divergence of actual prices from their fundamental values, but... do not leave a statistical trace and so cannot be identified' (Summers, 1986, p. 347).

Johansen (1991) finds that no co-integration between dividends and prices might not be due to bubbles but by the absence of co-integration caused by other factors. Evans (1991) argues that co-integration tests cannot identify bubbles based upon fundamentals as they follow the same evolutionary process as expected dividends (Evans, 1991, p. 347).

Thus, stationarity and co-integration tests do not provide completely reliable results for the identification of bubbles. The tests face small sample bias problems, and the models tested may be mis-specified. Nevertheless, these tests provide the best (or least the worst) basis for analysis of long-run relationships between observed and fundamental prices. The presence of a long-term relationship between dividends and prices can be an indication of bubble absence, but the tests greatly depend on the method employed to construct fundamental values. An appropriately specified model for constructing fundamental values must be based on a well-specified model of dividend prediction.

In long-run equilibrium, the capital-to-income ratio should equal the inverse of the user cost, that is, the initial yield. We extend the model of Dunse *et al.* (2007) to link the real property market via the inclusion of key demand variables such as finance and business services output and/or GDP. We estimate a yield model where

$$IY = f(\Delta RRVI, GY, LEP, EA) \tag{8.14}$$

where IY is the initial yield, $\Delta RRVI$ is the real rental value growth index, GY is the gross redemption yield on long dated gilts, LEP is the inverse of the price–earnings ratio, and EA is economic activity. The model is estimated for key office (and retail) locations covering the five key centres and London. A panel estimation approach is adopted.

In essence, the model attempts to identify fundamental and expectations for yields. Any remaining mispricing may be attributed to a 'bubble'. Following model estimation, estimated values for yields are calculated for each city. These are then compared with actual values, and the greater the difference, then the greater the over- or under-pricing of the asset.

Results for the office market are presented later in Table 8.8. The model is constructed as a fixed effects panel model. The individual city impacts are listed separately; however, while statistically significant, they are not significantly

Table 8.8 Office market initial yield panel regression model.

Dependent variable: office initial yield				
Method: pooled EGLS (cross-section SUR)				
Total pool (balanced) observations: 150				
Line estimation after one-step weighting matrix				
Variable	**Coefficient**	**Std. error**	**t-statistic**	**Prob.**
Gross redemption yied	0.203256	0.104033	1.953763	0.0528
Rental value growth	−0.978152	0.103956	−9.409291	0.0000
Rental deviation	0.919904	0.130400	7.054500	0.0000
Real dividend	0.424685	0.146702	2.894875	0.0044
Real dividend deviation	−0.248855	0.179196	−1.388732	0.1672
Fin & bus services	−0.172853	0.064732	−2.670285	0.0085
Fin & bus services deviation	−0.120378	0.109608	−1.098252	0.2740
Fixed effects				
City of London	3.913587	0.832175	4.702840	0.0000
Birmingham	3.609793	0.676033	5.339670	0.0000
Edinburgh	3.507257	0.664043	5.281674	0.0000
Glasgow	3.549299	0.661244	5.367609	0.0000
Leeds	3.552841	0.662950	5.359136	0.0000
Manchester	3.718352	0.717103	5.185243	0.0000
Weighted statistics				
R^2	0.495573	Mean dependent var		7.582459
Adjusted R^2	0.451390	S.D. dependent var		5.398719
S.E. of regression	0.944577	Sum squared resid		122.2349
f-statistic	11.21629	Durbin-Watson stat		1.020183
Prob(f-statistic)	0.000000			
Unweighted statistics				
R^2	0.390716	Mean dependent var		1.907098
Sum squared resid	2.940124	Durbin-Watson stat		0.387643

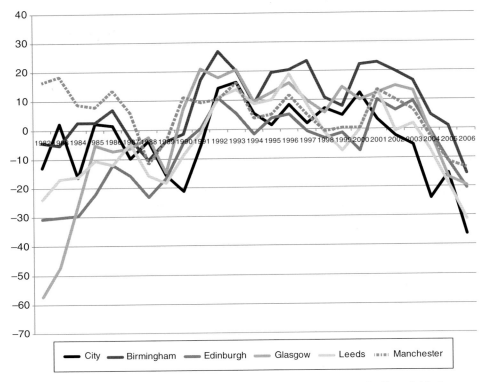

Figure 8.12   Percentage differences between actual and estimated office yields for individual cities 1981–2006.

different from each other. We capture mean reversion by using a moving average model for the real rent, dividend and economic activity from trend. We also measure the deviation from 'equilibrium' for these variables by using errors from random walk models estimated for each variable within each city.

We expect there to be a positive relationship between the initial yield and the gross redemption yield, although the variable is marginally insignificant at the 5% level. Rental value growth is negatively related to the initial yield and is statistically significant with the correct sign. The rental deviation is also significant and correctly signed. The economic activity variable, finance and business services output is significant and, again, correctly signed. Its deviation is not significant. Overall, the model performs broadly in accord with *a priori* expectations.

Estimated values for the initial yield can be calculated from this model and compared against actual values. If the model has adequately captured the drivers of initial yields, then any remaining differences should reflect bubbles in pricing. Figure 8.12 shows the difference between actual and estimated initial yields based upon the model presented in Table 8.8.

The figure suggests that mispricing is common. Examining the period before the recent financial crisis suggests actual yields were too low (the estimated value was higher leading to a negative difference) and thus that prices were too high. Evidence of prices being too high also appears in the late 1980s boom. Mispricing is not isolated to particular locations but appears across all the aforementioned markets. The cyclicality evident in the results suggests correlations in market sentiment by market participants – a 'bandwagon' effect or universal myopia. Thus, it implies correlation in risk assessment such that risk is underestimated in boom/growth periods and overestimated in troughs.

The implication of the preceding text is that prices may become too low – below fundamentals in weaker periods and above fundamentals in stronger markets as pricing expectations begin to embody past price changes rather than, or in addition to, information on market fundamentals.

Remarks on regional markets research

In the preceding text, we have attempted to discuss issues in market analysis that are relevant to investment decision making. This is particularly apposite as investors, especially international investors, have tended to focus on London and not looked further afield for investment opportunities in real estate. Market models have been estimated using a reduced-form error correction framework. These have indicated slow market adjustment taking approximately 3 years in most cities. Applying these models to forecasting shows their limited success, resulting essentially from an inability to predict changes in trend performance of demand or supply side factors.

Efficient frontiers have been calculated for retail and office markets, showing how weightings change across different markets. Offices show a higher risk-adjusted return combination than retail across the cities in the sample.

There is also evidence that the variance underestimates risk as ARCH effects are present across some of these markets. Further, there is evidence that such volatility can impact on the mean path of returns in some cities but not in others.

Finally, we identify bubbles in asset markets and show that there has been considerable mispricing in real estate markets across different cities, suggesting that market participants are making correlated inaccurate judgments.

From an investment perspective, there are a number of interesting findings from the preceding text:

(1) The shape of the efficient frontiers is similar to but in a number of ways different from the theoretical depiction normally provided by textbook

analysis. This will in part reflect the nature of property and the limited number of locations covered in the sample.

(2) Also in relation to efficient frontiers, only a subset of cities was chosen by the model for the optimal risk/return combinations reflected by the frontiers: two cities for offices and three for retail. The portfolio weightings across the cities then changed as the risk/return combination changed. This may suggest targeting of individual cities rather than spreading investment across locations.

(3) As ARCH effects exist, risk can be underestimated, and investors need to consider not just the volatility of markets but whether future returns are affected by this. Also the presence of ARCH effects affected cities in different ways, and thus, examining individual cities and local market characteristics is again of importance.

(4) The bubble behaviour of prices shows that prices diverged from fundamentals. This raises a number of issues. Investment timing and holding period become important in the context of a market where significant mispricing exists.

One of the issues in analysing regional markets is the availability of data. While this has improved substantially, there is still an opportunity to build more sophisticated models in the future as datasets become larger and statistical robustness can be increased.

While we have discussed bubbles and volatility, we really only observed the most recent period of price increases as one in which there is a sharp divergence between transaction prices and fundamental values. Some bubble literature suggests that there may be many bubbles in markets that go undetected which may seem incongruous with the definitions of bubbles that have been made. The late 1980s may also reflect bubble components to transactions values although the period of price increase was shorter in many markets than the most period of price rise until the financial crisis.

The last point leads on to issues relating to long-run values. If recent events affect lending behaviour to the market where debt has been an important source of funds, then long-run equilibrium values can change, and hence, adjustment processes will be towards these new long-run values. Detecting change in long-run values requires consideration of structural breaks in modelling without which estimated coefficients would be biased and adjustment processes inaccurately estimated.

Such changes against the background of volatile markets suggest that careful monitoring of market performance will continue to be necessary. It also raises issues related to the best ways to forecast future values given the complexity of what remains an inefficient market.

Bubbles in asset markets

As an alternative to the method of testing indicated earlier, using dividend discount methodology and following Shiller (1981), fundamental value can be written as

$$p_t^f = \sum_{n=1}^{T} \left(\frac{1}{(1+i)^n} d_{t+n} + \frac{1}{(1+i)^{T-n}} P_{1/X} \right) \tag{8.15}$$

where the fundamental price to be estimated is on the left-hand side, i is the discount rate, d_t is the period t dividend and $P_{1/X}$ is the truncation approximation of all out of sample dividends, X being the truncation date. Essentially, this approach suggests that fundamental values are dependent on dividend and price information only and that the investor has perfect foresight (the rational expectations error term here would always be 0 in each time period) for dividends and the discount rate. For the variance bounds test to be accurate in identifying bubbles, the aforementioned formula would need to be accurate at identifying fundamental values.

Fundamental values may also be constructed by the Gordon growth model which takes the following form:

$$P_t^f = \frac{1+g}{g-i} D_{t-1} \tag{8.16}$$

where g is the growth rate of the dividend.

Results in the literature suggested that variance bounds tests often suggested the presence of bubbles. However, the model in Equation (8.15) assumes market efficiency in predicting future cash flows in the cutoff year and that the dividend-generating process would be unchanged for out of sample dividends (Brooks *et al.*, 2001).

Excess volatility measured by the variance tests may not reflect bubbles (Kleidon, 1986) but rather may be because of non-rational expectations on the part of investors (not unreasonable in a real estate market characterised by information asymmetry) or be due to mis-specified models of fundamental values.

Flood and Garber (1980) suggest that modelling fundamental prices is fraught with difficulty and consequently models may be mis-specified and therefore prices identified may not reflect fundamental values. They argue that models of fundamental prices are not based upon the information sets that investors would face. Further, non-stationarity in dividend and price time series makes it difficult to accurately measure unconditional volatility of each series which could bias results. The consequence of the development of co-integration[3] analysis in macroeconomic time series analysis to account for the presence of unit roots has essentially made variance bounds tests redundant.

Risk management

Theoretical developments discussed previously reflect methodological advancements in research and market analysis. However, the next question is whether or not they are applied on a routine basis when it comes to risk management of asset portfolios. Do fund managers and investors apply modern portfolio theory or consider the possibility that there is a divergence between observed and fundamental prices? Are they aware of mean reversion and will they, due to myopia, make the same mistakes again?

Newell *et al.* (2004) examined international real estate research priorities and showed that portfolio and investment risk management were among the most important research areas in Australia (second) and the United Kingdom (third), and it was the most important research area in Germany. However, the research that has been undertaken is largely concerned with theoretical to empirical applications and methodological developments rather than being for direct application in the practice of risk management.

Apgar (1976) is one of the first of relatively few research papers to examine controlling risk in real estate from a more practical and theoretically less abstract perspective. The Investment Property Forum (IPF) (2000) surveyed the understanding and management of risk in the UK real estate sector. This survey identified key factors considered by fund managers in the process of risk management. It highlighted the specific issues that fund managers considered in the risks attached to investing in high-unit-value (lumpy) assets and potential risks associated with undiversified portfolios. Risk ranking was raised as an important tool in management strategies by Van der Schaaf and de Puy (2001).

IPF (2007) examines how fund managers control risk in real estate investments. It showed that sophisticated risk management strategies were not being adopted by real estate investors. This was due to methodological problems caused by the unique characteristics of real estate assets and lack of data that prevented techniques being applied. Schwenzer (2008) states that, for Germany, risk management systems were only in place to meet statutory obligations.

As indicated previously, lumpy assets imply potential problems for portfolio diversification. Byrne and Lee (2001) suggest that 400–500 properties are needed in a real estate portfolio to reduce risk sufficiently to bring it down to market levels. This implies that a fully diversified property portfolio would be highly expensive. Byrne and Lee (2007) suggest that while diversification benefits are increased with portfolio size, risk is not necessarily significantly reduced. Property characteristics of heterogeneity, indivisibility and transactions costs make it more difficult to directly apply standard portfolio models that would have more straightforward applicability to other financial assets.

The use of derivatives has become an issue in managing risk in real estate investment. Lecomte (2007) considers derivative markets for effectively hedging commercial real estate assets. Baroni *et al.* (2008) consider related pricing issues for designing derivatives, and Fabozzi *et al.* (2010) examine derivatives in European real estate and investigate the development of structured interest rate swaps.

Donner (2010) surveys approaches to risk management by different real estate investors. Focusing on Germany but with a sample covering German and non-German investors, Donner examines different investment vehicles available in real estate, including, Real Estate Investment Trusts, investment funds/open-end funds, closed-end funds, private equity investors and institutional investors plus specialist investors in real estate.

The survey results reveal that risks associated with changes in rents and vacancy rates are weighted most highly by investors followed by macroeconomic risks, although these two categories of risk may be highly correlated. Investors were more concerned with these factors than, for example, risks associated with changing micro-location. However, Donner also finds that there is incomplete risk management because some risks are exogenous and difficult for investors to control. Further, he finds that sophisticated or advanced methods to monitor and control risk were used only infrequently. Monte Carlo Simulation was used much less than 'gut feeling'. Financial instruments, like derivates, were also only infrequently adopted to manage risk. This in part may reflect the lack of available indices. Only 16% of the sample of investors used specialised risk management software for risk identification. The majority of investors also thought that risk rating agencies were poor or very poor.

The survey also revealed that around half of the investors sampled thought that it was difficult to apply modern portfolio theory in real estate. A minority consider the impact of new real estate assets on portfolio risk. 'Hence, it can be concluded that the majority of investors are still relying on naïve diversification in order to minimise risk' (Donner, 2010, p. 35).

Overall, these results would indicate that there is a gap between theory and practice. This could be related to the complexity of real estate assets in comparison to other asset classes. Factors of heterogeneity, limited information, transactions costs, indivisibility and illiquidity (of unsecuritised real estate) make application of standard finance approaches more difficult.

Combined with lack of data, this means that the real estate sector will lag behind other asset classes in terms of risk management.

Observations and conclusions

The previous discussion suggests that there are difficulties transferring risk management techniques from other asset classes into commercial real estate markets. Hence, investors may not fully evaluate investment risks in property. This would be compounded with a failure to understand market adjustment processes, particularly mean reversion in the real estate market. Given supply constraints and information asymmetry, such adjustment processes can be protracted and would not be fully observed in any one single time period. Against this background, it is possible to understand how bubbles could develop and be misunderstood to represent changes in fundamental values rather than divergence from them.

The last few decades have seen significant change in investment vehicles available in real estate, and in many countries, both securitised and unsecuritised vehicles exist that were absent previously. Thus, it could be argued that financial innovation has taken place in real estate markets across the globe. However, it is still the case that these markets often lag behind other asset markets in adoption of new financial products. Often, as indicated in the preceding text, this reflects information limitations due perhaps to thin markets, few transactions and comparables. This further implies that in particular locations where there is a concentration of real estate and markets are deeper, we might first see adoption of new methods of investing and financial product innovation. This leads to the idea that key cities across the globe will become important attractors for real estate investors. Newer markets in Asia such as Shanghai have become major destinations for real estate investors. London, New York and Tokyo also remain significant markets for attracting international real estate investors (although to varying extents). We have also seen an increasing focus on 'hub' locations within 'global regions'. For example, Singapore in Southeast Asia is a key investment destination. Along with Hong Kong, these are two of the most transparent markets in Asia for real estate investors.

The concern that investors have expressed in relation to risk of rental change and void or vacancy periods indicates concern for both endogenous development cycles and exogenous macroeconomic cycles. Yet it is clear that many if not all were caught out by the recent financial crisis. Of course, a focus on rents and vacancies is important, but a consideration of the relative performance of other asset classes is also relevant since occupation and investment markets can reflect divergent trends (at least for a time).

Investors face signal extraction problems if expectations of price appreciation affect values, but the impact of these expectations on values has not been correctly evaluated. The investor then may assume that the fundamental and observed prices are the same. As noted from the literature, testing for bubbles in real estate has not followed more standard techniques in other asset classes, and there remains the problem of identification of fundamental value. However, as dataset becomes longer, it should theoretically become easier to estimate more robust tests for bubbles. These tests, however, would only show what has happened historically from past data. The key question is whether factors creating bubbles can be identified from the past so that investors can use these factors and changes in these factors to help predict when bubble might form. Yet, even this may prove insufficient to prevent bubbles from gaining momentum. Self-interested investors who have more market knowledge than other economic actors (due to information asymmetry) may play the market to make higher returns from the bubble period itself. Even if their investments are debt financed, then timing market entry and exit can maximise returns. A debt is only a bad debt if it cannot be repaid, and that would only happen if the investor got the timing wrong.

The issues surrounding volatility were examined in the research on regional city markets. While this research is currently limited to the United Kingdom, it can in principle be extended to regional city markets in other countries where there are data time series available. Results from this aforementioned research pointed to ARCH processes in some markets. We see that, for example, London and Birmingham display ARCH effects. However, in contrast to Birmingham, London remains an attractive location for investment, especially international investment, suggesting that liquidity risk is a concern for investors. The smaller the market, the more illiquid it is and the higher is the perceived risk of investment.

In a post-financial crisis era, debt finance, at least in the short term, has become limited. In the longer run, it is probable that debt finance will become more important again. This would again feed into asset price inflation and possible divergence of fundamental and observed values. The spillover to the macroeconomy would be higher investment and consumer expenditure levels that would generate stronger growth conditions, and we are then into the story of heightened cyclical amplitude of fluctuation. The internationalisation and globalisation of the real estate investment market and finance market, in general, causes these effects to become a global phenomenon with only local market conditions causing differentiation of response. In less sophisticated markets with less information, there may be greater and more costly mistakes made in investment decisions.

However, financial innovation will continue in the real estate sector. It is reasonable to expect further significant growth in investment in real estate assets, especially in Asia and South America. Countries that currently do not have highly developed investment markets will create the legal systems that permit the development of direct and indirect vehicles as their economies develop, and they design policy frameworks to attract inward investment. This is not to say that each country will be the same. However, it is to say that countries increasingly recognise those characteristics of successful economic systems, and these usually contain a range of investment vehicles that aid inward investment and economic growth.

Notes

1   This section is based upon original research for Scottish Widows Investment Partnership (SWIP) on 'Investment in Regional Real Estate Markets', the final report for which was sent to SWIP in February 2012.
2   Formally:
    A series with no deterministic trend and which has a stationary and invertible ARMA representation after differencing d times, but which is not stationary after differencing $d-1$ times, is said to be integrated of order d.
    The components of a vector x_t are said to be co-integrated of order d, b, if x_t is $I(d)$ and there exists a nonzero vector α such that $\alpha^T x_t$ is $I(d-b)$, $d > = b > 0$. The vector α is called the co-integrating vector.
    In our models, we are looking for co-integrating relationships among variables that are individually integrated of order 1, so the deviation from the equilibrium relationship is integrated of order 0, that is, it is stationary (Banerjee *et al.*, 1993).
3   A series with no deterministic trend and which has a stationary and invertible ARMA representation after differencing d times, but which is not stationary after differencing $d-1$ times, is said to be integrated of order d. The components of a vector x_t are said to be co-integrated of order d, b, if x_t is $I(d)$ and there exists a nonzero vector α such that $\alpha^T x_t$ is $I(d-b)$, $d > = b > 0$. The vector α is called the co-integrating vector.

References

Ambrose, B. and Nourse, H. (1993) Factors influencing capitalization rates. *Journal of Real Estate Research*, **8**, 221–237.

Apgar, M. (1976) Controlling the risks in real estate. *Business Horizons*, **19** (2), 55.

Ball, M. (2002) Cultural explanations of regional property markets a critique. *Urban Studies*, **39** (8), 1453–1469.

Ball, M., Lizieri, C. and MacGregor, B. (1998) *The Economics of Commercial Property Markets*. Routledge, London.

Banerjee, A., J. Dolado, J. W. Galbraith and D. F. Hendry (1993) *Co-integration, Error-Correction, and the Econometric Analysis of Non-Stationary Data*. Oxford University Press, Oxford.

Barkham, R.J. and Geltner, D.M. (1994) Unsmoothing British valuation-based returns without assuming an efficient market. *Journal of Property Research*, **11**, 81–95.

Baroni, M., Barthélémy, F. and Mokrane, M. (2008) Is it possible to construct derivatives for the Paris residential market? *Journal of Real Estate Finance and Economics*, **37** (3), 233–264.

Barras, R. (1994) Property and the economic cycle: building cycles revisited. *Journal of Property Research*, **11**, 183–197.

Barras, R. (2005) A building cycle model for an imperfect world. *Journal of Property Research*, **22** (2), 63–96.

Baum, A., Crosby, N. and MacGregor, B. (1996) Price formation, mispricing and investment analysis in the property market. *Journal of Property Valuation and Investment*, **14** (1), 36–49.

Björklund, K. and Söderberg, B. (1999) Property cycles, speculative bubbles, and the gross income multiplier. *Journal of Real Estate Research*, **18** (1), 151–174.

Black, A., Fraser, P. and Hoesli, M. (2006) House prices, fundamentals and bubbles. *Journal of Business Finance and Accounting*, **33** (9–10), 1535–1555.

Brooks, C., Katsaris, A., McGough, T. and Tsolacos, S. (2001) Testing for bubbles in indirect property price cycles. *Journal of Property Research*, **18** (4), 341–356.

Brown, G.R. and Matysiak, G.A. (2000) *Real Estate Investment. A Capital Market Approach*. Pearson Education Ltd., Harlow, UK.

Byrne, P.J. and Lee, S. (2001) Risk reduction and real estate portfolio size. *Managerial and Decision Economics*, **22** (7), 369–379.

Byrne, P.J. and Lee, S. (2007) An exploration of the relationship between size, diversification and risk in UK real estate portfolios: 1989–1999. *Journal of Property Research*, **20** (2), 191–206.

Chen, J., Hudson-Wilson, S. and Nordby, N. (2004) Real estate pricing spreads and sensibilities: why real estate pricing is rational. *Journal of Real Estate Portfolio Management*, **10**, 1–22.

Crosby, N. (2000) Valuation accuracy, variation and bias in the context and expectations. *Journal of Property Investment and Finance*, **18** (2), 130–161.

Dehesh, A. and Pugh, C. (1999) The internationalization of post-1980 property cycles and the Japanese 'bubble' economy, 1986–96. *International Journal of Urban and Regional Research*, **23** (1), 147–164.

Dehesh, A. and Pugh, C. (2000) Property cycles in a global economy. *Urban Studies*, **37** (13), 2581–2602.

Dehesh, A. and Pugh, C. (2001) Theory and explanation of international property cycles since 1980. *Property Management*, **19** (4), 265–297.

Diba, B.T. and Grossman, H.I. (1988a) The theory of rational bubbles in stock prices. *Economic Journal*, **98**, 746–757.

Diba, B.T. and Grossman, H.L. (1988b) Explosive rational bubbles in stock prices? *American Economic Review*, **78**, 520–530.

Donner, M. (2010) Risk management in the aftermath of Lehmann Brothers – results from a survey among German and international real estate investors. *Journal of Property Research*, **27** (1), 19–38.

Dunse, N., Jones, C. and White, M. (2012) *Investment Issues and Opportunities in Regional Office Markets*, Report to Scottish Widows Investment Partnership, Edinburgh.

Dunse, N., Jones, C., White, M., Trevillion, E. and Wang, L. (2007) Modelling urban commercial property yields: exogenous and endogenous influences. *Journal of Property Research*, **24** (4), 1–20.

Evans, R. (1990) A transfer function analysis of real estate capitalization rates. *Journal of Real Estate Research*, **5**, 371–379.

Evans, G.W. (1991) Pitfalls in testing for explosive bubbles in asset prices. *American Economic Review*, **81**, 922–930.

Evans, A.W. (1995) Property market – ninety per cent efficient. *Urban Studies*, **32**, 5–29.

Fabozzi, F., Shiller, R. and Tunaru, R. (2010) Property derivatives for managing European real estate risk. *European Financial Management*, **16** (1), 8–26.

Fama, F.E. (1970) Efficient capital markets: a review of theory and empirical work. *Journal of Finance*, **25** (2), 383–417.

Fama, F.E. and French, K.R. (1988) Permanent and transitory components of stock prices. *Journal of Political Economy*, **96**, 246–273.

Flood, R.P. and Garber, P. (1980) Market fundamentals versus price level bubbles: the first tests. *Journal of Political Economy*, **88**, 745–770.

Glosten, L., Jagannathan, R., and Runke, D. (1993) Relationship between the expected value and the volatility of the nominal excess return on stocks. *Journal of Finance*, **48**, 1779–1801.

Greene, W.H. (1993) Econometric Analysis. Prentice Hall, Pearson Education Inc, NJ.

Gunnelin, Å., Hendershott, P.H., Hoesli, M. and Söderburg, B. (2004) Determinants of cross-sectional variation in discount rates, growth rates and exit cap rates. *Real Estate Economics*, **32** (2), 217–238.

Hendershott, P.H. (1996) Rental Adjustment and Valuation in Overbuilt Markets: Evidence from the Sydney Office Marke. *Journal of Urban Economics*, **39**, 51–67.

Hendershott, P.H. (2000) Property asset bubbles: evidence from the Sydney office market. *Journal of Real Estate Finance and Economics*, **20** (1), 67–81.

Hendershott, P.H. and MacGregor, B.D. (2005a) Investor rationality: evidence from UK capitalization rates. *Real Estate Economics*, **33** (2), 299–322.

Hendershott, P.H. and MacGregor, B.D. (2005b) Investor rationality: an analysis of NCREIF commercial property data. *Journal of Real Estate Research*, **27** (4), 445–474.

Hendershott, P.H., Lizieri, C.M. and Matysiak, G.A. (1999) The workings of the London office market. *Real Estate Economics*, **27** (2), 365–387.

Hendershott, P.H., MacGregor, B.D. and Tse, R.Y.C. (2002a) Estimation of the rental adjustment process. *Real Estate Economics*, **30** (2), 165–183.

Hendershott, P., MacGregor, B. and White, M. (2002b) Explaining commercial rents using an error correction model with panel data. *Journal of Real Estate Finance and Economics*, **24** (1), 59–87.

Hendershott, P.H., Hendershott, R.J. and Ward, C.R.W. (2003) Corporate equity and commercial property market 'bubbles'. *Urban Studies*, **40** (5–6), 993–1003.

Henneberry, J. (1999) Convergence and difference in regional office development cycles. *Urban Studies*, **36** (9), 1439–1465.

Hetherington, J. (1988) Forecasting of Rents. In: *Property Investment Theory*, A MacLeary and N. Nanthakumaran (eds.), London: D & F.N. Spon., 97–107.

Himmelberg, C., Mayer, C. and Sinai, T. (2005) Assessing high house prices, bubbles, fundamentals and misperceptions. *Journal of Economic Perspectives*, **19** (4), 67–92.

Hutchison N, Adair A and McWilliam J (2007) Covenant strength and the initial yield: an explicit and calibrated risk?. Paper presented to *the European Real Estate Society Annual Conference*, Cass Business School, City University, London, June 2007.

IPD, Investment Property Databank (2003) Valuation and Sale Price Variance Report 2003. RICS, London.

IPD, Investment Property Databank (2004) Valuation and Sale Price Report 2004. RICS, London.

IPD, Investment Property Databank (2006) Valuation and Sale Price Report 2006. RICS/IPD, London.

IPD, Investment Property Databank (2007) Valuation and Sale Price Report 2007. RICS/IPD, London.

IPD, Investment Property Databank (2008) Valuation and Sale Price Report 2008. RICS/IPD, London.

IPD, Investment Property Databank (2009) Valuation and Sale Price Report 2009. RICS/IPD, London.

IPF, Investment Property Forum (2000) The Assessment and Management of Risk in the Property Investment Industry. IPF, London.

IPF, Investment Property Forum (2007) Risk Management in UK Property Portfolios. IPF, London.

Johansen, S. (1991) Estimation and hypothesis testing of cointegrating vectors in Gaussian vector autoregressive models. *Econometrica*, **59**, 1551–1580.

Ke, Q. and White, M. (2013) Investigating the dynamics of, and interactions between, Shanghai office submarkets. *Journal of Property Research*, **30** (1), 1–20.

Ke, Q. and White, M. (2009) An econometric analysis of Shanghai office rents. *Journal of Property Investment and Finance*, **27** (2), 120–139.

Key, T., MacGregor, B.D., Nanthakumaran, N. and Zarkesh, F. (1994) *Understanding the Property Cycle*. RICS, London.

Kindleberger, C.P. (1987) 'Bubbles'. In: *The New Palgrave. A Dictionary of Economics*, edited by J. Eatwell, M. Milgate and P. Newman, MacMillan, London.

Kleidon, A. (1986) Variance bounds tests and stock price valuation models. *Journal of Political Economy*, **94**, 953–1001.

Lecomte, P. (2007) Beyond index-based hedging: can real estate trigger a new breed of derivatives market? *Journal of Real Estate Portfolio Management*, **13** (4), 345–378.

Miles, W. (2008) Boom-bust cycles and the forecasting performance of linear and non-linear models of house prices. *Journal of Real Estate Finance and Economics*, **36** (3), 249–264.

Mouzakis, F. and Richards, D. (2007) Panel data modelling of prime office rents: a study of 12 major European markets. *Journal of Property Research*, **24** (1), 31–53.

Newell, G., Worzala, E., McAllister, P. and Schulte, K.-W. (2004) An international perspective on real estate research priorities. *Journal of Real Estate Portfolio Management*, **10** (3), 161–170.

Quan, D. and Quigley, J. (1989) Inferring and investment return series for real estate from observations on sales. *American Real Estate and Urban Economics Association Journal*, **17** (2), 218–230.

Schwenzer, J. (2008) *Untersuchung zur Bedeutung und Ausprägung des Risikomanagements von Immobilien [Investigation of the Meaning and Development of Risk Management from the Perspective of an Accounting Firm]*. Braunschweig Technical University, Braunschweig.

Shiller, R.J. (1981) Do stock prices move too much to be justified by subsequent changes in dividends. *American Economic review*, **71**, 421–436.

Sivitanidou, R. and Sivitanides, P. (1999) Office capitalization rates: real estate and capital market influences. *Journal of Real Estate Finance and Economics*, **18**, 297–322.

Sivitanides, P., Southard, J., Torto, R. and Wheaton, W. (2001) The Determinants of Appraisal-Based Capitalization Rates. *Real Estate Finance*, **18**, 27–37.

Smith, M.H. and Smith, G. (2006) Bubble, bubble, where's the housing bubble? *Brookings Papers on Economic Activity*, Brookings Institute, Washington, DC.

Summers, L. (1986) Does the stock market rationally reflect fundamental values? *Journal of Finance*, **41**, 591–603.

Van der Schaaf, P. and de Puy, L. (2001) CRE portfolio management: Improving the process. *Journal of Corporate Real Estate*, **3** (2), 150–160.

Viezer, T.W. (1999) Econometric Integration of Real Estate's Space and Capital Markets. *Journal of Real Estate Research*, **18**, 503–19.

Wheaton, W.C., Torto, R.G. and Evans, P. (1997) The cyclic behaviour of the Greater London office market. *Journal of Real Estate Finance and Economics*, **15** (1), 77–92.

Wheaton, W.C., R.G. Torto, R.S. Sivitanides, J.A. Southard, R.E. Hopkins and J.M. Costello (2001) Real Estate Risk: A Forward-Looking Approach. *Real Estate Finance*, **18** (3), 20–28.

9

International Financial Innovation and Real Estate Market Performance

Introduction

Innovations in new product development have changed the face of the finance market. We see this earliest in the United States; however, many of these products or instruments have appeared subsequently in markets in other countries. In recent years, the focus of attention has been on the use and impact of debt products. Therefore, this chapter will examine mortgage markets and how these have evolved with the development of mortgage pass-through securities, collateralised mortgage obligations and derivative securities.

Mortgage product development

Mortgage products are most commonly known in the housing market where there are many borrowers undertaking house purchase and that often requires borrowing on a long-term basis. Mortgage terms often range between 25 and 30 years for the repayment of interest and principal. Mortgage lenders have to consider how to price a mortgage given demand for funds from alternative investments and the characteristics of the borrower. The mortgage price will take into consideration the prevailing central bank base rate that reflects the minimum that investors would seek to earn from

Real Estate Finance in the New Economy, First Edition. Piyush Tiwari and Michael White.
© 2014 John Wiley & Sons, Ltd. Published 2014 by John Wiley & Sons, Ltd.

investing in the marketplace. The lender would also consider inflation and expected inflation to avoid making real losses. Generally, nominal interest rates are higher in countries with higher actual and expected inflation. Likewise, mortgage products would be expected to have a higher nominal interest rate in the context of a higher inflation environment. However, if inflation is unanticipated, the lenders' real return will be reduced as this cannot be factored into mortgage pricing decisions.

Lenders also face the possibility that mortgages are repaid before their terms have reached completion. On average, borrowers in the United Kingdom repay mortgages within 7 years of issue rather than the usual 25-year terms on these products. In these circumstances, lenders lose the expected interest payments had the mortgage been kept full term. Alternatively, rather than prepaying the mortgage, borrowers may default on their payments.

Thus, the risks of inflation, early repayment and default will need to be evaluated by the lender. Many mortgage products have adjustable or variable interest rates that reduce inflation risks. However, as inflation erodes the principal in real terms, then if wages remain at least constant in real terms, the possibility of early repayment increases. Default risk also rises as the interest rate increases.

Lenders have historically required borrowers to make sizeable downpayments to reduce the loan-to-value and loan-to-income ratios. This would reduce risk of default as repayments would be smaller and more manageable for households. The downpayment constraints would also work to exclude lower-income households (and more volatile-income households) from the mortgage market. Terms were also relatively short, around 5 years. This is in contrast to mortgage bonds that can have last for over 40 years in some countries. Shorter terms also mean less room for capitalisation and hence a restraint on house price inflation.

Longer-term mortgages developed in the post-war period against a background of economic growth and increasing household incomes and wealth. The mortgage market grew as home ownership increased and as fewer housing units became available for rent. This changed the composition of mortgage borrowers which now began to encompass lower-income households and households with greater default risk. As house prices kept increasing in real and nominal terms, housing began to be seen as an asset for investors. Against this background are the development of more complex mortgage products and increasing debt finance in commercial real estate markets.

Why use debt?

The main motivation for debt usage is to purchase assets where the investor has insufficient capital or equity to afford the asset outright. Alternatively, debt may permit purchasing more than one asset and hence can aid in port-folio diversification. There may be tax advantages to borrowing in mortgage markets that makes this more attractive than other sources of finance. In addition, debt permits borrowers to benefit from financial leverage. Brueggeman and Fisher (2008) define financial leverage as 'benefits that may result for an investor who borrows money at a rate of interest lower than the expected rate of return on total funds invested in a property' (p. 348). When the property's investment return exceeds the debt interest rate, 'the return on equity is magnified' (Brueggeman and Fisher, 2008, p. 348). However, extra debt brings with it extra risk.

Lenders to the commercial real estate market will consider additional factors to the housing market mortgage in order to control risk. A widely used benchmark is the debt coverage ratio (DCR). This is the ratio of net operating income (NOI) to the mortgage payment. Lenders will want this to be significantly above 1, probably around 1.2, to provide a cushion against reductions in NOI before borrowers find it difficult to make the mortgage repayment.

Commercial property lenders may also impose prepayment penalties or require lockout clauses that prevent the sale of properties within a given time period following the initial mortgage issue.

However, while these and various other requirements may exist, the debt market has still remained popular as a source of funds for borrowers. Lenders are attracted to this market in part because commercial property has characteristics that distinguish it from the housing market. 'The income from [commercial] real estate...may be expected to increase substantially over the investment holding period for several reasons. First, in an inflationary environment income may be expected to rise – especially when the lease is structured to allow the lease payments to increase each year. Second, the income for a building that was just developed may be expected to increase for several years because of the time required to lease the new space. Third, the income may be expected to increase because the property has below-market leases at the time it is purchased. If these leases...expire during the investment holding period, the investor may project that income will rise as the leases are renewed at the higher projected market rate' (Brueggeman and Fisher, 2008, p. 362).

These preceding factors may have implications for the structure of the mortgage. Fixed rate, constant or level payments may not be suitable as they could imply a very low DCR since NOI is below its long-term level initially. The mortgage would possibly require payments to be lower initially and then be increased in the future. Lenders may also receive income from the income generated by the borrower in the form of an equity participation loan. In return for this, the lender charges a lower rate of interest. Such loans are subject to the specific circumstances of each mortgage transaction.

A borrower may enter a participation loan agreement with a lender because the motivation of a lower interest rate particularly in the initial loan period may be advantageous. Also, if the agreement to share equity doesn't happen until a particular level of cash flow is generated, then there is some time before the loan begins to take effect. Both lender and borrower can find that this approach helps to reduce risk in the mortgage transaction.

Risk analysis

Investments that have higher risk should provide a higher expected return. So, for example, index-linked government debt may be the least risky asset with the lowest expected return. Risk then begins to increase until we come to stocks that are regarded as the most risky asset class and therefore should carry with them the highest expected return. In general terms, real estate is seen to lie somewhere between government bonds and stocks with respect to their risk-expected return combination. As an asset class, mortgage-backed securities are seen to be riskier than government debt but less risky than corporate bonds and real estate. Different types of risk are considered by investors when they decide upon different assets.

In real estate, the income that a commercial property produces depends upon the occupation rate which can vary over an economic cycle. Even if tenants have long leases, some may go bankrupt and the investor's income stream is therefore reduced. With turnover rents, there is a stronger relationship between the investment income stream and the economic cycle. This risk may be referred to as business risk. The more varied is the tenant base of a commercial property (perhaps in relation to the markets they serve), the greater is the possibility of reducing business risk particularly if the different markets have a low correlation with respect to their performance.

Financial risk is incurred if there is debt finance for the commercial property investment. This type of risk is also affected by the cost and structure of the debt. Another risk is that arising when there are few transactions in the market – liquidity risk. This makes the asset more difficult to liquidate and is often a concern for investors in thinner property markets. These thinner markets can occur spatially or temporally, spatially if the investable real estate market is very small with few properties coming on to the market at any given point in time or temporally when the market is in recession such as the early 1990s or after the financial crisis in 2008.

Risks also arise with unexpected inflation which can erode the real value of payments where these are fixed in nominal terms. Higher inflation in the past was one of the key factors leading to the shortening of lease lengths in the United Kingdom. This contrasts with more recent forces tending to reduce lease length that have been occupier driven.

In real estate, investors must also take management risk into consideration. This is because, in contrast to other asset classes, real estate must be managed, and such management can have an impact on the returns generated by the property investment. Management strategies will vary with the real estate sector. For example, shopping centres would require consideration of the mix of outlets to maintain and increase footfall. Office occupiers in key financial centres would potentially be more similar and 'fix' would possibly be less relevant although a more diversified occupier base within a building reduces the impact of sector-specific recessions.

Asset values will be affected by interest rate changes, and hence, there are risks attached to interest rate movements. Highly levered real estate investments would experience significant changes in payments as interest rates changes (for variable rate debt).

Finally, real estate is also subject to legislative and environmental risk. Legislation can affect investment returns and planning restrictions can impact on land cost and hence the profitability of new development. Increased concerns regarding the environment have affected legislation that has also impacted on construction costs that in turn impacts on new development and refurbishment.

Variable risk

While different types and sources of risk are outlined earlier, risk is often measured using the standard deviation of returns in standard mean–variance analysis. However, investment returns may be more volatile in one-time period than in another. Standard mean–variance analysis may underestimate volatility if autoregressive conditionally heteroscedastic (ARCH) effects are present. These ARCH processes have a conditional volatility greater than that measured by the unconditional variance. The importance of this effect is amplified during periods of high volatility in prices.

Further, the inefficiency of the property market and associated information problems could imply that 'large and small forecast errors [would] appear to occur in clusters, suggesting a form of heteroscedasticity in which the variance of the forecast error depends on the size of the preceding disturbance' (Greene, 1993, pp. 438–439).

If ARCH effects exist, then the conditional variance will be larger than the unconditional variance for certain time periods and risk will be higher than that indicated by the unconditional variance alone (see Miles, 2008). ARCH models essentially try to capture the higher volatility missed by the standard mean–variance approach. An ARCH process has a conditional mean and variance. The condition mean follows an ARMA (p, q) process. Hence,

$$X_t = \sum_{i=1}^{p} \varphi_i X_{t-i} + \sum_{i=1}^{q} \theta_i \varepsilon_{t=i} \tag{9.1}$$

If the disturbances had constant variance, as assumed by the classical model, the unconditional variance would be constant over time. However, many series display volatility clustering such that they are more volatile in some consecutive time periods than in others. The error variance is therefore time-varying and can be written as a function of its lagged values. Thus,

$$\varepsilon_t^2 = \alpha_0 + \sum_{i=1}^{q} \alpha_i \varepsilon_{t=i}^2 + \mu_t \tag{9.2}$$

where ε^2 is the variance of the error term and μ is a stochastic disturbance. A generalised autoregressive conditional heteroscedasticity (GARCH) model begins by estimating conditional variance from an ARMA model as in Equation (9.1) and then is specified as

$$\varepsilon_t = \alpha_0 + \sum_{i=1}^{q} \alpha_i \varepsilon_{t-1}^2 + \sum_{i=1}^{p} \gamma_i \varepsilon_{t-1} \tag{9.3}$$

The coefficient α (commonly known as the ARCH effect) captures the tendency for the conditional variance to cluster, while the γ (commonly known as the GARCH effect) captures the tendency for shocks to have a persistent influence on the conditional variance. ARCH models, where the presence of ARCH effects affects the future path of mean returns (ARCH-M), have also been developed and would be of particular interest to investors.

The secondary mortgage market

The secondary mortgage market was developed to permit mortgage originators to (re)sell mortgages. It permitted funds to flow to where demand existed for them and for sellers to raise funds and issue new loans based upon those funds. Regulatory change has had a significant impact on these markets, and while early developments in the market occurred in the United States, deregulation in many countries saw product innovation in mortgage markets.

In the United States, federal legislation created Government-Sponsored Enterprises (GSEs) in the mortgage market. Possibly, the most well known of these, outside the United States, is the Federal National Mortgage Association (Fannie Mae). Its objectives have been to '[enhance]...secondary market operations in federally insured and guaranteed mortgages;... [manage]...direct loans...and [liquidate]...properties and mortgages acquired by default; [manage]...special-assistance programs, including support for subsidised mortgage loan programs' (Brueggeman and Fisher, 2008, p. 555). Initially, interest rates were regulated to encourage home ownership. Fannie Mae would 'raise capital by issuing debt when necessary to purchase mortgages, thereby replenishing capital to originators during periods of rising interest rates' (Brueggeman and Fisher, 2008, p. 556). These mortgages would then be sold at a profit when interest rates were lower. This would provide Fannie Mae with monies to reduce debt that was incurred when the mortgages were initially purchased. Hence, Fannie Mae had a key role in maintaining liquidity in the mortgage market. By its actions, it also took on interest rate risk. Over time, it was assumed that Fannie Mae would 'earn a "spread" between interest earned on mortgages and interest paid on its bonds...' (Brueggeman and Fisher, 2008, p. 556).

Further legislative changes in 1968 and the establishment of the Government National Mortgage Association (or 'Ginnie Mae') proved significant in the development of the secondary mortgage market in the United States. The new legislation guaranteed repayment of principal and interest on mortgage pools issued by GSEs. This helped to overcome problems that had arisen previously when borrowers defaulted on their repayments requiring claims to be made for payments in arrears and remittance of loan balances. The consequent unpredictability of ash flows was disliked by investors.

The new guarantee programme caused substantial growth in the secondary mortgage market. It permitted mortgage originators to package mortgages and then issues (pass-through) securities where the investor could buy a 'security interest in a pool of mortgages with interest and principal passed through to investors as received from borrowers' (Brueggeman and Fisher, 2008, p. 557).

As these assets were essentially back by federal government, investors were attracted by their low perceived default risk. The securities had bond-like characteristics with the exception that the principal could be repaid at any time.

The changes made by legislation set the background against which mortgage-related securities pools developed. One of the key aspects of this is the behaviour of mortgage originators who are now able to shift interest rate risk onto different types of investor. Debt-based securities include mortgage-backed bonds (MBBs), mortgage pass-through securities (MPTs), and collateralised debt obligations (CDOs).

Mortgage-backed bonds

Issuers of MBBs create a pool of mortgages and issue bonds. The bond issue usually comes with a fixed-coupon rate and maturity. Such bond issues are overcollateralised to ensure that interest and principal payments can be met. This also allows for the possibility of default by mortgage borrowers and early or prepayment of mortgage principal. Mortgage issuers must replenish the pool of mortgages to keep the level of overcollateralisation constant. 'Mortgage-backed bonds, like all mortgage-related securities, are usually underwritten by investment banking companies, given an investment rating by an independent bond rating agency, and sold through an underwriting syndicate' (Brueggeman and Fisher, 2008, p. 561).

The investment rating given to the MBBs is affected by the quality of mortgages comprising the pool, diversification and mortgage interest rates; the probability of prepayment; the degree of overcollateralisation; and, for commercial mortgages, the DCR and value from appraisal of the properties concerned.

The quality of mortgages will vary inversely with loan-to-value ratio and default risk (these two latter may also be directly related). Also, mortgage pools undiversified by location may be exposed to greater risk due to local economic fluctuations, for example, than pools covering different locations with economic bases that have lower correlations with each other. The investment rating will then determine pricing of the bond issue and the return investors receive for holds the MBBs. Riskier pools will be cheaper and have a higher yield attached to them.

Mortgage pass-through securities

An MPT provides an undivided ownership interest in a pool of mortgages. As with MBBs, there is a trustee designated as the pool owner who ensures that payments are made to investors or security owners. Cash flows are passed through to investors by mortgage issuers. Coupon rates on pass-through securities will typically be lower than the mortgage rate to pay for the servicing fee charged. Unlike the MBB, with MPTs, the security holds must carry prepayment risk. This is not the case with the MBBs where the overcollateralisation requirement shifts this risk to the issuer.

Collateralised mortgage obligations

Collateralised mortgage obligations (CMOs) are issue against a mortgage pool that is used as collateral. The issuer of a CMO maintains ownership of the pool of mortgages. Like MPTs, the bond purchaser carries prepayment risk. 'The main difference between CMOs and the other mortgage-backed securities is that CMOs are securities issued in multiple classes against the same pool of mortgages' (Brueggeman and Fisher, 2008, p. 582). The maturity of the securities varies (e.g. 5 or 7 years) that have the benefit of being better able to meet the needs of investors for varying maturity dates. The securities with different payment streams and maturity dates may be very different from the characteristics of the mortgage product terms upon which they are based.

By prioritising payments of interest income and principal across the different classes of debt securities in the issue of the CMO, prepayment risk to the investor is reduced. CMOs are issued in classes named *tranches* that have different maturity dates. Some make payments that make them like bonds, while in others cash flow can be deferred to the future for a higher return but with the price of some exposure to prepayment risk. These derivative products have been in demand from investors and have multiplied since their first inception.

Commercial mortgage-backed securities

Commercial mortgage-backed securities (CMBSs) bear many similarities to their residential counterparts. However, commercial mortgages are taken out on investable real estate or income-generating property assets across retail, office and industrial sectors. Thus, there is the added concern on the viability of the occupier in commercial space to pay rent.

A commercial mortgage-backed security offering (CMO) has some distinctive features. Firstly, the mortgages in the pool have relatively short maturities and make only interest payments. Principal is only repaid at the maturity date. 'Two major classes of debt securities are usually offered as a [CMO]; *senior* and *subordinated* tranches. Sometimes these are referred to as the "A piece" and "B piece" respectively. In practice there will be several subclasses within each of these major classes. The distinction between the two classes is largely based on the priority of claims on all payments flowing the pool, with the senior tranche receiving the highest priority and the subordinate tranche coming second. .... [if] the senior tranche is subordinated by 30 percent because the subordinate tranche is 30 percent of the securities, ... there can be up to 30 percent loss in value of the mortgage pool before the senior tranche will incur any loss' (Brueggeman and Fisher, 2008, p. 605).

Commercial mortgage borrowers often refinance their mortgage before its maturity date. However, there is always some probability that this will not happen. If so, then repayments to CMO investors will be delayed. This risk of being unable to refinance is referred to as extension risk.

Securities created from commercial mortgages are given a credit rating by the credit rating agencies. As commercial mortgages rely on income from property assets, the worst case scenario is assumed in calculating the credit rating in relation to tenants going bankrupt, void periods and correlation in local markets. The rating agency usually only gives an investment grade rating to the senior tranche. The subordinate tranche would always have a lower rating or even be unrated. It is the accuracy of such ratings that have been seriously called into question in the financial crisis that spread from the subprime mortgage market in the United States and through interlinkages in the international financial system to other countries and banking systems.

Collateralised debt obligations (CDOs)

These are a variation of the products discussed earlier. They are a logical extension of development of these 'family' of assets. CDOs use a wider range of collateral than CMBSs including debt from REITs and other debt sources deemed too risky for CMBSs. The mortgages in a CDO are a mix of different types of debt. Various classes of securities can be issued with different levels of risk attached to them. CDOs may include mezzanine financing loans. This type of loan acts as a bridging loan to cover the time gap between mortgage debt and equity investment. CDOs have become very flexible products. Managed CDOs can be very flexible, allowing the issuer to swap collateral backing the CDO and reinvest mortgage principal.

Institutions and market performance

The aforementioned discussion has sought to outline the developments in debt financing that have occurred and that have provided a significant source of liquidity for the purchase of real estate assets in different countries across the world. Examining the recent financial crisis, commentators have suggested that not only has the deregulated market model failed, but the institutions that regulate this market have also failed. As Adams *et al.* (2005) state, 'As the rules, norms and regulations are created by society to enable the market to function properly, institutions reflect prevailing power and interests. Yet, to be successful, institutions must be effective in generating "workable mutuality" out of the formal and informal processes of conflict resolution from which they develop (Rutherford, 1994). In this context, what is legally or culturally feasible may deserve as much attention as what is technologically feasible' (Keogh and D'Arcy, 1999). The objective of letting markets allocate resources and removing 'barriers' has been a central tenet of government policy for a generation. Yet, the crisis suggests that regulation may be needed as market participants make mistakes and enough of them make the same mistakes sufficient to cause severe economic problems.

Self-interested individuals with imperfect information all making the same mistakes and misunderstanding market signals or perhaps not being able to identify when the signal is corrupted with noise (or bad debt) can make mistakes that lead to crises. However, this is not a new phenomenon. Collecting information in imperfect markets can be seen as a transaction cost (Adams *et al.*, 2005), and such costs have implications for market adjustment.

Dehesh and Pugh (2000) argue that 'deregulation and the ensuing intensification of competition between the banking sector and capital markets narrowed margins and led to excessive lending to the property sector. But the overinvestment in the property sector in the upturn was unsustainable and turned into non-performing loans in the inevitable downturn, thus increasing risks to the banking sector and threatening the stability of financial systems. This has drastically curtailed the ability of the banking sector to provide capital to finance recovery' (p. 2581). They further argue that 'movement of international finance capital increased liquidity in domestic markets and led to rises in asset prices, including property' (Dehesh and Pugh, 2000, p. 2581).

Much of the arguments made by Dehesh and Pugh (2000) are applicable to the financial crisis from 2007/2008 onwards. They use examples from the case of Japan to the Asian financial crisis in 1997. Yet, while there are many similarities, the most notable aspect of the most recent crisis is that nobody seems to have been able to learn from the immediate past and apply it to the 2007/2008 crisis. Of course, it can be argued that there are characteristics of the global financial crisis that are unique; there are enough similarities that should have raised concern. Indeed, there is statistical evidence that market repricing began to happen to some extent and in some markets just prior to the onset of the financial crisis as yields began to increase in some commercial real estate markets (e.g. London offices show yield increases before the crisis).

Dehesh and Pugh (2000) highlight the role of the internationalised economic system as a source of property market instability. This arises as a consequence of the integrated global financial system before which property were driven by domestic macroeconomic and property market characteristics. The international connectedness adds extra uncertainty and volatility. The authors discuss the role of financial services which has grown with economic structural change. This sector, they argue, has influenced real estate markets particularly in those locations that have an economic concentration of international and domestic financial firms (e.g. London, New York). Capital mobility has increased and the flows of finance have increased substantially as investors chase 'excess' profit and arbitrage opportunities. Feeding into this has been the increasingly varied array of financial products, some of which were discussed earlier. Dehesh and Pugh suggest that this in turn can lead to overinvestment in boom periods and underinvestment in recessions increasing the amplitude of cyclical fluctuations.

This is consistent with the view that risk is undervalued and buildings overvalued in boom periods and the opposite in slumps. Information asymmetry in imperfect markets may be one of the root causes of these divergences from fundamentals so that short-run fluctuations affect behaviour influencing expectations formation and then leading to bubbles, market participants making mistakes in the same direction and the generation of excessive cyclical volatility. Against this background, it is easy for financial institutions to lend without giving adequate consideration to default risks. The debt lending to property then can create a debt overhang in recessionary periods which makes these periods more protracted.

Dehesh and Pugh (2000) use Japan as an example in their paper. The story highlights the role of financial innovation and liquidity in driving asset prices. But it also shows a role for institutional change that happened in many countries and suggests that institutions shape markets and thus impact on market outcomes. In considering the role of institutional economics in helping to understanding land and property markets, Adams *et al.* (2005) state that 'Institutional economics...opposes the simple neoclassical notion that resources are allocated merely by market processes since it holds that markets both reflect and help to operationalise the institutional structure of society' (Samuels, 1995).

Japan was one of a number of countries that introduced policies of financial liberalisation – thus changing the institutional structure and framework

Table 9.1   Financial liberalisation, fiscal and monetary policies.

Country	Timing of deregulation in financial markets	Property sector impact of tax changes	Peak of monetary expansion	Asset price inflation	Scale of asset price inflation
USA	Starting since late 1970s	Housing investment	1983–1988	1985–1989 land	Medium
UK	Starting in 1980	Limited	1983–1988	1983–1989 land	High
Japan	Starting in 1985	Property investment for firms, inheritance tax	1985–1989	1985–1989 land	High
Germany	Interest rates 1967–1969	Large housing investments	1985–1988	1990 onwards land	Low
Sweden	1985	Housing investment	1986/1987	1985–1989 land	High
				1988/1989 stock	
Norway	1984/1985	Housing investment	1984–1986	1986–1989 land	High

Source: Adapted from Dehesh and Pugh (2000). Reproduced by permission of Sage Publications Ltd.

within which market participants operated. Table 9.1 in the following text lists some of the countries that deregulated their financial markets in the 1980s.

Thus, similar institutional change was occurring across many developed countries and across countries which were those with the largest and most valuable investable real estate markets (e.g. the United States accounts for approximately half of the total value of commercial real estate transactions in the world in any given year. The United Kingdom on average contributes 10% of total transaction value).

In the language of new institutional economic theory, 'the rules of the game' (North, 1990) were changing, or as Hamilton (1932) described, institutions, 'a way of thought or action of some prevalence, which is embedded in the habits of a group or the customs of people' and thus 'institutions [that] fix the confines of and impose structure upon the activities of human beings' (Hamilton, 1932, p. 84), were changing. Keogh and D'Arcy (1999) conceptualise real estate markets as networks of formal rules (lease laws), conventions (information sharing) and relationships (perhaps market actors possessing asymmetric information and expectations of market performance). Deregulation changed the formal rules in which property markets operated in different countries.

In the countries listed in Table 9.1, policies of monetary expansion are pursued against the new deregulated background. In most cases, there is significant asset price change (except in the case of Germany). This however does not occur immediately; there is usually time lag in the transmission process. In the case of the United Kingdom where deregulation began in 1980, there is a delay of at least 3 years before expansionary monetary policy and asset inflation. While this will reflect the impact of recession in the early 1980s, market participants' expectations of future value growth will also be changing. In the recession, expectations of future growth may be subdued. Positive growth may be needed to change investors' outlooks. Thus, the impact of deregulation will only impact macroeconomic performance and asset values when expectations of value growth change.

Adaptive expectations were part of the reason for increasing speculation in many property markets, contributing to bubbles as discussed in earlier chapters. Urban regeneration in Tokyo saw increased demand for office space against a background of vacancy rates of less than 1%. As prices rose, this fed into expectations of future price accumulation. Particular institutional characteristics of the funding mechanism for large Japanese companies affected the supply of debt finance during this period.

Deregulation had permitted companies to borrow from overseas and domestic capital markets in addition to the bank borrowing. To maintain market share, banks began lending to other groups including smaller and medium-sized companies. Often, the funds raised were to purchase intermediate goods to be used in the production process, but some portion was also used to buy financial assets. This enabled companies to hedge against the possibility of reduced competitiveness of exports as the yen appreciated against other currencies. Monetary expansion and the performance of the services sector also encouraged the diversion of funds to other sectors. Land held by firms also rose in value and smaller firms increased land holdings, expecting future value gains. Land held as assets almost doubled in the decade after 1984 (see Dehesh and Pugh, 2000). These forces drive land values to the point where they are five times that of the United States.

But the bubble burst in 1991, leaving a debt burden overhanging the economy which has persisted now for two decades. Economic growth has been negligible, national debt has ballooned, and consumers have been cautious, preferring to increase their savings rather than spend or speculate.

The next financial crisis was in Southeast Asia in 1997. Thailand, Indonesia, Malaysia and also South Korea had all seen strong economic growth driven by exports. However, banking sectors had tended to be relatively underdeveloped. They lacked transparency, criteria for loan approval were less than objective, and they were undercapitalised. The sector had witnessed bankruptcies and was exposed to short-dated overseas finance. Hence, it was exposed to speculative attack if investors became nervous. Furthermore, macroeconomic policy was concerned with exports being reduced by adverse currency movements against the U.S. dollar. Thus, currencies were fixed against the dollar. When it began to appreciate, countries devalued their currencies against the dollar in order to maintain competitiveness. However, this increased dollar debt in local currency terms and precipitated international capital outflows and put downward pressure on already devalued currencies. This came after a period of rapid economic growth that had seen significant capital inflows, high increases in rental values in commercial space and an institutional framework that was characterised by close relationships between state governments, the financial sector and real estate market participants.

Growth in values had built up expectations of future value increases. Access to credit and asset inflation led to similar interlinkages between real estate and the macroeconomies of Southeast Asian nations as had been seen earlier in Japan. The outcome of the Asian financial crisis has been that economic growth in Malaysia has never returned to pre-crisis levels although it has continued to grow and has not seen the low growth rates of Japan. Other countries in the region fare better. Singapore was least exposed to the problems of its neighbouring states has a more robust and transparent financial system. Most of the countries required support from the International Monetary Fund (IMF) that required reforms to be introduced.

Dehesh and Pugh (2000, p. 2598) state that 'post-1980 international property cycles which occurred in countries such as the US, the UK, Australia, Japan, the Nordic countries and some Asian economies have been significantly influenced by the evolving condition of the post-Bretton-Woods international "non-system". Clearly, some countries experienced more acute cycles than other and, in countries where property cycles were exceptional, for example in Japan, they made the two-way interdependence between the property sector and the macroeconomy, via various transmission mechanisms, more significant than cycles typically found in earlier times'.

The authors go on to note the consequences of such cycles which in their aftermath leave behind protracted recessions, nonperforming loans and debt overhang. They note that in many economies, banks made mistakes regarding the credit worthiness of borrowers' ability to repay loans. Of course, when asset values risk, default risk is reduced as borrowers can more easily sell assets above purchase price and repay any outstanding debt. In a recession, borrowers may not be able to sell assets due to lack of demand or may only be able to sell at reduced prices such that some element of principal still remains to be repaid. Thus, recession increases default risk. The cyclical correlations across loans may imply that all loans are potentially good in boom periods but potentially bad in recessions. This is consistent with risk being underrated in boom periods and overrated in slumps which in turn implies mispricing will take place in both booms (too high) and slumps (too low).

Cycles in real estate and the availability of finance

Real estate cycles cannot be avoided. They are a recurring feature of the real estate market. Examining the construction sector in different economies also suggests that this sector is highly volatile, more so than the macroeconomy itself. As an intermediate good in the production process, commercial space can be seen as fixed investment, and this industry commonly experiences wide swings in activity. It links to the concept of the accelerator in the macroeconomy, and in cycles, the accelerator and multiplier processes will interact. A constant change in output will mean no more change in the construction industry, and hence, the accelerator value will fall to 0 (peak) before the macroeconomy reaches its cyclical peak. If the economy is not changing rapidly, then the commercial development sector only responds to replacement investment and covering depreciation of existing stock. Only endogenous cycles within the property market will exist and be relatively subdued.

The large fluctuations in rents and capital values seen in many countries not only reflect demand and supply imbalance in user markets, plus exogenous macroeconomic changes that may include structural changes to economies, but also have occurred against a background of deregulation in financial markets. As an asset, flows of investment will impact on value change and add to the cyclical volatility in the market. Disconnects have emerged between investor sentiment and use values. For example, the weakness of the London office market from 2001 to 2004 reflected uncertainty from occupiers. Investors however still found this asset to be attractive, and investment flows continued especially from Eurozone investors who could earn a higher return in London offices than the cost of servicing their debt-financed investments.

Deregulation permits such flows of finance. As an asset in itself, expectations of future values become important, and as discussed earlier, these expectations have not always proved accurate. Indeed, given the recurring events after the boom of the late 1980s and crash of the early 1990s followed by the Asian financial crisis, it become more difficult to explain why investors did not think that they should consider the risks attached to a long run up in values before 2007.

In a market with information asymmetries and imperfections, investors may adopt a strategy of examining the limited information available which in the case of the real estate market may be limited to a short history of price movements for the asset in question. These adaptive expectations are then used in decision making and in a changing market will make systematic mistakes. However, the question still remains as to why investors seem to ignore past market cycles.

In the previous chapter, we had said that property cycles are mean reverting. They must adjust towards their long-run equilibrium or fundamental values. Given the limited information in the property market, the issue is then one of what precise information is contained in value signals. An investor who observed increasing real values over consecutive time periods may reasonably assume that real estate assets are becoming relatively more valuable than in the past. In this case, it makes sense to invest. It might also be the case that the fundamental value itself increases. This may be due to economic change that changes the structure of the economy. There may be institutional change that affects the balance of demand and supply (e.g. supply may become permanently less elastic due to policy decisions). Thus, the price information signal is not clean and separate influences on the observed price cannot be disentangled by the investor. This signal extraction problem will be pervasive in real estate. We have seen that it is relevant in markets where information flows are greater (such as the United Kingdom and the United States) and also where there is less market information (such as Thailand and also Japan – see the Jones Lang LaSalle transparency index).

The imperfect real estate market is then set in a context of a globally integrated deregulated financial sector in which real estate has become an asset class and for which debt finance has been an attractive route into real estate for investors. Some of the debt vehicles were discussed previously and elsewhere in this text.

The flow of funds to which real estate is now exposed has increased greatly and is greater today than it would have been without financial deregulation. These financial flows make it difficult for governments to follow monetary and fiscal policies that the market does not believe are credible. And just as debt products have a rating, national government ratings provide investors with information about credit worthiness. However, this rating clearly failed prior to the financial crisis.

Correlation of risks during the cycle means that problems are exacerbated when markets turn. Mispricing led to too much being paid for real estate assets during the boom and this unravelled in the slump. Four years after the beginning of the 2007 crisis, there remains a significant debt overhang, most of it transferred to public sector accounts which in turn has raised concerns in relation to sovereign debt. The same rating agencies that made such errors before the financial crisis are the same ones rating government debt. If they were unable to accurately price risk before the crisis (and by having too high rating on debt, they underestimated risk), the question arises as to whether they are overestimating risks in the recession and thus making it more costly than it needs to be (with respect to fundamentals) for governments to service debt. The latter of course increases the risk of default since default risk rises with the cost of debt servicing.

The cycles in the 1980s in Europe, Japan, the United States and Australia were the first to occur in a deregulated world finance system. As indicated earlier, there are similarities with the Asian financial crisis in 1997. Between then and 2007, the world economy grew, but this was partly funded by expansionary monetary policy especially after 2001. The U.S. government policy also played a role as it encouraged what would ultimately turn out to be sources of bad debt to enter the debt market.

Conclusions

This chapter has examined developments in debt vehicles for investment purposes in real estate markets. While not all markets are the same or as well developed in each country, the international connectedness of the financial system enables debt-backed investors in one country to invest in others.

Complicated debt instruments have permitted significant borrowing that has inflated real estate asset values around the world. Risks have been ignored since as long as asset values continue to rise, then there is no incentive for lenders to be cautious and they can permit high multiples for borrowers who also cannot lose. For many investors who have chosen the 'right' time to buy and sell, debt usage has enabled them to increase their profits. However, when the timing is wrong, default risk rises and, through contagion effects, values fall. Lenders become unwilling to lend and liquidity disappears. This further exacerbates the fall in values.

The tap of debt turned on in the boom and off in the slump increases the amplitude of fluctuation of property cycles across the globe. However, the movements are not symmetric as the resultant unpaid debt in the slump leaves the financial sector undercapitalised and unwilling to lend which further lengthens the slump itself.

The experience of developed economies since 2007 is one where the debt overhang from the bursting of the real estate bubble has left them in stagnation. There persist high levels of indebtedness in government finances in many countries partly as a consequence of policymakers trying to compensate for the weakness in financial institutions exposed to the real estate sector. Financial innovation has made real estate markets more volatile, and there are stronger interlinkages with the macroeconomy making it too more volatile.

The excess debt has also led to caution by lenders and investors. Expectations for future value increases are weakened and via wealth effects reduce consumption growth. This extends the length of the stagflation or recessionary phases. Countries that have seen the most rapid price growth tend to be those with the largest economic problems related to debt overhang and recession. The divergence between short-run and fundamental values has been heightened by the flow of liquidity from the financial sector. This increased divergence may also make signal extraction more difficult and hence make the market more inefficient and pricing more inaccurate. In case of high conditional volatility where ARCH processes are present, potentially costly mistakes can arise.

Thus, the overall impact of financial deregulation is one that makes values more volatile and recessions deeper and longer. As imbalances can persist, investors' expectations may be inaccurate and result in future cycles as they may inaccurately interpret observed prices and price changes being unable to separate fundamental values from transitory effects. The cycles in the post-financial-deregulation era suggest that cycles cannot be avoided. If the institutional structure of the global system remains as it is now, large cycles may be expected as funds continue to flow across borders, chasing the best risk-adjusted return.

References

Adams, D., Dunse, N. and White, M. (2005) Conceptualising state-market relations in land and property: the growth of institutionalism – extension or challenge to mainstream economics. In: *Planning, Public Policy and Property Markets* (eds D. Adams, C. Watkins, and M. White). Blackwell, Oxford.

Brueggeman, W.B. and Fisher, J.D. (2008) *Real Estate Finance and Investments*, 13th edn. McGraw Hill, New York.

Dehesh, A. and Pugh, C. (2000) Property cycles in a global economy. *Urban Studies*, **37** (13), 2581–2602.

Greene, W.H. (1993) *Econometric Analysis*. Prentice Hall, Pearson Education Inc, NJ.

Hamilton, W. (1932) 'Institution' in Encyclopedia of the Social Sciences, eds. E. Seigman and A. Johnson, 8th ed., Macmillan, New York.

Keogh, G. and D'Arcy, E. (1999) Property Market Efficiency: An Institutional Economics Perspective. *Urban Studies*, **36**, 2401–14.

Miles, W. (2008) Boom-bust cycles and the forecasting performance of linear and non-linear models of house prices. *Journal of Real Estate Finance and Economics*, **36** (3), 249–264.

North, D. (1990), *Institutions, Institutional Change and Economic Performance*. Cambridge: Cambridge University Press, UK.

Rutherford, M. (1994) *Institutions in Economics: The Old and the New Institutionalism*, Cambridge University Press, Cambridge.

Samuels, W. (1995) The Present State of Institutional Economics. *Cambridge Journal of Economics*, **19**, 569–90.

10

Real Estate in the New Economy

Introduction

The economic background against which this book has been written is one following the most significant financial crisis in post-war history. It has also been a crisis in which real estate assets have played a pivotal role in different economies. The crisis has helped to highlight the links between property markets and the macroeconomy. It has revealed imperfect expectations mechanisms and hence inaccurate decision making based upon false assumptions (or hopes) of future asset values. It has shown up weaknesses in institutional structures and both in relation to the context within which the financial system operates and the policies adopted both before and after the crisis. It has shown how contagion can spread in interlinked financial markets across the globe and has shed light on divergence between transaction values and fundamental values. Amplitude of fluctuation in macroeconomic cycles has increased due to debt exposure in the real estate sector and because asset wealth has been translated into consumption expenditure due to deregulation.

The past 30 years has seen a process of deregulation and economic liberalisation that have changed institutional structures in many countries. This reflected the desire of many nations to increase their GDP and living standards. It could be argued that there is an implicit assumption that only the market can best allocate resources. While it has been argued that it is

Real Estate Finance in the New Economy, First Edition. Piyush Tiwari and Michael White.
© 2014 John Wiley & Sons, Ltd. Published 2014 by John Wiley & Sons, Ltd.

more efficient than centrally planned systems, there is another implicit assumption in that the market is able to always solve imbalances. Critics suggest that the financial crisis shows how badly the market can get it wrong, and Keynes (1936) implies that equilibrium in markets can be one with persistent imbalances with no tendency for further market correction.

In this final chapter, we discuss what we mean by the term 'new economy'. We then examine the changes that have taken place in real estate investment and in investment decision-making processes. We broaden out the debate to examine the political economy of response to the financial crisis and potential short- and longer-term responses. Finally, we consider future real estate investment and the interlinkages between the real estate sector and economy.

The new economy and world economic structure

In Chapter 5, the new economy was defined as being the name given to those industries benefitting directly and indirectly from the latest revolution in information and communication technologies, the extensive use of the latest electronic systems, advanced software, digitalisation and the internet (Chorafas, 2001). The new economy is also seen to open up global competition for financial institutions, encouraging innovation and, possibly, risk-taking. This innovation has been seen in an increasing array of financial products used to invest in real estate assets. Also new has been the increasing importance of international debt finance and with this further integration of the world financial system.

This new economy has been heavily debt financed, although since the financial crisis in 2008, the regime in which it operates may be changing. However, Chapter 5 also suggests that in a highly indebted environment, property market volatility increases and there is a heightened risk of an increased frequency of extreme events. The post-financial crisis world is characterised by high indebtedness of national governments, many of whom have taken on the bad debts in the financial sector. Some monetary authorities have attempted to increase money supply to absorb bad debts, while others have resisted this and have faced loss of investor confidence in the repayment abilities of highly indebted nations. Consequent austerity policies run the risk of making deficits worse as economic growth is either weak of non-existent.

Events in financial markets and subsequently in public debt markets raise the issue of whether or not there will be structural breaks in market performance. The economic cycle since 2008 has not been similar to cycles in the early 1990s, the early 1980s or the mid-1970s, but the debt overhang and slow growth may mean that adjustment towards the 'normal' or historically observed long-run growth trajectories do not materialise. This would have implications for capital values and investment return performance on real estate and other assets in those countries most affected by recent market turbulence.

Of course, there have been market adjustments, particularly in the foreign exchange market which, given the liquidity of currencies and fully integrated markets, have shouldered much of the burden of adjustment before other markets (e.g. labour and product markets) can react. Table 10.1 shows the extent to which exchange rates have moved. The data are effective exchange rate indices with 2005 as the base year.

The data cover countries that have been exposed to a greater or less extent to real estate asset value bubbles, financial crises and public debt crises. For some countries, there has been only a limited impact from the financial crisis on their macroeconomies (such as Australia and Norway). In contrast, Iceland faced significant exposure to the financial crisis with bad debt in Icelandic banks significantly exceeding the country's GDP. Of all the countries listed, Iceland has seen the largest fall in its effective exchange rate. The United Kingdom and New Zealand have sent their effective exchange rates fall by around 20% and 15%, respectively, since 2005.

In the Eurozone, however, there is a complete contrast in that countries experiencing large property asset price bubbles have not had exchange rate movements to cushion adjustment in their real economies. Thus, in the cases of Ireland and Spain, their effective exchange had increased by 2009 by approximately 10% and 4%, respectively. Thus, not only is the exchange rate not depreciating but is actually appreciating, putting further pressure for adjustment on their real economies.

The crises in financial and real estate markets have also impacted on public debt positions as shown in Table 10.2. The financial crisis begins to put pressure on public finances towards the end of 2007 and into 2008 and onwards. By 2009, all countries show a deterioration with many become highly indebted. Even Norway, which retails a healthy surplus, finds that this surplus is significantly reduced as a proportion of GDP. General government deficits exceed 10% of GDP by 2010 in Greece, Ireland, the United Kingdom and the United States. These high deficits add to national debt, and markets have become concerned with the ability of domestic authorities to service high debt levels. Government debt as a proportion of GDP is shown in Table 10.3.

Examining the debt statistics reveals that Japan has the highest ratio of national debt to GDP at just over 212%. Some countries have debt to GDP ratios above 100%. These are Belgium, Greece, Iceland, Ireland, Italy, Portugal and the United States. While the United States, Iceland and Japan have their own currencies and therefore their own central banks, the other

Table 10.1 Effective exchange rates, 1997–2009.

	1997	1998	1999	2000	2001	2002	2003	2004	2005	2006	2007	2008	2009
Australia	96.0	89.0	89.4	83.0	77.7	80.8	90.3	97.5	100.0	98.6	104.8	102.6	98.0
Austria	95.0	96.9	97.2	95.0	95.4	96.2	99.6	100.7	100.0	100.1	100.8	101.3	102.3
Belgium	92.4	94.7	94.4	90.6	91.7	93.6	98.6	100.4	100.0	100.2	101.6	103.7	104.6
Canada	87.1	82.9	82.7	83.5	81.0	79.7	88.1	93.5	100.0	106.6	111.3	110.7	104.8
Chile	119.5	115.6	107.8	105.0	94.0	92.0	86.8	94.5	100.0	103.6	100.6	98.2	95.3
Czech Republic	78.5	79.7	79.2	80.1	84.2	93.9	93.8	94.1	100.0	105.0	107.4	119.7	114.9
Denmark	94.1	96.5	95.8	91.8	93.4	94.9	99.5	100.9	100.0	99.9	101.2	103.2	105.7
Estonia	80.7	85.7	93.7	91.4	92.8	94.8	99.3	100.8	100.0	99.8	100.9	102.4	106.1
Finland	88.6	91.4	93.9	89.6	91.5	93.5	98.9	100.8	100.0	99.9	101.6	103.7	106.0
France	93.7	96.1	95.4	91.8	92.7	94.3	99.0	100.5	100.0	100.1	101.5	103.2	103.9
Germany	91.2	94.5	94.4	90.2	91.3	93.2	99.0	101.1	100.0	100.1	101.6	103.0	104.6
Greece	101.4	98.1	98.3	91.6	92.5	94.4	99.2	100.9	100.0	100.0	101.3	103.2	104.2
Hungary	108.8	98.4	94.7	89.7	91.4	97.8	97.4	99.5	100.0	93.7	99.2	99.6	90.6
Iceland	91.8	94.2	95.5	96.3	82.1	84.8	89.0	89.9	100.0	89.7	90.7	65.8	47.7
Ireland	98.6	96.0	93.3	86.8	87.9	90.1	97.9	100.2	100.0	100.2	102.6	107.9	110.1
Israel	126.3	120.3	113.3	122.9	124.3	109.1	104.9	101.1	100.0	100.3	103.7	115.6	109.9
Italy	92.9	94.9	94.6	91.0	92.3	94.3	99.1	100.8	100.0	100.1	101.4	102.9	104.1
Japan	83.9	86.4	99.4	108.0	99.5	95.6	98.9	103.1	100.0	92.6	87.5	97.5	111.2
Korea	106.6	76.7	88.3	94.5	87.3	90.3	89.8	89.8	100.0	107.4	106.8	86.0	73.4
Luxembourg	97.0	97.7	97.5	94.7	95.1	96.2	99.5	100.6	100.0	100.2	101.6	102.8	102.4
Mexico	136.9	121.6	116.1	118.6	122.0	118.5	103.4	97.2	100.0	99.3	97.3	94.6	78.7
Netherlands	90.4	93.6	93.3	88.3	89.6	91.8	98.2	100.7	100.0	100.1	102.0	104.0	104.6
New Zealand	93.8	83.8	81.1	73.4	72.3	78.4	89.3	95.5	100.0	92.4	98.8	92.4	84.8
Norway	95.5	92.6	92.3	90.2	93.2	101.2	99.1	95.8	100.0	99.5	101.0	100.9	97.8
Poland	102.3	100.3	93.4	96.1	105.9	101.5	91.4	89.5	100.0	103.1	106.8	116.3	95.5
Portugal	98.1	98.0	97.5	95.1	96.0	97.1	99.8	100.5	100.0	100.0	100.8	101.9	102.5
Slovak Republic	97.0	96.3	89.2	90.6	88.5	88.9	94.0	98.1	100.0	103.1	113.6	122.6	131.3
Slovenia	117.0	118.5	117.4	107.6	102.3	100.1	101.7	101.3	100.0	99.8	101.0	102.2	104.5
Spain	94.6	96.1	95.6	92.5	93.6	95.4	99.3	100.5	100.0	100.2	101.3	102.9	104.0
Sweden	101.1	101.0	100.7	100.9	92.7	95.1	100.7	102.5	100.0	100.4	101.6	99.6	91.4
Switzerland	86.9	91.2	91.9	90.1	93.8	98.7	100.4	100.8	100.0	98.6	96.1	101.6	107.2
Turkey	910.1	548.7	361.9	263.0	148.1	110.3	97.4	95.0	100.0	93.2	95.3	91.4	81.4
United Kingdom	91.3	97.2	97.7	100.0	99.1	100.6	96.9	101.5	100.0	100.6	102.4	89.5	79.5
United States	95.9	105.5	105.2	107.7	113.3	113.9	107.3	102.6	100.0	98.3	94.0	90.6	95.7
Euro area	85.7	90.6	89.7	81.5	83.5	87.0	97.7	101.6	100.0	100.2	103.4	107.1	109.6

Source: Reproduced by permission of the OECD (2009).

Table 10.2 General government financial balances (as % of GDP) 1993–2011.

	1993	1994	1995	1996	1997	1998	1999	2000	2001	2002	2003	2004	2005	2006	2007	2008	2009	2010	2011
Australia	-4.9	-4.7	-3.9	-2.6	-1.0	0.8	1.2	0.4	-0.5	0.7	1.3	1.0	1.2	1.3	1.4	-0.2	-4.9	-5.9	-2.8
Austria	-4.4	-4.9	-5.9	-4.2	-2.0	-2.5	-2.4	-1.9	-0.2	-0.9	-1.7	-4.6	-1.8	-1.7	-1.0	-1.0	-4.2	-4.6	-3.7
Belgium	-7.5	-5.2	-4.5	-4.0	-2.3	-1.0	-0.7	-0.1	0.4	-0.2	-0.2	-0.4	-2.8	0.1	-0.4	-1.3	-6.0	-4.2	-3.6
Canada	-8.7	-6.7	-5.3	-2.8	0.2	0.1	1.6	2.9	0.7	-0.1	-0.1	0.9	1.5	1.6	1.4	0.0	-5.5	-5.5	-4.9
Czech Republic	–	–	-13.4	-3.3	-3.8	-5.0	-3.7	-3.7	-5.6	-6.8	-6.6	-2.9	-3.6	-2.6	-0.7	-2.7	-5.8	-4.7	-3.8
Denmark	-3.9	-3.4	-2.9	-2.0	-0.6	-0.1	1.3	2.2	1.2	0.3	-0.1	1.9	5.0	5.0	4.8	3.3	-2.8	-2.9	-3.8
Estonia	–	–	1.1	-0.3	2.2	-0.7	-3.5	-0.2	-0.1	0.3	1.7	1.6	1.6	2.4	2.5	-2.9	-1.8	0.1	-0.5
Finland	-8.3	-6.7	-6.2	-3.5	-1.4	1.5	1.6	6.8	5.0	4.0	2.3	2.1	2.5	3.9	5.2	4.2	-2.9	-2.8	-1.4
France	-6.4	-5.5	-5.5	-4.0	-3.3	-2.6	-1.8	-1.5	-1.6	-3.2	-4.1	-3.6	-3.0	-2.3	-2.7	-3.3	-7.5	-7.0	-5.6
Germany	-3.0	-2.3	-9.7	-3.3	-2.6	-2.2	-1.5	1.3	-2.8	-3.6	-4.0	-3.8	-3.3	-1.6	0.3	0.1	-3.0	-3.3	-2.1
Greece	-11.9	-8.3	-9.1	-6.6	-5.9	-3.8	-3.1	-3.7	-4.4	-4.8	-5.7	-7.4	-5.3	-6.0	-6.7	-9.8	-15.6	-10.4	-7.5
Hungary	–	–	-8.7	-4.6	-6.0	-7.9	-5.4	-3.0	-4.0	-8.9	-7.2	-6.4	-7.9	-9.3	-5.0	-3.6	-4.4	-4.2	2.6
Iceland	-4.5	-4.7	-3.0	-1.6	0.0	-0.4	1.1	1.7	-0.7	-2.6	-2.8	0.0	4.9	6.3	5.4	-13.5	-10.0	-7.8	-2.7
Ireland	-2.7	-2.0	-2.1	-0.1	1.4	2.3	2.6	4.8	1.0	-0.3	0.4	1.4	1.6	2.9	0.1	-7.3	-14.3	-32.4	-10.1
Israel	–	–	–	–	–	-8.0	-6.3	-4.0	-6.4	-8.2	-8.3	-6.1	-4.9	-2.5	-1.5	-3.7	-6.4	-5.0	-3.7
Italy	-10.1	-9.1	-7.4	-7.0	-2.7	-3.1	-1.8	-0.9	-3.1	-3.0	-3.5	-3.6	-4.4	-3.3	-1.5	-2.7	-5.3	-4.5	-3.9
Japan	-2.5	-3.8	-4.7	-5.1	-4.0	-11.2	-7.4	-7.6	-6.3	-8.0	-7.9	-6.2	-6.7	-1.6	-2.4	-2.2	-8.7	-8.1	-8.9
Korea	1.7	2.3	3.5	3.2	3.0	1.3	2.4	5.4	4.3	5.1	0.5	2.7	3.4	3.9	4.7	3.0	-1.1	0.0	0.5
Luxembourg	1.5	2.5	2.4	1.2	3.7	3.4	3.4	6.0	6.1	2.1	0.5	-1.1	0.0	1.4	3.7	3.0	-0.9	-1.7	-0.9
Netherlands	-2.8	-3.5	-9.2	-1.9	-1.2	-0.9	0.4	2.0	-0.3	-2.1	-3.2	-1.8	-0.3	0.5	0.2	0.5	-5.5	-5.3	-3.7
New Zealand	-0.4	2.7	2.5	2.5	0.9	0.0	-0.2	1.8	1.5	3.6	3.8	4.1	4.7	5.3	4.5	0.4	-2.6	-4.6	-8.5
Norway	-1.4	0.3	3.2	6.3	7.6	3.3	6.0	15.4	13.3	9.2	7.3	11.1	15.1	18.4	17.5	19.1	10.5	10.5	12.5
Poland	–	–	-4.4	-4.9	-4.6	-4.3	-2.3	-3.0	-5.3	-5.0	-6.2	-5.4	-4.1	-3.6	-1.9	-3.7	-7.4	-7.9	-5.8
Portugal	-7.5	-7.1	-5.0	-4.5	-3.4	-3.5	-2.7	-2.9	-4.3	-2.9	-3.1	-3.4	-5.9	-4.1	-3.2	-3.6	-10.1	-9.2	-5.9
Slovak Republic	–	–	-3.4	-9.9	-6.3	-5.3	-7.4	-12.3	-6.5	-8.2	-2.8	-2.4	-2.8	-3.2	-1.8	-2.1	-8.0	-7.9	-5.1
Slovenia	–	–	-8.4	-1.1	-2.4	-2.4	-3.0	-3.7	-4.0	-2.5	-2.7	-2.3	-1.5	-1.4	-0.1	-1.8	-6.0	-5.6	-5.6
Spain	-7.3	-6.8	-6.5	-4.9	-3.4	-3.2	-1.4	-1.0	-0.7	-0.5	-0.2	-0.4	1.0	2.0	1.9	-4.2	-11.1	-9.2	-6.3
Sweden	-11.2	-9.1	-7.3	-3.3	-1.6	0.9	0.8	3.6	1.6	-1.5	-1.3	0.4	1.9	2.2	3.6	2.2	-0.9	-0.3	0.3
Switzerland	-3.5	-2.8	-2.0	-1.8	-2.8	-1.9	-0.5	0.1	-0.1	-1.2	-1.7	-1.8	-0.7	0.8	1.7	2.3	1.2	0.5	0.6
Turkey	–	–	–	–	–	–	–	–	–	–	–	–	–	0.8	-1.2	-2.2	-6.7	-4.6	-3.3
United Kingdom	-8.0	-6.8	-5.8	-4.2	-2.2	-0.1	0.9	3.7	0.6	-2.0	-3.7	-3.6	-3.3	-2.7	-2.8	-4.8	-10.8	-10.3	-8.7
United States	-5.1	-3.7	-3.3	-2.3	-0.9	0.3	0.7	1.5	-0.6	-4.0	-5.0	-4.4	-3.3	-2.2	-2.9	-6.3	-11.3	-10.6	-10.1
Euro area	-5.8	-5.0	-7.5	-4.3	-2.7	-2.3	-1.4	-0.1	-1.9	-2.6	-3.1	-3.0	-2.6	-1.4	-0.7	-2.1	-6.3	-6.0	-4.2
Total OECD	-5.1	-4.3	-4.8	-3.3	-1.9	-2.2	-1.0	0.1	-1.4	-3.3	-4.1	-3.4	-2.8	-1.3	-1.3	-3.3	-8.2	-7.7	-6.7

Source: Reproduced by permission of the OECD (2010).

Table 10.3 General government gross financial liabilities (as % of GDP) 1993–2011.

	1993	1994	1995	1996	1997	1998	1999	2000	2001	2002	2003	2004	2005	2006	2007	2008	2009	2010	2011
Australia	30.3	39.6	41.3	38.6	37.0	32.0	27.6	24.6	21.8	19.8	18.3	16.5	16.1	15.3	14.2	13.6	19.4	25.3	29.3
Austria	62.1	65.4	69.7	70.2	66.7	68.4	71.2	71.1	72.1	73.0	71.2	70.8	70.9	66.6	63.1	67.3	72.6	78.6	80.0
Belgium[1]	140.7	137.8	135.4	133.4	128.0	123.2	119.7	113.7	112.0	108.4	103.5	98.5	95.9	91.7	88.1	93.3	100.5	100.7	100.7
Canada	96.3	98.0	101.6	101.7	96.3	95.2	91.4	82.1	82.7	80.6	76.6	72.6	71.6	70.3	66.5	71.3	83.4	84.2	85.9
Czech Republic	–	–	–	–	–	–	–	–	–	32.8	34.7	34.5	34.3	33.9	33.7	36.3	42.4	46.6	49.3
Denmark	92.4	85.8	81.7	79.1	74.8	72.4	67.1	60.4	58.4	58.2	56.6	54.0	45.9	41.2	34.3	42.6	52.4	55.5	57.1
Estonia	–	–	13.3	12.3	11.3	10.0	10.9	9.4	8.9	10.2	10.8	8.5	8.2	8.0	7.3	8.3	12.4	12.1	15.2
Finland	57.8	60.9	65.3	66.2	64.8	61.2	54.9	52.5	50.0	49.6	51.5	51.5	48.4	45.5	41.4	40.6	52.1	57.4	62.7
France	51.0	60.2	62.7	66	68.8	70.3	66.8	65.6	64.3	67.3	71.4	73.9	75.7	70.9	72.3	77.8	89.2	94.1	97.3
Germany[2]	46.2	46.5	55.7	58.8	60.3	62.2	61.5	60.4	59.8	62.2	65.4	68.8	71.2	69.3	65.3	69.3	76.4	87.0	87.3
Greece	–	–	101.1	103.1	100.0	97.7	101.5	115.3	118.1	117.6	112.3	114.8	121.2	115.6	112.9	116.1	131.6	147.3	157.1
Hungary	91.6	91.4	88.1	75.6	66.0	64.0	66.3	60.8	59.1	60.2	61.3	65.0	68.5	71.7	71.8	76.3	84.7	85.6	79.8
Iceland	–	–	–	–	–	77.3	73.6	72.9	75.0	72.0	71.0	64.5	52.6	57.4	53.3	102.0	120.0	120.2	121.0
Ireland	–	–	–	–	–	62.1	51.2	39.4	36.9	35.2	34.1	32.8	32.6	28.8	28.8	49.6	71.6	102.4	120.4
Israel	–	–	–	–	–	100.9	94.9	84.5	89.0	96.6	99.2	97.4	93.5	84.3	77.7	76.7	79.2	76.1	73.5
Italy	116.3	120.9	122.5	128.9	130.3	132.6	126.4	121.6	120.8	119.4	116.8	117.3	120.0	117.4	112.8	115.2	127.8	126.8	129.0
Japan[3]	73.9	79.0	86.2	93.8	100.5	113.2	127.0	135.4	143.7	152.3	158.0	165.5	175.5	172.1	167.0	174.1	194.1	199.7	212.7
Korea[4]	–	–	–	–	–	–	–	–	–	19.2	19.3	22.6	24.6	27.7	27.9	29.6	32.5	33.9	33.3
Luxembourg	–	–	9.5	10.1	10.2	11.2	10.0	9.2	8.2	8.4	7.9	8.6	7.6	12.1	11.7	16.4	14.7	19.7	20.5
Netherlands	96.5	86.7	89.6	88.1	82.2	80.8	71.6	63.9	59.4	60.3	61.4	61.9	60.7	54.5	51.5	64.5	67.6	71.4	74.3
New Zealand	–	56.8	50.7	44.3	41.7	41.6	39.0	36.9	34.9	33.0	30.9	28.2	26.9	26.6	25.7	28.9	34.5	38.7	45.8
Norway	37.8	34.6	37.9	33.6	29.7	28.0	29.1	32.7	31.6	38.8	48.2	51.0	47.9	59.4	57.4	54.9	48.0	49.5	56.1
Poland	–	–	51.6	51.5	48.4	44.0	46.8	45.4	43.7	55.0	55.3	54.8	54.7	55.2	51.7	54.5	58.4	62.4	65.6
Portugal	–	–	66.8	66.5	65.3	63.3	60.5	60.2	61.7	65.0	66.8	69.3	72.8	77.6	75.4	80.6	93.1	103.1	110.8
Slovak Republic	–	–	38.2	37.6	39.0	41.2	53.5	57.6	57.1	50.2	48.2	47.6	39.1	34.1	32.8	31.8	39.9	44.5	48.7
Slovenia	–	–	–	–	–	–	–	–	33.7	34.8	34.2	35.0	33.9	33.8	30.0	29.7	44.2	47.5	52.9
Spain	65.5	64.3	69.3	76.0	75.0	75.3	69.4	66.5	61.9	60.3	55.3	53.4	50.4	45.9	42.1	47.4	62.3	66.1	73.6
Sweden	78.2	82.5	81.1	84.4	83.0	82.0	73.2	64.3	62.7	60.2	59.3	60.0	60.8	53.9	49.3	49.6	52.0	49.1	45.4
Switzerland	42.9	45.5	47.7	50.1	52.1	54.8	51.9	52.4	51.2	57.2	57.0	57.9	56.4	50.2	46.8	43.7	41.5	40.2	38.7
United Kingdom	48.7	46.8	51.6	51.2	52.0	52.5	47.4	45.1	40.4	40.8	41.5	43.8	46.4	46.1	47.2	57.0	72.4	82.4	88.5
United States	71.9	71.1	70.7	69.9	67.4	64.2	60.5	54.5	54.4	56.8	60.2	61.2	61.4	60.8	62.0	71.0	84.3	93.6	101.1
Euro area	69.0	69.9	75.4	79.8	80.8	81.5	78.1	75.8	74.3	75.2	75.9	77.1	78.1	74.5	71.6	76.5	86.9	92.7	95.6
Total OECD	68.8	69.9	72.4	73.9	73.5	74.2	72.5	69.8	69.6	71.6	73.4	74.9	76.3	74.5	73.1	79.3	90.9	97.6	102.4

Source: Reproduced by permission of the OECD (2010).

countries are members of the Eurozone with independent monetary policy. Hence, they have limited room for manoeuvre with respect to policy instruments. As a consequence of a loss of monetary policy, they are unable to use debt maturity transformation by central banks to alleviate the short-term pressure that such deficits and debts place upon their credit ratings and hence are exposed to higher borrowing costs to service the debt which in turn raises default probabilities that itself makes borrowing even more expensive.

Table 10.4 shows the 10-year (or equivalent) government bond yields. Countries with their own monetary policies and central banks have lower yields on their debt than the more indebted countries within the Eurozone. For example, Japan that has the highest ratio of debt to GDP has a bond yield of 1.3% in 2011. This contrasts with much higher yields in Greece and Ireland.

From the preceding text, we can see that the new economy contains many indebted nations. Part of this indebtedness reflects the fall in asset values and income streams after the credit and property bubbles have burst.

Countries that have been less exposed to the financial crisis include many in East Asia. Northern Europe has also proved to relatively resilient and has avoided high national debt and deficits that have affected southern and western fringes of the European Union. In North America, Canada has also avoided the more extreme cycle experienced in the United States. Further, countries such as Brazil, Russia, India and China have in general performed well with China continuing to grow strongly.

Since the crisis has not been met by a wave of currency controls or restrictions on capital flows, the world economy has continued to see high levels of cross-border finance flows and FDI. As Asia has been the main beneficiary, then the question arises as to whether we are seeing a permanent shift towards the East for future economic growth and development.

Blankenburg and Palma (2009, p. 531) state that 'global financial assets rose from US$12 trillion in 1980 to US$196 trillion in 2007'. They also note that 'outstanding credit default swaps (CDS) today amount to no less than US$60 trillion' (Blankenburg and Palma, 2009, p. 531).

Crotty (2009) provides an analysis of the institutional structures that contributed to the global financial crisis. He argues that the crisis is a consequence of the process of financial deregulation to which policymakers have blindly ascribed. He defines the term 'New Financial Architecture' to reflect the integration of financial markets and light regulation by government and notes that deregulation leads to financial innovation that stimulates financial booms that then end in loss of money or economic recessions. The authorities then respond with bailouts and the process begins again. Financial markets have grown larger since deregulation began making financial crises bigger and having a greater impact on macroeconomies around the globe.

Table 10.4 Long-term interest rates (% per annum), 1996–2011.

	1996	1997	1998	1999	2000	2001	2002	2003	2004	2005	2006	2007	2008	2009	2010	2011
Australia	8.2	7.0	5.5	6.0	6.3	5.6	5.8	5.4	5.6	5.3	5.6	6.0	5.8	5.0	5.4	5.7
Austria	6.3	5.7	4.7	4.7	5.6	5.1	5.0	4.2	4.2	3.4	3.8	4.3	4.4	3.9	3.2	3.7
Belgium	6.3	5.6	4.7	4.7	5.6	5.1	4.9	4.1	4.1	3.4	3.8	4.3	4.4	3.8	3.3	4.2
Canada	7.2	6.1	5.3	5.5	5.9	5.5	5.3	4.8	4.6	4.1	4.2	4.3	3.6	3.2	3.2	3.4
Chile	–	–	–	–	–	–	–	–	–	6.0	6.1	6.1	7.0	5.7	6.3	7.0
Czech Republic	–	–	–	–	–	6.3	4.9	4.1	4.8	3.5	3.8	4.3	4.6	4.8	3.9	4.2
Denmark	7.2	6.3	5.0	4.9	5.7	5.1	5.1	4.3	4.3	3.4	3.8	4.3	4.3	3.6	2.9	3.6
Finland	7.1	6.0	4.8	4.7	5.5	5.0	5.0	4.1	4.1	3.4	3.8	4.3	4.3	3.7	3.0	3.6
France	6.3	5.6	4.6	4.6	5.4	4.9	4.9	4.1	4.1	3.4	3.8	4.3	4.2	3.6	3.1	3.7
Germany	6.2	5.7	4.6	4.5	5.3	4.8	4.8	4.1	4.0	3.4	3.8	4.2	4.0	3.2	2.7	3.3
Greece	–	9.9	8.5	6.3	6.1	5.3	5.1	4.3	4.3	3.6	4.1	4.5	4.8	5.2	9.1	13.5
Hungary	–	–	–	–	8.6	7.9	7.1	6.8	8.3	6.6	7.1	6.7	8.2	9.1	7.3	7.3
Iceland	9.2	8.7	7.7	8.5	11.2	10.4	8.0	6.7	7.5	7.7	9.3	9.8	11.1	8.0	5.0	3.4
Ireland	7.2	6.3	4.7	4.8	5.5	5.0	5.0	4.1	4.1	3.3	3.8	4.3	4.6	5.2	6.0	9.6
Israel	–	4.1	4.9	5.2	5.5	4.8	5.3	4.7	7.6	6.4	6.3	5.6	5.9	5.1	4.7	5.4
Italy	9.4	6.9	4.9	4.7	5.6	5.2	5.0	4.3	4.3	3.6	4.0	4.5	4.7	4.3	4.0	4.8
Japan	3.1	2.4	1.5	1.7	1.7	1.3	1.3	1.0	1.5	1.4	1.7	1.7	1.5	1.3	1.1	1.3
Korea	10.9	11.7	12.8	8.7	8.5	6.9	6.6	5.0	4.7	5.0	5.2	5.4	5.6	5.2	4.8	5.2
Luxembourg	6.3	5.6	4.7	4.7	5.5	4.9	4.7	3.3	2.8	2.4	3.3	4.5	4.6	4.2	3.2	3.7
Mexico	34.4	22.4	24.8	24.1	16.9	13.8	8.5	7.4	7.7	9.3	7.5	7.6	8.1	5.8	4.9	5.0
Netherlands	6.2	5.6	4.6	4.6	5.4	5.0	4.9	4.1	4.1	3.4	3.8	4.3	4.2	3.7	3.0	3.6
New Zealand	7.9	7.2	6.3	6.4	6.9	6.4	6.5	5.9	6.1	5.9	5.8	6.3	6.1	5.5	5.6	5.5
Norway	6.8	5.9	5.4	5.5	6.2	6.2	6.4	5.0	4.4	3.7	4.1	4.8	4.5	4.0	3.5	4.0
Portugal	8.6	6.4	4.9	4.8	5.6	5.2	5.0	4.2	4.1	3.4	3.9	4.4	4.5	4.2	5.4	8.7
Slovak Republic	9.7	9.4	21.7	16.2	9.8	8.0	6.9	5.0	5.0	3.5	4.4	4.5	4.7	4.7	3.9	4.4
Slovenia	–	–	–	–	–	–	–	6.4	4.7	3.8	3.9	4.5	4.6	4.4	3.8	4.5
Spain	8.7	6.4	4.8	4.7	5.5	5.1	5.0	4.1	4.1	3.4	3.8	4.3	4.4	4.0	4.2	5.3
Sweden	8.1	6.7	5.0	5.0	5.4	5.1	5.3	4.6	4.4	3.4	3.7	4.2	3.9	3.2	2.9	3.5
Switzerland	4.0	3.4	3.0	3.0	3.9	3.4	3.2	2.7	2.7	2.1	2.5	2.9	2.9	2.2	1.6	2.2
Turkey	–	–	–	–	36.9	95.2	65.0	46.5	25.2	16.5	17.9	18.3	19.2	11.6	8.4	8.8
United Kingdom	7.8	7.1	5.6	5.1	5.3	4.9	4.9	4.5	4.9	4.4	4.5	5.0	4.6	3.6	3.6	3.8
United States	6.4	6.4	5.3	5.6	6.0	5.0	4.6	4.0	4.3	4.3	4.8	4.6	3.7	3.3	3.2	3.5
Euro area	7.2	6.0	4.8	4.7	5.4	5.0	4.9	4.2	4.1	3.4	3.8	4.3	4.3	3.8	3.6	4.4

Source: Reproduced by permission of the OECD (2009).

The neoclassical view that the market will resolve problems also implies that assets are correctly priced and expected risk-adjusted returns are accurate. If this is the case, then there is no need for burdensome regulation that if it existed would make the market less efficient and cause that industry to move to less regulated economies. Monetary policy in this environment should only be about controlling inflation (inflation targeting), and authorities should ignore asset price inflation, exchange rate movements or the quality of credit (Leijonhufvud, 2009).

Crotty (2009) argues that in this deregulated financial world, perverse incentives are created that cause excessive risk-taking. He uses mortgage securitisation as an example. The process of securitisation generates fee income for '...banks and mortgage brokers who sold the loans, investment bankers who packaged the loans into securities, banks and specialist institutions who serviced the securities and rating agencies who gave them their seal of approval. Since fees do not have to be returned if the securities later suffer large losses, everyone involved had strong incentives to maximise the flow of loans through the system whether or not they were sound' (Crotty, 2009, p. 565). Possibly, contracts could be written that change the burden of risk, but that has not happened and is beyond the scope of this discussion. Although it is not inconceivable that policy changes, it is difficult to envisage a regulatory authority taking such a step.

In boom periods, Crotty (2009) notes that this is when maximising debt financing enhances profits and potential bonuses. Even when significant losses were made, wiping out over a decade of earnings in the case of Merrill Lynch, bonuses were still being paid out. Bonuses in 2008 during the financial crisis were as high as they had been in 2004. For individuals within the sector, it was sensible to take on high-risk strategies 'even if they [understood] that their decisions [were] likely to cause a crash in the immediate future. Since they [did] not have to return their bubble-year bonuses when the inevitable crisis [occurred] and since they [continued] to receive substantial bonuses even in the crisis, they [had] a powerful incentive to pursue high-risk, high-leverage strategies' (Crotty, 2009, p. 565).

The perverse incentives evident within this system also extended to credit rating agencies. Capital requirements of banks had to reflect their risk-weighted assets. However, rating agencies determine asset risk and risk weights. More highly rated assets had lower capital requirements under Basel II rules. As major institutions hold only triple A rated assets, they would be in a position to reduce their capital requirements and increase lending and profits. 'Ratings agencies are paid by the investment banks whose products they rate' (Crotty, 2009, p. 566). Therefore, they have an incentive to rate the assets of those institutions highly. Given the few (three) rating agencies, it would not make sense for any one of them to give an asset a low rating as the institution could go to another that would award a higher rating and (the rating agency would) earn income. Thus, there was a perverse incentive for the rating agencies to provide high quality ratings on assets that may not have earned them. 'The recent global financial boom and crisis might not have occurred if perverse incentives had not induced credit rating agencies to give absurdly high ratings to illiquid, non-transparent, structured financial products such as MBSs, CDOs and collateralized loan obligations' (Crotty, 2009, p. 566).

The complexity of newer financial instruments has made markets less transparent, made pricing more difficult, reduced the accuracy of market information and therefore has made the market less efficient. The axiomatic concept that the market accurately sets prices on these assets is further called into question as a large proportion of the value of these complex assets are sold through private transactions. This further implies that risk is not accurately priced.

In addition to the development of complex financial products discussed in Chapter 9, product innovation has involved further complications to these instruments. Investors can buy tranches of mortgage-backed collateralised debt obligations (CDOs) that (as outlined in Chapter 9) have different risk profiles. Thousands of mortgages may be included in a single MBS and up to 150 MBSs can be held in a CDO. Further financial engineering has created CDOs squared. This is based upon a CDO that is made from other CDO tranches. A yet further variation is the higher-power CDO in which 'mortgages appear in more than one of the underlying CDOs' (Crotty, 2009, p. 567). All of this implies that it is difficult to price the CDO. As the number of mortgages increases, it becomes significantly harder to arrive at a calculation for default risk and hence product price. In addition, changes in mortgage value can create significant and unexpected changes in the values of CDOs. The use of black-box simulation methodologies to attempt to estimate the CDO price has caused mispricing of these complex assets. Financial engineering has thus led to less transparency and to more pricing inaccuracy.

Nevertheless, CDOs were highly rated assets during the boom period. However, when homeowners defaulted on mortgage payments, these assets quickly lost their attractiveness, and their values collapsed. Liquidity also dried up as institutions became concerned about their asset base. This was contrary to the assumption that finance would always be available. Banks refused to lend to each other and the interbank offered rate increased dramatically. By 2009, approximately 50% of CDOs had defaulted, an incredible proportion for a highly rated asset.

Banks were also holding risky MBSs and CDOs for a number of reasons. They wanted to convince investors that the assets were safe so they held usually the riskiest of them (the toxic assets). However, the assets were held off balance sheet and had no reserve requirements. When the market crashed, banks were holding MBSs and CDOs and faced huge losses as a consequence of their collapse in value.

The behaviour of banks can in part be explained by the institutional context within which they were operating. The particular institutional context was created under Basel I by which capital requirements differed for loans and for assets that the banks held for trading purposes and hence would not be held for long time periods. These latter had much lower capital requirements. Thus, the regulatory environment provided an incentive for banks to hold CDOs for trading purposes. However, in the market crash, banks still had significant exposure to these assets with little or no capital set aside to protect against the losses they faced. Banks had in fact not been trading the assets. Bank holdings of MBSs and CDOs were the main reason why on-balance-sheet assets more than doubled between 2000 and 2006 to US$23 trillion.

The role played by insurance products in this market is also one that seems to have increased moral hazard. Credit default swaps (CDSs) permit insurance against loss from default on loans by payment of an insurance premium. This potential hedging instrument became another asset that was traded, and most CDSs were used in a form of gambling (speculation) rather than hedging. 'No regulator objected when AIG guaranteed $440 billion worth of shaky securities with no capital set aside to protect against loss apparently because both the securities and AIG were triple A rated' (Crotty, 2009, p. 569). The U.S. government intervened to save AIG in order to avoid the losses that other domestic and foreign companies would have faced if their contracts with AIG had become void. Hence, the moral hazard is underwritten by the state under the motto of 'too big to fail'. The consequence of this and similar policies in other countries is that the moral hazard remains, the perverse incentive mechanism is intact and public debt has multiplied. Government also paid the face value of CDOs to banks rather than their lower market values. In this scenario, the perverse incentive mechanism produces the biggest pay-off.

Another institutional failure in the deregulated financial world has been that the Bank for International Settlements told regulators to permit banks to self-evaluate risks and thus capital requirements. This was to be based upon Value at Risk (VAR) measured by using historical data. However, this approach has a number of flaws. Generating reliable estimates over time is tricky. In boom periods, risk would be underestimated as defaults are low but systematic risks remain. Also, correlation between asset classes can vary, and historic information may not reflect future degrees of correlation in asset return performance. It is argued that the use of VAR left banks undercapitalised. The regulation was ineffective and open to abuse.

The globally integrated financial system was supposed to be able transfer risk to those who were risk-takers and who could manage it. However, this has not happened. Instead, risk-taking has been excessive in a system that is weakly regulated, and the cost of loss is minimised as public authorities become providers of liquidity should the system itself fail. Risk has not been unpacked by new financial products but rather has been repacked to become more difficult to evaluate.

The aftermath of the resulting financial crisis has been stagnation. Minsky (1977, 1986) argues that financial markets cause instability in economies. He argues that financial systems have an inherent tendency to degenerate towards Ponzi financing schemes that make the system fragile and easily prone to crises. The policy response as mentioned earlier has been to intervene to prevent depression. But there is no obvious source of economic growth that will effectively erode the newly enlarged government deficits.

Leijonhufvud (2009) argues that as a consequence of the financial crisis, economies are facing 'balance sheet' recessions. Debt exposure on balance sheets in the private sector and especially within financial institutions has to be remedied before sustained economic growth can return. Leijonhufvud argues that policymakers in Japan failed to adequately deal with these issues after their real estate bubble burst in 1990 and that this subsequently led to a long period of slow or no growth extending right up until the 2008 financial crisis. He states that '[the] Japanese government did not act to repair the balance sheets of the private sector following the crash. Instead it chose a policy of keeping [the] bank rate at near zero so as to reduce deposit rates and let the banks earn their way back into solvency. This proved ineffectual' (Leijonhufvud, 2009, p. 745). Traditional fiscal remedies were also tried (e.g. infrastructure investment), but this simply created much more public debt. Even after the property bubble burst in Japan, some banks still failed in the late 1990s. Only in 2002 did the government begin to implement measures to deal with bad debt in the banking system. Evidence suggested that firms were not borrowing for investment either because they were unwilling or that funds in the banking were not available due to the banks trying to recapitalise after their exposure to bad loans. '...once the credit system had crashed a central bank policy of low interest rates could not counteract this intertemporal effective demand failure' (Leijonhufvud, 2009, p. 746). The very low interest rate policy did not effectively stimulate the economy or open up closed channels of credit. Instead, it permitted banks to very slowly improve their balance sheets.

Real estate bubbles that occurred at around the same time as that of Japan, in Finland and Sweden did not lead to the same long periods of stagnation. Government policy in these countries acted swiftly to sort out the problem with bad loans in the banking system. Both economies subsequently experienced growth rates about the European average and have performed relatively well through the 2008 financial crisis. 'The lesson to be drawn from these examples is that deficit spending will be absorbed into the *financial sinkholes* in private sector balance sheets and will not become effective until those holes have been filled' (Leijonhufvud, 2009, p. 746). The 'sinkhole' left in the aftermath of the 2008 crisis is substantial and will take considerable time to fill. Leijonhufvud argues that governments will need to take on the bad debt of the financial sector before any demand management Keynesian-style policy has a chance of working in the macroeconomy. The scale of the task is enormous, and public finances are under pressure due to the financial debacle even before finding the funds required for fiscal stimulus. In many countries, fiscal policy has taken an opposite route and is contractionary in nature since deficits are too big to finance at affordable interest rates. Of course, the policy prescription still has not avoided moral hazard that has let the financial sector off the hook for its excessive risk indulgence.

Of course, the financial crisis has had an impact on (and possibly undermined) the theoretical basis used to justify policy over the past 30 years. The role of economic authorities has changed out of recognition. Intervention has been geared towards preventing depression and hence has covered a range of partly related financial interventions. The previous position supported by different governments was that central banks should focus on inflation targeting to the exclusion of all else. This is a policy prescription that has its origins in the rules versus discretion debate that goes back to intellectual differences between Monetarists and Keynesians that rose to the surface in the 1970s. Monetarists began to have a significant impact on policy from the 1980s onwards, and their more liberal economic stance has been reflected in policies such as inflation targeting by monetary authorities as being the main role of the central bank, which with operation independence from government ensures predictability and credibility of monetary policy rules. This reductionist policy view is consistent with the idea that the real and monetary economies are separate and hence the central bank cannot influence real values of output and employment permanently through discretionary monetary policies that would have been adopted in the Keynesian era. So interest rates are changed to ensure that the inflation target is met.

But such policies ignored the rapid inflation in asset prices. Since general inflation as measured by the consumer price index (CPI) or the retail price index (RPI) was low, the inflation target had been met, and the authorities did not intervene to address the growth of bubbles in asset values, particularly in real estate. The simplistic policy approach ignored structural factors restricting general price inflation and policy myopically looked at only one variable among a sea of pricing information. This is somewhat more surprising since the policy was drawn from the neoclassical economic world in which full information is assumed.

Nevertheless, the policies pursued in many countries followed similar lines with the prevailing dogma of minimum intervention in a model dominated by neoclassical thinking of economic systems. However, 'a few economists challenged the assumption of rational behaviour, questioned the belief that financial markets can be trusted and pointed to the long history of financial crises that had devastating economic consequences. But they were swimming against the tide, unable to make much headway against a pervasive and, in retrospect, foolish complacency' (Krugman, 2009). The Ponzi scheme which describes the financial system just prior to collapse will collapse but only once it is recognised as such. In a neoclassical world, this cannot be the case as markets are transparent and have full information. Clearly, the two are incongruent.

The debts that accumulated would have to be repaid, and this has led to financial retrenchment by households that places downward pressure on asset prices and reduces tax revenues. This force has led to public finances deteriorating in addition to public policy responses to banking failures. For the general public and for direct investors in real estate, property has played a major role in the financial collapse.

Institutional inertia has been a key component in setting the background against which the financial crisis occurred. Even in the face of problems in asset markets where mispricing occurred, authorities failed to change the system having difficulty of swimming against the free market mantra that was strongly supported by policymakers who set up the institutional framework in the first place. Galbraith (2009) further argues that these failings reflect failures in the teaching of economics which he suggests has become dominated by the neoclassical school of thought to the exclusion of all else.

Real estate in the new economy

The real estate market has experienced significant volatility in values over the period from 2001 to 2011. The extent of volatility in peak to trough variation has varied across locations within countries as well as between countries. In addition, the extent of this volatility has varied over time through different economic cycles in different countries. In the United Kingdom, comparisons have been made with the large cycle in the real estate market in the late 1980s and early 1990s which also coincides with the last recession. Lack of new supply in the market recently has prevented values falling further and placed a floor on rental value declines as well as impacting on yield movements. However, the debt overhang from the credit bubble has weakened growth and led to weakness in occupier markets that may persist. Some commentators suggest that the situation is similar to that experienced by Japan after its property market bubble burst in 1990 leaving it with very low growth rates for two decades. From the investors' perspective, low growth would impact on expected (risk-adjusted) return performance and encourage them to look elsewhere.

From the aforementioned debate, we cannot assume that we simply describe the behaviour of atomistic individual economic actors acting in a policy vacuum or one in which institutions will only ever behave in the way we have thus far observed. Predicting future movement in the real estate sector in global markets can be conditional on the status quo. However, if the latter changes, then all predictions become irrelevant. Any debate on the new economy is complicated by changes to the understanding of the role of markets and institutions. The new economy may be the brave new world of the free market and limited intervention by policymakers who through globalisation have become weaker. This then reinforces the view of the neoclassical school of economic thought that policy is irrelevant. However, political economy cannot be ignored as the distributional impact of the free market may cause governments to change institutional structures. In addition, the scale of impact of financial crises is vast and long lasting, placing pressures on private and public budgets that a return to the previous status quo would seem short-sighted.

The interlinkages between the real estate sector and the macroeconomy reveal significant multiplier effects and feedback effects increasing volatility and in bubble markets show the impact that real estate speculation can have on financial markets and macroeconomic instability. If the new economy of strong interlinkages between markets and integrated financial flows dominates, then it is reasonable to expect future contagion of financial crises to occur. The outlook is then one of more macroeconomic instability and imbalances on account balance sheets. Given the increased probability of extreme events and the significant cost that these impose, the implication might mean that institutional change is inevitable and the apparent victory of the neoclassical economic doctrine is no longer assured.

From an investment perspective, globalisation and world economic integration has increased the number of investment opportunities. This is of course reflected in the increased size of international financial flows between countries as investors seek to place funds to maximise their returns. Real estate has become an important asset within investment strategies and portfolios reflecting its relatively low return correlation with other asset classes of shares and debt and hence the potential diversification benefits that it can offer. It has also been attractive due to its ability to act as an inflation hedge (Hudson-Wilson *et al.*, 2003).

International real estate investment has benefitted from an increased range of investment media especially with the development of indirect investment vehicles. This has made investment more attractive as it has reduced unit costs and made the market more liquid. Growth of real estate securities has been significant as more countries have introduced legislation to permit the creation of tax-efficient vehicles for investment. Between 2000 and 2007, publicly traded real estate securities grew from US$350 billion to US$945 billion (Yunus, 2009). The rapid increase in value and the relative performance of this asset have made it more attractive to institutional investors. However, performance measurement remains problematic due to market imperfections leading to information asymmetry.

Data sources for indirect vehicles have begun to improve due to collection of information providing a 20-year return history and property company share prices. These data have been compiled through the FTSE, the European Public Real Estate Association (EPRA) and the National Association of Real Estate Investment Fiduciaries (NAREIT) in the United States. They provide data on the United States, Europe and Asia. The information they provide is useful for the performance measurement and portfolio decision making.

As markets have become globalised, it is possible that they are all interrelated such that diversification benefits have been eroded. Yunus (2009) examines the relationship between major property markets including the United States, the United Kingdom, Australia, France, Hong Kong, Japan and the Netherlands over the period 1990–2007. Yunus considers whether global integration has caused market convergence over time, thus reducing diversification benefits. Increasing convergence is tested by examining whether the number of co-integrating relationships increases as the time period under examination is lengthened. This statistical approach is built upon the work of Hansen and Johansen (1999) and the application to other asset markets in Rangvid (2001) and in Rangvid and Sørensen (2002). The method of analysis permits identification of common trends and finds the long-run drivers of the market plus factors that have only short-term impacts (see Gerlach *et al.*, 2006; Wilson *et al.*, 2011). Thus, the approach identifies valid long-run relationships via co-integration, and the common trends component identifies drivers that link the markets in different countries.

The aforementioned is important from an investor's perspective if he/she is looking to identify diversification benefits of international investment. Country variation is important, but the length of the holding period is also important if the diversification benefit from investing in different countries is only short term, and in the long term, countries behave more similarly due to global increased economic integration (Kasa, 1992; Tarbert, 1998).

Wilson and Okunev (1996) examined property market integration between the United Kingdom, the United States and Australia. They found that the markets were segmented and hence that diversification benefits existed. A later study by Wilson and Zurbruegg (2001) tested markets in the United Kingdom, the United States, Australia and Japan. In contrast to the previous study, they suggest that these property markets are related and that there is therefore no diversification benefit for investors. Yang *et al.* (2005) examine public property markets in Eurozone countries. They argue that larger countries in the monetary union show closer integration and that the smaller countries have not displayed integration.

Yunus (2009) shows that cross-correlations in weekly real estate returns between countries are low. This might be taken to suggest that diversification opportunities exist for international investors. Next, unit root and co-integration tests are conducted. The results indicate that 'only the property markets of the United States, Australia, France, Hong Kong, Japan, and the United Kingdom are part of the long-run cointegrating relationships' (Yunus, 2009, p. 400). 'Overall, the results show that the US public property market shares long run linkages with the property markets of Australia, France, Hong Kong, Japan and the [UK]' (Yunus, 2009, p. 401).

If the number of co-integrating vectors increases over time, then as per Hansen and Johansen (1999), the real estate markets will become more closely integrated. Yunus finds this to be the case among the markets of Australia, France, Japan, Hong Kong, the United Kingdom and the Unites States. Since the Netherlands is not part of the long-run co-integration, there will be diversification benefits with it. The source of common trends seems to be the United States and Japan which are driving the other markets with which there is co-integration. Thus, there is evidence of increasing convergence in many real estate markets that is consistent with findings from research on stock markets across the globe.

Investors thus examine real estate in the same way as they examine other asset classes. The 'new economy' thus applies the same methods to analyse any asset in any country. The role played by institutions is assumed to be passive in the sense that it is seen to set the background to the new integrated global economy.

Overview and conclusions

At the beginning of this text, we set out the topics for discussion and the key objectives to be addressed. These included providing a discussion on the developments in real estate's financial structure and examining how real estate finance interacted with the macroeconomy in different countries. Our initial chapters set the scene with respect to internationalisation strategies and flows of finance across the globe. Chapter 3 provided more detail on flows of funds, financing systems, financial intermediaries and the importance of debt in the commercial real estate market. Chapter 9 discusses financial innovation that has led to the creation of a wide range of debt-based products.

The concept of the new economy was discussed in Chapter 5. The integrated world economy and financial system was seen to potentially increase volatility of cycles in addition to adding to the number of cycles. One of the consequences of the debt-based system is increased probability of asset bubbles where values diverge from fundamentals. This is discussed in Chapter 6 and again in more detail in Chapter 8.

At the time of writing this book, the financial crisis of 2008 is still having a major impact on real estate markets across the globe. Debt-financed real estate investment which saw rapid growth remains significantly constrained almost 4 years after the crisis began. Public sector deficits that ballooned after the crisis have caused market panic and have constrained the ability of governments to create a fiscal stimulus. Monetary policy has involved asset purchases and quantitative easing in many monetary zones. However, the balance sheets of financial institutions remain weak.

Changes in yields in real estate markets suggested that economic actors had begun to re-price assets before the crisis began. However, the complexity of debt instruments meant that their prices were unreasonably high and the income streams (further weakened by defaults) could never justify the capital values sought on investment vehicles that covered large numbers of individual mortgages.

The scale of borrowing against expected future values has been enormous. Icelandic bank debt exposure was massively greater than the total GDP of the country. UK and U.S. banks have been hugely exposed and have required government support to remain in operation. Irish banks have also been greatly affected by exposure to a real estate bubble that has burst.

As time moves on since the crisis and economic growth has remained elusive since the bubble burst, many economies are witnessing their worst period of sustained weakness in GDP growth. Previous post-war recessions usually ended with a return to growth after at most 2 years. In the aftermath of the 2008 financial crisis, there has been no significant economic growth in many developed economies for over 3 years. This has caused more parallels to be drawn to the 1929 market crash. This led to depression throughout the 1930s. Leijonhufvud (2009) argues that because of the impact such crises have on the balance sheet of banks, then standard fiscal and monetary policy will not be sufficient. The first step should be to recapitalise the banking system. Only then will lending and confidence improve.

Of course, recapitalisation itself could be argued to be a moral hazard and raise the issue of whether or not banks are too big to let fail. If they know this in advance, then their behaviour is even more difficult to control. Crotty (2009) discusses in detail the problems with the financial sector. There have been repeated financial crises and each time regulation has not changed the rules sufficiently or has been ineffective. Institutional economists point to regulatory failings and vested interests controlling policy in such a manner that makes true reform impossible leaving the economies of the world subject to further turbulence due to the behaviour of the unstable financial system. They might be further concerned by the growth of finance degrees that have become popular in universities across the world. Beguiled by the beauty of equilibrium equations, the inherent flaws in the financial system remain hidden and more importantly not taught. So in a full information market of liquid products, nobody knows the true measure of risk or can calculate it or therefore calculate price.

Theoretical models have gone beyond simple mean–variance analysis and developed approaches to considering conditional risk, and further applications have considered over- and underestimation of risk in slumps and booms, respectively. Investor herd mentality has also been examined. However, fundamental questions remain on the ability of markets to adjust after shocks. Real estate markets are inefficient and adjustment processes can be protracted – taking years in many cases.

In the new economy of integrated markets, low barriers to financial flows and more countries linking into the world economy system, there is no evidence to suggest that markets are less volatile. Mature and transparent real estate markets in Australia, Canada, the United States, the United Kingdom and the Netherlands, Ireland, Sweden, Benelux, France and Germany still experience cycles in capital values, rents, vacancy rates and yields. Less transparent markets in tier 1 cities in China also exhibit significant cyclical value movements.[1] Hence, the high degree of openness of mature markets has meant that large financial flows reflecting investor sentiment can strongly impact the market in addition to imbalances in demand and supply due to the development lag. Thus, while imbalances are an inevitable consequence of the nature of the supply response in the commercial real estate market, there is in addition a speculative element funded by debt and international financial flows that can add more volatility to value change. Without this, markets would be less volatile, and the macroeconomic impacts would therefore be less volatile.

However, there is evidence that investors can play the market by buying at the trough and selling at the peak (if their predictions are correct) and hence making a larger return. However, even if their expectations are correct, they can only sell illiquid unsecuritised real estate if there is another high-value purchaser. The strategy therefore works only in larger markets (e.g. London) where the direct market is relatively big. In thin markets, buyers are scarce, and it may be difficult to realise higher returns from this type of strategy. This may imply that larger markets will become more volatile than smaller ones due to this type of strategy being employed. It also implies that more liquidity means more volatility.

Real estate in the new economy could therefore be seen as an asset class that has contributed to economic volatility. Access to finance and international financial flows has linked markets together making it easy to chase potentially good deals in many countries. Literature suggests that prices have deviated from fundamental values across the globe to a greater or lesser extent. Housing and commercial property price bubbles have been of concern in many countries including the United States, the United Kingdom, China, Spain, Ireland and Denmark. Thus, the financial system's contribution to instability is not location specific, nor is it isolated to more transparent markets. As methods of investing in real estate expand, particularly through the expansion of indirect vehicles, it would seem likely that real estate will continue to add volatility in the new world economy. If we consider markets such as China where the investable stock is less than 25% of total stock, then there is scope for significant increases in investment. In addition, as the nation continues to grow, the total stock itself will also expand. Investment opportunities will therefore increase.

However, if this investment contributes to GDP and higher living standards, extra volatility may be a price worth paying. But there is a difference between an increase in fundamental values of assets and asset price increases due to bubbles (unsupported by real economic factors). The evidence suggests that bubbles precede financial crises such as the 2008 crisis. The full impact of this is still being felt, and the long-term consequences cannot yet be accurately identified.

Over the past 30 years, policymakers have embraced a liberal economic model that has encouraged deregulation in financial markets and global economic integration. Wealth has increased globally, but there are significant imbalances in the global economy with Western economies being burdened with debt, often in both the public and private sectors, and economies in Asia running surpluses and often buying debt issued by Western nations that consume their products. Such imbalances cannot persist in the long run particularly in the face of market integration. Policy credibility comes into question. The world economy faces structural change, and there is pressure for regulatory change. Thus, the direction of the new economy becomes less clear and less certain.

Evidence suggests that the role of real estate has been significant in cyclical fluctuations. Coupled with the openness in the new economy and the array of financing methods, real estate will continue to cause macroeconomic fluctuations. Of course, these are never symmetric or easily predictable as they interact with other exogenous variables. The challenge is not simply to model the past but to be able to identify and capture empirically the impact of the new economy on the ways in which different sectors of national economies (including real estate) and the new international economy interact.

Note

1   See Jones Lang LaSalle's 2010 transparency index for discussion of country rankings and index components.

References

Blankenburg, S. and Palma, G.J. (2009) Introduction: the global financial crisis. *Cambridge Journal of Economics*, **33** (4), 531–538.

Chorafas, D.N. (2001) *Managing risk in the new economy*, Chapter 1, New York Institute of Finance, Prentice Hall Press.

Crotty, J. (2009) Structural causes of the global financial crisis a critical assessment of the 'new financial architecture'. *Cambridge Journal of Economics*, **33** (4), 563–580.

Galbraith, J.K. (2009) Who are these economists anyway? *Action and Thought*, 85–97.

Gerlach, R., Wilson, P. and Zurbruegg, R. (2006) Structural breaks and diversification: the impact of the 1997 Asian financial crisis on the integration of Asia-Pacific real estate markets. *Journal of International Money and Finance*, **25**, 974–991.

Hansen, H. and Johansen, S. (1999) Some tests for parameter constancy in cointegrated VAR models. *Econometrics Journal*, **2**, 306–333.

Hudson-Wilson, S., Fabozzi, F.J. and Gordon, J.N. (2003) Why real estate? *Journal of Portfolio Management*.

Kasa, K. (1992) Common stochastic trends in international stock markets. *Journal of Monetary Economics*, **29** (1), 95–124.

Keynes, J.M. (1936) *The General Theory of Employment, Interest and Money*. Palgrave Macmillan, UK.

Krugman, P. (2009) How did economists get it so wrong? *New York Times Sunday Magazine*, September 6.

Leijonhufvud, A. (2009) Out of the corridor: Keynes and the crisis. *Cambridge Journal of Economics*, **33** (4), 741–757.

Minsky, H.P. (1977) A theory of system fragility. In: *Financial Crises: Institutions and Markets in a Fragile Environment* (eds E.I. Altman and A.W. Sametz). New York, John Wiley & Sons.

Minsky, H.P. (1986) *Stabilizing an Unstable Economy*. Yale University Press, New Haven.

OECD (2009) 'Statistical Annex', OECD Economic Outlook, Volume 2009 Issue 1, OECD Publishing. http://dx.doi.org/10.1787/eco_outlook-v2009-1-47-en.

OECD (2010) 'Statistical Annex', OECD Economic Outlook, Volume 2010 Issue 2, OECD Publishing. http://dx.doi.org/10.1787/eco_outlook-v2010-2-47-en.

Rangvid, J. (2001) Increasing convergence among European stock markets? A recursive common stochastic trends analysis. *Economic Letters*, 71, 383–389.

Rangvid, J. and Sørensen, C. (2002) Convergence in the ERM and declining numbers of common stochastic trends. *Journal of Emerging Market Finance*, **1**, 183–213.

Tarbert, H. (1998) The long run diversification benefits available from investing across geographical regions and property type: evidence from cointegration tests. *Economic Modelling*, **15**, 49–65.

Wilson, P. and Okunev, J. (1996) Evidence of segmentation in domestic and international property markets. *Journal of Property Finance*, **7**, 78–97.

Wilson, P. and Zurbruegg, R. (2001) Structural breaks, diversification, and international real estate markets – some new evidence. *Briefings in Real Estate Finance*, **1**, 348–366.

Wilson, P., White, M., Dunse, N., Cheung, C. and Zurbruegg, R. (2011) Modelling price movements in housing micro-markets: identifying long-term components in local housing market dynamics. *Urban Studies*, **48** (9), 1853–1874.

Yang, J., Kolari, W. and Zhu, G. (2005) European public real estate market integration. *Applied Financial Economics*, **15**, 895–905.

Yunus, N. (2009) Increasing convergence between US and international securitised property markets: evidence based on cointegration tests. *Real Estate Economics*, **37** (3), 383–411.

Index

Figures are indicated by *italic page numbers*, Tables by **boldface numbers**, and notes by suffix 'n' (e.g. '28n2' indicates note 2 on page 28)

WILEY Blackwell

Also available from Wiley Blackwell

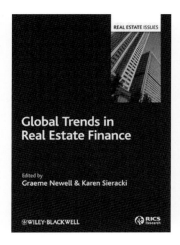

Global Trends in Real Estate Finance
Newell & Sieracki
978-1-4051-5128-3

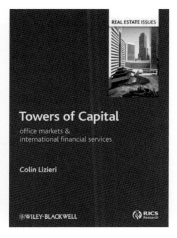

Towers of Capital: Office Markets & International Financial Services
Lizieri
978-1-4051-5672-1

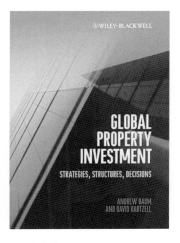

Global Property Investment
Baum & Hartzell
978-1-4443-3528-6

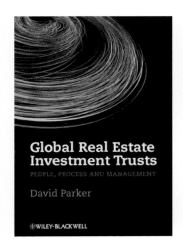

Global Real Estate Investment Trusts
Parker
978-1-4051-8722-0

Real Estate and Globalisation
Barkham
978-0-470-65597-9

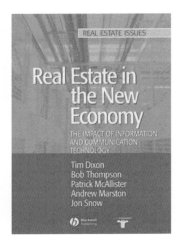

Real Estate in the New Economy
Dixon, Thompson, McAllister, Marston & Snow
978-1-4051-1778-4

www.wiley.com/go/construction